A POLITICAL HISTORY OF POSTWAR ITALY

MODERN ITALY

A
Political
History
of
Postwar
Italy

NORMAN KOGAN

FREDERICK A. PRAEGER, *Publishers*
New York · Washington

Published in the United States of America in 1966
by Frederick A. Praeger, Inc., Publishers
111 Fourth Avenue, New York, N.Y. 10003, U.S.A.

© 1966 by Frederick A. Praeger, Inc.
Library of Congress Catalog Card Number: 66-18905
Printed in the United States of America

To
MERYL

Preface

My introduction to Italy took place a little more than two decades ago, as a result of wartime experiences. I have been fortunate in being able to return a number of times since. This book was finished during my most recent visit. But it is to Mr. Frederick A. Praeger that I owe the suggestion to write this survey of postwar Italian life. My primary intention was to provide a narrative description of the major events of the period. Naturally, I wrote about what I considered the principal issues, and since my interests are primarily political and economic, this book is, first of all, a political and economic history of the country. Little attention is devoted to literary, cultural, or artistic movements and trends.

The changes in Italian life over the years have been enormous, the continuities striking, and in the following pages I have elaborated at some length on them. Although I was mainly concerned with narration, I am constitutionally incapable of withholding my opinions. Consequently, the following pages are peppered with judgments. The basic orientation behind these judgments could be characterized in Italy as falling within the "democratic, lay left" (*sinistra, democratica e laica*). This not only is revealed explicitly in a number of places but is also implicit in some of the themes which recur a number of times.

I wish to thank the University of Connecticut for its encouragement of my interest in Italy over the years. It, and the Research Foundation of the University, provided the time and money to enable me to spend the year 1964/65 in Italy working on this project. I wish to thank Harvard University Press for permission to reproduce the map of the Venezia Giulia–boundary proposals, which originally appeared in Robert Lee Wolff, *The Balkans in Our Time*. Thomas Y. Crowell Company kindly permitted me

vii

to use the map of modern Italy, which appeared in my book *The Government of Italy*. My wife, Meryl, gave to this enterprise the indispensable practical aid and moral support of the academician's wife. Needless to say, I take the usual, and sole, responsibility for the contents.

NORMAN KOGAN

Storrs, Connecticut
Spring, 1966

Contents

Tables

Maps

A POLITICAL HISTORY OF POSTWAR ITALY

1

World War II and Its Consequences

Italy entered World War II as a member of the Axis and emerged from it as a cobelligerent of the Allies. With few exceptions its wartime record on the side of Nazi Germany was mediocre. Benito Mussolini brought his country into the war on June 10, 1940, militarily and economically unprepared, in the belief that Germany had already won. There was little public support for his intervention, and when his calculation proved to be mistaken, the inadequacy of his war preparations was exposed.

The invasion of Greece turned into a disaster; Hitler had to send troops into that beleaguered country to bail Mussolini out. For reasons of prestige, an Italian expeditionary corps was sent to Russia, where it was eventually decimated. The occupation of Dalmatia and Croatia was made so trying by Yugoslav partisans that a cousin of King Victor Emmanuel III's, put on the throne of Croatia, never dared enter that Axis-created country to establish his reign. The Italian Navy and Air Force failed to establish control over the Mediterranean Sea and close it off to the British. In North Africa, a combined Italian-German Afrika Korps could not quite take Egypt, and after their defeat by the British at El Alamein, their days were numbered. The Anglo-American invasion of French North Africa in November, 1942, threatened the forces under General Erwin Rommel from the rear. By May, 1943, Italy's African empire was completely lost.

In July, the Anglo-American forces invaded Sicily. On July 25,

3

1943, Mussolini's Fascist regime was overthrown by a *coup d'état* carried out by generals under the authority of Victor Emmanuel. The King proclaimed a new government of military leaders and civilian technicians led by Marshal Pietro Badoglio, who in turn announced that Italy would continue fighting at the side of Nazi Germany.

Italian hopes of withdrawing from the war with the permission of both Germany and the Allies were deflated when German troops in large numbers began to cross the Brenner Pass into the peninsula. In August, while continuing to deal with the Germans, the Italian Government sent out emissaries to Tangier and Lisbon to approach the Allies for terms of a settlement. The Allies responded by insisting on an unconditional military surrender, though at the same time indicating that the peace settlement would be honorablè. Rome then sent General Giuseppe Castellano to Lisbon to negotiate with military aides to General Dwight D. Eisenhower, the Allied supreme commander in the Mediterranean theater of war. Castellano soon made it clear that Italy hoped to execute a reversal of alliances without surrendering, thereby saving what could be saved from a lost war by joining the erstwhile enemy. The Anglo-American representatives refused to countenance anything short of unconditional surrender, but then gave Castellano an *aide-mémoire* stating that the armistice terms could be modified depending on the contributions of the Italian Government and people during the remainder of the war.

Castellano's return to Rome at the end of August coincided with increasing unrest among the people over the absence of peace. The Italian Government delayed in giving the Allies an answer, countering with a request that Allied divisions be landed north of Rome to draw German troops away from the capital, thereby saving the royal family, the Vatican, and the government. The Allies gave Italy until midnight, September 3, to accept the armistice and offered to send an airborne division to protect Rome against a German reaction if the Italians could guarantee the airfields for the landing. The Italian Government gave in, accepted the Allied terms, approved the airborne operation, and on September 3, 1943, General Castellano signed the armistice at Cassibile, Sicily. Announcement of the surrender was to be withheld to coincide with the invasion of peninsular Italy and the rescue of Rome.

The Rome operation was messed up thoroughly. Badoglio, fearful of Nazi capture, tried to call off the armistice at the last minute. The Allies canceled the airborne mission and threatened Badoglio with the dissolution of his government and the destruction of his country. Reluctantly, on the evening of September 8, coinciding with the American landing at Salerno, the Italian Government announced its surrender.

Italian troops were now in France, the Balkan States, and Italy, and most of them were thrown into confusion by the announcement. After an initial disorientation, the Germans reacted quickly; in a few days they disarmed sixty-one demoralized Italian divisions. On September 9, German troops started to move into Rome. The King, his family, and some of his aides and military ministers fled the unprepared and unprotected city for safety behind the slowly advancing Allied lines in the south. This flight enraged the people in central and northern Italy and was probably the final straw in destroying the monarch's reputation, already shaky because of the ruin brought about after twenty years of complicity with Fascism. A few days later, the Germans rescued the imprisoned Mussolini, and safe behind German lines, he established the Fascist Social Republic of Italy. Italy was cut in two, the battleground of contesting foreign armies and competing Italian governments.

Allied expectations of a rapid German retreat never materialized, and in the fall and winter of 1943 the war bogged down in southern Italy. Italian efforts to organize a recovery and to contribute to the war against the Nazis, upon which future hopes for ameliorated armistice conditions and for a generous peace settlement depended, were blocked by two critical factors. Recovery, both civilian and military, would depend on Allied contributions of supplies and equipment, but for economic and political reasons, the Allies were little disposed to do much. Italy had a low priority on the supplies, equipment, and resources needed by numerous countries all over the globe. The British, especially, were not inclined to support an Italian revival after three years of war in the Mediterranean, and were thinking of a postwar future in which Italy would be kept weak and innocuous.

On the Italian side, recovery would depend on the capacity of Italians to reorganize a government and unite to wage an anti-Nazi struggle. Unity and reorganization were blocked, however, by the refusal of the revived anti-Fascist parties to collaborate with the King and Badoglio, both of whom they identified with Fascism and Italy's ruin. Six parties—Liberal, Democratic Labor, Christian Democratic, Action, Socialist, and Communist—had joined together to form the Committee of National Liberation (CLN). The Neapolitan Committee, led by the distinguished philosopher Benedetto Croce and the returned exile Count Carlo Sforza, insisted on the abdication of Victor Emmanuel III and Crown Prince Humbert as the precondition for collaboration in a reformed Italian government. They would accept a regency for the young Prince of Naples as an expedient until the issue of Monarchy *vs.* Republic could be settled after the war. The King refused to abdicate. The Allies would not pressure him, and efforts to organize a political government collapsed. Badoglio reinstituted his cabinet of technicians, but this unsatisfactory substitute failed to resolve the problem.

In the early spring of 1944, American pressure for a solution increased. The United States Government was willing to abandon Victor Emmanuel, who had a staunch protector, however, in Winston Churchill. In March, Russia recognized the King's government. At the beginning of April, Palmiro Togliatti, leader of the Italian Communist Party, returned from exile in Russia to announce that the Communists would drop their opposition to the King in the interests of unity and the prosecution of the war. The other anti-Fascist parties and the United States were both outmaneuvered. A compromise was reached whereby the King agreed to turn over his powers to Crown Prince Humbert as Lieutenant-General and retire from active life once Rome was recaptured. The anti-Fascist parties in the CLN reluctantly agreed, and on April 24, 1944, the six parties formed a new government with Badoglio (desired by the British) as Prime Minister. The ministers took a pledge to the crown, and made two pledges to the Allies: (1) they would not upset the Lieutenancy until after the war, when the people would decide the issue; (2) they would postpone their social goals and radical objectives and concentrate on providing for the population's minimum needs. They were also informed that the armistice obligations signed by the earlier government were binding on them. Thus, anti-Fascism bound itself to pay for the crimes of Fascism.

In the late spring, the Allies mounted their offensive and on June 4, 1944, they reached Rome. The American Government forced Victor Emmanuel to keep his pledge and to proclaim the Lieutenancy. The Roman anti-Fascist political leaders, now emerged from hiding, indignantly rejected Badoglio as a suitable government leader. A new government was formed under the leadership of Ivanoe Bonomi, chairman of the Central Committee of National Liberation. Churchill tried to have Badoglio restored as Prime Minister, but failed when the Americans backed Bonomi. He did succeed in blocking Sforza as Foreign Minister, for he considered the Count the man principally responsible for crystallizing the opposition to the King.

By fall, the Allied offensive had ground to a halt north of Florence, along the line of the Apennines. Another miserable winter was in store for all concerned: the south was overrun by Allied troops and the civilians starved along on minimum rations; the north, dominated by German troops and their Fascist cohorts, was the scene of a desperate struggle by the partisans. The political situation in Rome deteriorated. Attempts to purge Fascist bureaucrats and military leaders were blocked by conservative political leaders and Allied officials. The authority of the CLN was challenged at both national and local levels. Demands for economic, agricultural, and social reform were made by restive left-wing parties. Internationally, Italy's anomalous position as cobelligerent remained unchanged despite every effort to become a full-fledged Ally.

The Roosevelt Administration, motivated by concern over deteriorating conditions in Rome and by consideration of the forthcoming election at home, pressured a reluctant British Government into accepting economic concessions but could not bring them to accept any major political ones. On September 26, 1944, in an announcement from the Roosevelt home at Hyde Park, New York, England and America jointly proclaimed that they were committed to the current and postwar rehabilitation of Italy. (It was understood that America would pay most of the bill.) Allied controls over the Italian Government would be relaxed. The United Nations Relief and Rehabilitation Administration (UNRRA) would provide medical supplies. Italy did not get Allied status, however; it was still a defeated enemy, recognized only as a cobelligerent. The United States announced that ambassadors would be exchanged with the Italian Government, but Britain refused to go along.

The publication of the Anglo-American concessions bolstered the political regime in Italy and restored some harmony. These results were only temporary, however, for the aid for civilian reconstruction could not be forthcoming until after the war; UNRRA had no medical supplies to give; American promises of more wheat for bread turned out to be meaningless. The Allied Control Commission changed its name to the Allied Commission, but relaxed no controls. The issues which were dividing the cabinet reasserted themselves: the purge, Monarchy *vs.* CLN, agrarian reform.

Bonomi, moving steadily to the right in a promonarchist position, precipitated the crisis by submitting his resignation as Premier directly to the Lieutenant-General, thus taking the initiative away from the CLN. He was forced to backtrack, however, when the Lieutenant-General discovered that there were no political forces of any consequence other than the CLN upon which to base a cabinet. Bonomi then agreed to re-establish a CLN cabinet. The British once again vetoed Sforza as Foreign Minister. This time the issue broke into the open and Britain was publicly criticized by the United States. The Socialist and Action parties, resentful at Bonomi's weakness and inability to resist British pressure, refused to enter a new cabinet. In addition, Bonomi continued to insist that his authority came from the Lieutenant-General, not from the CLN. The Communists were willing to accept his concept, anxious to remain in the cabinet under any circumstances.

The settlement of the crisis was facilitated by the realization that the government would be a temporary caretaker, useful until the war ended with the liberation of the north. In that northern region, behind the German lines, an extensive and well-organized resistance movement had developed, and engaged in bitter partisan warfare against both German occupiers and reconstituted military units of Mussolini's Fascist Social Republic. Under the leadership of the Committee of National Liberation of Upper Italy, a clandestine military and political movement was organized, posing threats both to eventual Allied military control of the north and to the political authority of the Rome government. The military contributions of the guerrillas, in addition to the combat action of the small Italian regular armed forces whose reconstitution the Allies had permitted, were of sufficient value to the Allies to warrant reaching agreement.

In August, 1944, the Allies had sent General Giuseppe Cadorna to the north to take over military control of the partisan armies, but the guerrilla leaders had not paid much attention to him. After the reorganization of the government at Rome in November, Allied High Command in the Mediterranean invited partisan leaders for conversations. On December 7, 1944, an agreement was reached by which the Allies and the Rome government specified the financial and military aid they would furnish to the underground. The partisans agreed to recognize the Allied Military Government as the sole authority in the north after the defeat of the Germans and to turn in all their arms. A later understanding specified that Allied Military Government officials would approve local and provincial appointments made clandestinely by the CLN, except in cases of grave security objections.

On December 26, 1944, the Bonomi government recognized the Committee of National Liberation of Upper Italy as its official representative in the north. The Committee agreed to act as the delegate of the Rome government and formally recognized that government as the only legitimate one and as the legal successor of the government that had signed the armistice for Italy.

The settlements of December, 1944, appeared to resolve major perplexities for the Italian Government and the Allies. Presumably there would be no revolution aimed at overthrowing the regime. The anti-Fascist leaders of the north, as well as those of the south, were now pledged to accept the surrender terms of monarchist Italy, even though many of them were revolutionary republicans.

The coming of spring in 1945 brought the last great military drive of the war in Italy, as elsewhere in Europe. In April, German resistance collapsed. Partisan formations took over the principal cities of the north, establishing temporary local governments and restoring municipal services, in many cases before Allied troops arrived. Mussolini was captured by a Communist band and shot, along with a few of his most faithful followers. Most, but not all, of the guerrillas' weapons were given over to the Allies as promised. Some were hidden for potential future needs; others were used to settle private vendettas and personal enmities, the inevitable concomitants of civil war.

Some of the left-wing partisan officers and men were ready to take direct action for a revolutionary republic, but most of the partisans wanted to go home. The top political leaders of the left were sober and responsible. In a speech in Milan on May 21, 1945, Palmiro Togliatti reminded northern Communists that the British had not hesitated to crush Greek Communist partisans in Athens just a few months earlier. There was no Red Army in Italy to protect a revolt, therefore the Italian Communist Party was to prefer the path of legality, to work for change through a constituent assembly, parliamentary practice, and participation in a CLN government.[1] Later, Pietro Nenni, leader of the Socialist Party, would make the same evaluation. "When the north fell," he said, "it was impossible to take direct action for a republic with the Allies in Italy. It would have meant risking a conflict with the Allied occupation armies that could only have ended unsuccessfully. Therefore all energy was concentrated on the Constituent Assembly."[2]

The temporary exhilaration on the morrow of the war's end soon evaporated and the Italian people were left to contemplate the aftermath. It was a bitter picture that they might view. They had fought on both sides, evoked the contempt of both sides, and could have little hope that their efforts between September, 1943, and May, 1945, would be much appreciated by their cobelligerents. Because of Mussolini's fatuous foreign policy, Italians had

---

[1] *L'Unità* (Milan), May 22, 1945.

[2] Mimeographed press release, Partito Socialista Italiano di Unità Proletaria (Italian Socialist Party of Proletarian Unity), 24th Congress (Florence, April, 1946).

died in Italy, France, Germany, the Balkans, Russia, and North and East Africa. Large parts of the Navy and most of the merchant marine were destroyed. Untold wealth had been squandered in dreams of imperial glory. Inside the country, food and basic raw materials were in short supply. Most of the transportation and communications networks had been ruined, although sections had already been reconstructed in the course of the Allied march northward. Housing, hospitals, public utilities, would all require vast sums for reconstruction.

As the country was divided militarily by the battle lines, so the same lines had divided it politically. The south, traditionally inert in politics, had been liberated rapidly and spared the bitter experience of German occupation and the concomitant civil war. Except for the "four days of Naples," there was no partisan experience to provide political, moral, and ideological sustenance. The center and north, with a traditionally keener political consciousness, had suffered not only Nazi occupation and Fascist reprisals but also Allied and German bombings, advances, and retreats. These opposite experiences of the war created an atmosphere of hostility, apprehension, and fear between the two parts of the country; one more legacy of division to be added to more remote historic differences.

To offset this dismal picture were a few important potential assets. One was the Italian capacity for hard work. Another was the relative survival of the country's industrial plant, located mainly in the north. While northern industry had suffered damage from bombing, a combination of factors had prevented the Germans from implementing a last-minute scorched-earth policy. At the end, the Nazi retreat had been too rapid, the partisans had taken measures in advance to counteract mass destruction, and Allied negotiators had induced the German SS commander in Italy to spare the factories. Even some raw materials and supplies were available to begin production. What would be required was a continuing inflow to supplement initial stocks.

Political assets were found in the leadership of the parties now coming to the fore. A combination of older pre-Fascists and younger underground anti-Fascists, the political leaders of Italy were of varying quality and temperament. Their internecine quarrels and maneuverings would eventually divide the parties of the CLN, and this split would be aggravated by external pressures of a growing Cold War. But in the immediate postwar period, they were able to unite sufficiently to lay the premises for reconstruction. Premises, however, were not enough. Massive foreign help would have to be added to them. Although Italy was surrounded by hostile European neighbors, victims of Fascist aggression, it had the important asset of American friendship and support. The Hyde Park declaration of September, 1944, promised aid for postwar Italian reconstruction. And the United States had the political and economic strength to make these promises effective.

2

Postwar Settlements

Two immediate postwar problems faced the Italian Government: to achieve a satisfactory peace settlement and to keep the population alive. The solutions of both depended on foreign, as well as Italian, intentions and deeds. Ever since the armistice in September, 1943, the Italian Government had sought to moderate the surrender terms and to obtain an acceptable peace settlement. The collaboration with the Allies during the period of economic, military, and political cobelligerency had undoubtedly achieved an amelioration of Allied controls by the end of the war. The military effort, especially, had earned the appreciation of the Allied military. Field Marshal Sir Harold Alexander, commander of the British forces in Italy, told a press conference on June 21, 1945, that in his opinion Italy had completely rehabilitated itself.[1] The American Army newspaper, *Stars & Stripes* (Mediterranean section), editorialized on the contributions of the northern partisans in the following language:

> Our advance guards and armored troops entered cities full of Italian patriots. They were there in an extraordinary number. The Allied soldiers have finally felt that they were fighting to liberate people who really wanted to be free. After long months of the winter war, in the mud and the rain and the ruins, finally the Allied soldiers have seen another Italy.[2]

[1] *Il Progresso italo-americano* (New York), July 30, 1945.
[2] "Italian News Bulletin" (mimeographed; U.S. Office of War Information, May 2, 1945).

On August 23, 1945, General Mark W. Clark, commander of American forces in Italy, cabled Ferruccio Parri, who had succeeded Bonomi as Prime Minister the previous June:

> On leaving Italy after two years of hard campaigns in your country, I wish to salute your people and thank them for the help and collaboration they always gave me in driving the enemy out of your country. . . .
>
> It was a great satisfaction to me that your people—soldiers, partisans and civilians—gave me such cordial help and played such an important part in the final campaign of the Po Valley where they completely annihilated the enemy, thus liberating your country.[3]

Hardheaded European politicians, however, were not likely to permit themselves the luxury of gratitude or forgiveness. They had demands to make on a defeated Italy; they had their own power positions to establish or to reinforce; they had vivid memories of Fascist aggression. Britain, France, Yugoslavia, Greece, Russia, Albania, to say nothing of Ethiopia, had all felt the effects of Mussolini's expansionist ambitions. They had territorial or financial or colonial claims to present to Italy for payment.

In addition to its contribution to the war against the Nazis, post-Fascist Italy had two other important assets. America wanted nothing material from Italy and was committed to its rehabilitation. Inside the United States there were influential Italian-American and Roman Catholic forces to plead Italy's cause. This attitude was also held by a number of Latin American countries, although their voice at the peace conference would be modest.

There was also a fear, among the Western Allies at least, that a harsh peace settlement might wreck Italy's fragile political and economic structure, perhaps bringing chaos to be followed by Communism or a revival of Fascism. As the Cold War evolved in the postwar period, and as the internal strength of the Italian Communist Party was revealed in its full electoral force, these considerations would become more pressing. But in the early period of peace negotiations, the rancors and resentments of past depredations, and the jockeying for future power positions, would dominate among the victors.

---

[3] *Nazioni unite* (New York), September 15, 1945, p. 2.

Italy participated in the peace conference but could not negotiate with the Allies. It was permitted to make oral and written
presentations of its position, but the peace conference was primarily a testing of strength among victors, not a settlement between victors and defeated. The Italians would, of course, try to
influence in any way possible the positions of the various victors,
through diplomatic and other channels, but in the end they
would have to accept the decision of the others.

Of the major issues of the peace settlement—boundaries, colonies, disarmament, and reparations—the drawing of territorial
boundaries was by far the most important. Yugoslavia, France,
and Austria demanded frontier revisions; the first two countries
were among the victors, the last was classified as a "liberated," not
an "enemy," state, although it had been absorbed by Germany
in 1938.

Before the end of the war, both the royal Yugoslav government-
in-exile and Marshal Tito's Communist partisan regime inside
Yugoslavia had publicly demanded all of the Italian region of
Venezia Giulia, including its key city of Trieste. In May, 1945,
Tito's partisans had overrun Trieste, occupying the city and most
of the surrounding region. Italy pleaded with the Allies to get the
Yugoslavs out, and under considerable British and American pressure, supplemented finally by Soviet advice, Tito reluctantly withdrew. A provisional occupation boundary, called the Morgan line,
was negotiated with Tito in June, 1945, leaving the cities of
Trieste and Pola (Pulj) in the hands of Anglo-American forces,
but most of the Istrian Peninsula under Yugoslav control.

All the Italian parties were behind the government's position.
Even the Communists, who had temporized for some time, publicly asserted the *Italianità* of Trieste in May, 1945. Count Sforza,
the most authoritative Italian foreign-affairs spokesman, had delivered a speech in August, 1944, that called for a return to the
1920 boundary, which he himself had negotiated, with Fiume
(Rieka) to be made a free city. By the summer of 1945, this position was no longer tenable. Foreign Minister Alcide De Gasperi
suggested in a letter to Secretary of State James F. Byrnes that the
Wilson line of 1919 would be an equitable boundary. He reaf-
firmed this position the following month in an address to the

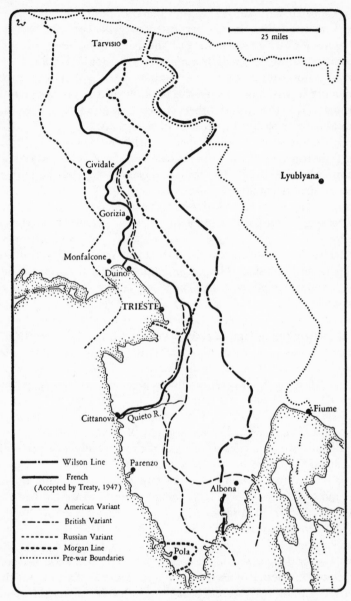

25 miles

Tarvisio

Cividale

Lyublyana

Gorizia

Monfalcone

Duino

TRIESTE

Fiume

Cittanova

Quieto R.

Parenzo

Albona

Pola

Wilson Line
French
(Accepted by Treaty, 1947)
American Variant
British Variant
Russian Variant
Morgan Line
Pre-war Boundaries

VENEZIA GIULIA–BOUNDARY PROPOSALS

Council of Foreign Ministers.[4] The Yugoslavs, with Russian backing, were demanding the entire region, claiming that it was solidly inhabited by Slavs except for enclaves of Italians in the coastal towns.

The dispute dragged on and the Foreign Ministers finally decided to send a four-power committee of experts to establish a boundary. The experts were instructed to draw a frontier relying mainly on the ethnic principle which would take into account local geographic and economic factors. The goal was to minimize the minorities that would inevitably remain. The committee, however, returned in April, 1946, with four different boundaries. None of them recommended the Wilson line, although the American boundary came closest to it. The Russian expert ignored instructions and drew a line equivalent to the extreme Yugoslav claim. The British and French lines lay in between. In May, 1946, the Italians retreated to the American line.

The Americans and the British retreated to the French line over vigorous Italian protests, and in June, 1946, after the French suggested setting up the Free Territory of Trieste as an additional concession, the Russians agreed. The French line would be the eastern boundary of the Free Territory. Italy's protests went in vain: the settlement remained unsatisfactory, leaving major headaches for the future. The Free Territory was subdivided into two zones, A and B, with Zone A, including the city itself, under Anglo-American occupation and Zone B under Yugoslav occupation. The occupation was supposed to be temporary, to last only until the United Nations Security Council could appoint a neutral governor for the Free Territory. The Council could not agree on a governor, however, so the occupation dragged on for years.

The Trieste settlement was Italy's biggest blow. Areas that were indisputably Italian were torn away. It left bitterness and rancor inside the country, for Trieste was the one foreign-policy issue

---

[4] The text of De Gasperi's letter to Brynes is printed in *United States and Italy, 1936–1946* ("Publications of the United States Department of State," No. 2669 [Washington, D.C.: Government Printing Office, 1946]), pp. 166–67; De Gasperi's statement to the Council of Foreign Ministers is reprinted in *Memorandum on the Italo-Yugoslav Frontier* (Rome: Ministry of Foreign Affairs, 1946), pp. 2–3.

really felt by large numbers of Italians, even those in small villages and remote rural areas. It became a weapon with which right-wing nationalist forces inside Italy attacked the Italian Government for its weakness, and the British and American governments for having sold out Italy's interests. And even though Russia forced the concessions that culminated in the Anglo-American retreat to the French line, the Italian Communists did not suffer. They pointed out that Russia knew how to fight for its friends and that if Italy were more friendly, it would benefit too.[5]

On February 28, 1945, Italy and France resumed diplomatic relations. At that time the French asserted they had no claims on Italian metropolitan territory. Nevertheless, in April, 1945, French troops crossed the Alps to occupy adjacent territory in Piedmont and the Val d'Aosta. French agents tried to win the French-speaking *Valdostani* over to the idea of annexation. Allied agreements made with Charles de Gaulle had permitted a restricted French occupation of Italian soil, but de Gaulle's troops had gone beyond the agreed limits. The British and the Americans could not permit a French occupation at the same time they were trying to push the Yugoslavs out of Trieste. De Gaulle was ordered to pull his troops out. He hesitated and President Truman threatened to cut off all supplies to France. De Gaulle retreated and by July, 1945, French troops were behind the frontier. The Italian Government immediately announced that linguistic autonomy would be granted to the Val d'Aosta (reversing Mussolini's policy of forcible Italianization) and that French-language schools would be instituted along with a limited degree of administrative autonomy.

At the Council of Foreign Ministers, the French gave up claims to the Aosta Valley and to stretches of the Italian Riviera, but demanded minor boundary rectifications in the Maritime Alps. The size of the territory demanded was not large, and the number of inhabitants was quite small, but several of the desired valleys were of both strategic and economic importance.

The Italian position was that the boundary should follow the

---

[5] During this period, bilateral negotiations between Italy and Yugoslavia were conducted with the aim of reaching a settlement, but they also failed.

watershed of the Alps. The French demands, if realized, would bring France down onto the Italian side of the mountains and eliminate natural barriers to invasion routes into the Po Valley. Also on French soil would be some major hydroelectric-power installations that provided substantial portions of electric current to such cities as Genoa and Turin.

Italian objections were overridden and the peace conference approved the French requests except for a few very minor territorial rectifications. Provisions were inserted in the final document to protect Italian rights to the water and electric power from the detached territories. In later years, the French Government was willing to return some of the seized territories, but the French Assembly refused to ratify a bill for their return.

Even more vexatious than the issue of French territorial claims was the clash over the South Tyrol. In 1919, at the end of World War I, Italy had acquired both the province of Trento and the province of Bolzano (South Tyrol) from Austria. The population of Trento was overwhelmingly Italian; the South Tyrol was predominately Austro-German in culture and language and less heavily populated. During the Fascist period, Mussolini had made efforts to Italianize the South Tyrol by importing Italian industries and labor into the province and by attempting to impose Italian language and culture on the indigenous inhabitants.

The South Tyrolese were rabid German nationalists and were later Nazi in orientation. But Hitler abandoned them in 1939 when he and Mussolini agreed that since the South Tyrol was "forever Italian," a plebiscite should be held among the German-speaking inhabitants that would require them to opt for Italy or the Third Reich. (It must be remembered that Austria had already been absorbed by Germany.) Those choosing Italy would accept Italianization; the others would be transferred to the Reich. Of the 266,885 persons who voted in the plebiscite the following year, 185,365—or almost 70 per cent—opted for transfer to Nazi Germany. The outbreak of the war slowed down the transfer of population, so that only 77,772 people had left the South Tyrol by 1943. The Italian surrender in September, 1943, led to a *de facto* German annexation of the area and the return of many of the optants.[6] Because of their bilingual capacities, the South Tyrolese Germans played a crucial part in the German rule over northern Italy in the next twenty months, earning the bitter hatred of partisans and other inhabitants alike. Austria, also, was unpopular, because ten of the Nazi divisions operating in Italy after September, 1943, were composed primarily of Austrians.

The main Italian claim to the South Tyrol was that Italy had fought toward the end of the war on the side of the victors, while Austria had stayed with Germany all the way. Even before November, 1945, when Austria put forth its claim for the return of the South Tyrol, the Italian position had been fully developed. The fundamental point was to play down the ethnic issue, which was the major Italian thesis in the Trieste dispute, and to substitute other arguments—strategic, economic, and geographic—as the controlling bases for debate. Therefore, at the same time the Italian Government thought the loss of some 350,000 Italians in the provinces of Trieste and Istria an outrage, it considered the inclusion of some 200,000 German-speaking inhabitants in Italy "a matter of minor importance."[7]

The Allies accepted these Italian arguments (not necessarily because of their compelling logic) and in March, 1946, the foreign ministers' deputies decided that the ethnic claim would not be controlling in the South Tyrol dispute. The Austrian Government then asked for border rectifications, but later these were also denied. The 1919 boundary was left untouched—the major Italian victory of the peace conference—although about two-thirds of the population of the South Tyrol was, and still is, ethnically German.

On September 5, 1946, the Italian and Austrian governments entered into an agreement concerning guarantees for the administrative, cultural, and economic autonomy of the South Tyrol.

---

[6] After September, 1943, the Germans also conducted a *de facto* annexation of Trieste and the Istrian Peninsula. There are indications that a German victory in the war would have led to the Italian loss of Venezia Giulia and the South Tyrol despite the fact that Hitler and Mussolini were allies.

[7] "Memorandum on the Question of the Italian Northern Frontier," in *The Italo-Austrian Frontier*, Vol. I: *Official Statements and Other Documents Presented to the Council of Foreign Ministers (February–June, 1946), with Foreword* (Rome: Ministero degli Affari Esteri, 1946), pp. 2–4.

Known as the De Gasperi–Gruber Accord, it became Annex IV of the final peace treaty. Ambiguities in the language, put in to help Foreign Minister Karl Gruber make it acceptable to the Austrians, however reluctantly, as well as disputes over its subsequent application by Italy, would lead to a revival of conflict in the area in the 1950's and 1960's. The conflict would be accompanied by acts of terrorism on the part of South Tyrolese extremists and severe repression on the part of Italian authorities.

The Italian positions on Trieste and the South Tyrol were completely contradictory. The arguments used in one case refuted the arguments used in the other. Aware of this, the Italians did not call for a plebiscite as a suitable means of resolving conflicting territorial claims in Venezia Giulia until after the South Tyrol agreement had been reached, in order to avoid justifying the Austrian request for a plebiscite in the province of Bolzano. The logic of Italy's position lay in its ambition to hold fast to all it could reasonably save. It was more powerful vis-à-vis Austria than a vis-à-vis France or Yugoslavia, so the Austrians lost their claim. From the Allied point of view, the South Tyrol was a compensation for some of the losses Italy was required to suffer elsewhere.

In the colonies, Italy's losses were practically total. All of its colonies were taken away from it. This, however, may have been the best thing that happened to Italy in the postwar period. When the agonies of the liquidation of the French, British, and other overseas empires are recalled, the Italians may be considered fortunate to have escaped them. In 1945 and 1946, however, no Italian government (and no other colonial power) saw the situation in this light. Although Italy's colonies had been an economic and financial drain on the limited resources of a chronically poor country, all efforts were made to hang on to them.

The Italians made a distinction between those colonies acquired before Fascism and those acquired by Mussolini. As early as August, 1944, Count Sforza had announced that Italy renounced the Fascist acquisitions of Albania and Ethiopia and would give the Dodecanese to Greece. He stated that Italy would claim the pre-Fascist colonies, however, unless other colonial

powers turned over their colonies to an international organization. One year later, August, 1945, in his letter to United States
Secretary of State James Byrnes, Foreign Minister Alcide De-
Gasperi again claimed the pre-Fascist colonies of Eritrea, Italian
Somaliland, and Libya, preferably under direct Italian sovereignty, but at least as trusteeships. He was ready to grant England strategic bases in Libya and to rectify the Eritrean frontier
to provide Ethiopia with an outlet to the sea. His main argument
was that the colonies were necessary to relieve Italy's surplus
population, although they had failed miserably in this function
in preceding decades.

England was unalterably opposed to the return of the colonies
to Italy and had committed itself on this issue to various African
chiefs, especially in Libya. Nor were the Russians and the Americans much more favorably disposed. Only France was on Italy's
side, for fear of the repercussions on its own colonial system. The
victorious Allies could not agree on how to dispose of the colonies,
however, and the peace treaty took them away from Italy without
a definitive solution. The United Nations General Assembly
wrestled with the problem for several years. During those years,
Italy pleaded, negotiated, and bargained in order to regain control of them and finally a piecemeal solution was reached. The
U.N. turned Eritrea over to Ethiopia, Libya was given independence under British sponsorship, advice, and assistance, and
Somaliland was granted to Italy as a United Nations trusteeship
for ten years. For that decade, Italy continued to pour some of
its limited resources into Somaliland's desolate and economically
backward land, and in return received only trouble, scandal, and
inferior bananas.[8]

The long-drawn-out colonial struggle, to a considerable extent
a question of *amour-propre* for Italy, had negative repercussions
on domestic Italian politics. Like the Trieste boundary settlement, it provided opportunities for nationalist, monarchist, and
neo-Fascist attacks on the government and on Italy's Western

---

[8] The Italian banana monopoly later became the object of Italian judicial
and parliamentary investigation for corruption and was abolished on January
1, 1965.

allies. It was the shortsightedness of the Italian Government in pursuing an unworthy and futile cause which opened it to these attacks. Even the Communists were able to parade as patriotic Italian nationalists once Russia abandoned its efforts to get a trusteeship for Tripolitania (part of Italian Libya). Unlike Trieste, however, there was little evidence that the colonies had any deeply felt meaning for the great masses of the peasants and workers, the inhabitants of rural and small-town Italy. The hullabaloo in Italy was due mainly to the exploitation of the issue by former colonial officials, political opportunists, and sufferers from nostalgia.

The commitment of the United States and Britain in September, 1944, to the postwar rehabilitation of the Italian economy logically implied the renunciation of demands for reparation as a part of the peace settlement. In 1945, the United States, Britain, and France formally renounced reparation claims. The Soviet Union and other, smaller victims of Fascist aggression—Yugoslavia, Greece, Albania, and Ethiopia—persisted, however, in demanding economic reparation for damage suffered.

Italy did not argue against the principle of reparation payments, for it had its own claims against Germany for damage sustained after September, 1943. It argued that its economic contribution to the war against the Nazis, and the economic damage suffered after September, 1943, valued at $5,543,900,000 and $13,462,200,000 respectively, should be accepted as a more than adequate economic contribution to the war. It pointed out, in addition, that a reconstruction and rehabilitation program could only be hindered by a requirement to make financial reparation, whether in money or goods and services.

Neither American pressure nor Italian arguments moved the Soviet Union and the other claimants. The final peace treaty imposed a bill on Italy of $5 million to Albania, $25 million to Ethiopia, $100 million to Russia, $105 million to Greece, and $125 million to Yugoslavia. The U.S.S.R. was allowed to seize Italian assets in Hungary, Bulgaria, and Rumania as part payment. (Italy would have lost these assets in any case, because of the nationalization policies followed by Eastern European countries in the postwar period.) In effect, the United States paid the Italian reparation bills through its postwar loans, grants, and gifts to Italy.

In addition to the reparation payments, the peace treaty granted the victors the right to confiscate Italian property in their own countries as compensation for the claims of their private citizens for property damage and unpaid debts. Britain, the United States, and France did not confiscate the property of Italian nationals permanently resident on their own soil. They waived the right to confiscate foreign assets of Italian individuals and firms resident in Italy by accepting flat payments from the Italian Government: $5 million to the United States and 15 billion lire to France, while Britain settled for the payment of debts owed by Italians to private persons and firms in the United Kingdom. The Italian Government paid the debts and then had the difficult job of collecting from the Italian debtors. As a result, all Italian assets abroad were saved, except those in Ethiopia and Eastern Europe.

Italy's claim to reparation from Germany was rejected. The Germans had seized Italy's entire gold reserve, and though it was recaptured by the Allies intact, Italy was forced to accept, instead of full restitution, a proportionate share of the total gold stolen by the Nazis from all occupied countries.

On the whole, the financial burden imposed on Italy by the peace settlement was moderate, and as mentioned above, it was largely borne by the United States. It is true that Italy indirectly made a substantial economic contribution to the Allies by bearing the burden of domestic inflation caused partly by the expenditure of Allied military lire inside the country. Again, the United States gave Italy a credit for some of these lire spent by American servicemen on Italian soil during the war.

The last major issue of the peace settlement was disarmament and demilitarization. The Allies were in unanimous agreement that the size of the postwar Italian armed forces was to be strictly limited to the minimum required for the local defense of the boundaries and for maintenance of domestic law and order.

Italian claims as to the number of the armed manpower necessary for effective defense were based on the general principles that a nation's power had to be relative to the power of its neighbors and that, therefore, no final figures could ever be established as to the "adequate" number of a country's armed manpower. Italy presented some provisional figures on the proposed size of its Army and asked to be permitted to retain whatever of its Navy and Air Force it had left. The Navy was a crucial issue: next to the boundary questions, it touched the sentiments and hearts of the Italian people. The Italians argued correctly that the remnants of the Navy had not surrendered in September, 1943, but had passed to the side of the Allies with flags flying: the Navy was not available for disposal.

These Italian arguments carried no weight. The major Allies had already agreed at the Teheran Conference to take the Italian Navy; and the peace treaty left Italy with two old battleships, four cruisers, four destroyers, sixteen torpedo boats, and twenty corvettes. Italy was forbidden in the future to build or buy battleships, aircraft carriers, and submarines. Personnel was to be limited to 25,000 men. The Army was limited to 250,000 men, including the Carabinieri (part of the domestic police force in peacetime). The Air Force was limited to 200 combat and 150 noncombat planes, bombers were prohibited, and personnel was limited to 25,000. Italy was required to destroy all fixed fortifications within twenty kilometers of its boundaries with France and Yugoslavia, and was prohibited from constructing new ones that could fire on these nations or their territorial waters. With the boundary changes that have already been mentioned, which eliminated the natural defenses of the mountain barriers, Italy was left vulnerable to invasion by land.

In addition, Italy was prohibited from constructing military installations on the Apulian coast, opposite Yugoslavia, Albania, and Greece. The coasts of Sicily and Sardinia were to be unfortified, and smaller islands, such as the base of Pantelleria, were to be demilitarized. Thus Italy was left vulnerable to invasion by sea. Since the British had been dominant in the Mediterranean in the past, and erroneously expected to be dominant in the future, the demilitarization of the Italian coastlines was conceived as an integral part of British postwar strategy for the reassertion of a pre-eminent role in that part of the world.

The Americans and the British later returned their share of the Italian fleet to Italy for scrap, as they had surplus vessels of their own. The gesture was received gratefully. France returned some of its spoils, but kept its best acquisitions. Greece, Yugoslavia and Russia returned nothing.

De Gasperi did not hesitate to point out to the peace conference that in its efforts to guard against future Italian aggression, it was leaving Italy defenseless. But the whole postwar balance of power was so changed that Italy could no longer be considered even nominally a first-class power. Any probable future aggression by Italy would most likely be part of a larger struggle; and the same could be said for any future attack against it.

For Italy was dependent on others for its security. American troops remained in occupation until the peace treaty was ratified by the victors in the autumn of 1947. And at the time of their withdrawal, President Truman publicly warned that the United States would not be indifferent to any threat to Italy's security. Two years later, Italy was a member of the North Atlantic Treaty Organization. Its allies then attempted to get the Soviet Union to agree to a revision of the clauses on armament, but the Russians demanded the exodus of Italy from NATO as their price for consenting to revision. At the peak of the Cold War, the Italian Government claimed that the Soviet refusal to approve Italy's admission to the United Nations justified Italy's escape from the obligations of the peace treaty. Thus, on February 8, 1952, Italy announced its intention to rearm beyond the treaty limitations. It was so economically and politically weak, however, that its rearmament was dependent on external—primarily American—military aid, which had already begun and which was continuing a decade and a half later.

The peace treaty was not finally signed until February 10, 1947, and not ratified until the autumn of that year. During the two years that had elapsed between the end of hostilities and the completion of the treaty, Italy's international position had changed drastically. In September, 1945, in his first appearance before the Council of Foreign Ministers, De Gasperi had entered a hall filled with hostility and rancor. Only Secretary of State Byrnes demonstrated any kindliness toward him. Memories of Fascist aggression were still sharp among Europeans and Africans. By 1947, the emerging Cold War and the internal Italian vulnerability to the extreme left had changed the international picture. Although England was still wavering between a policy of keeping Italy weak and therefore less of a threat in the Mediterranean and a policy of bolstering Italy the better to enable it to resist internal and external pressures, France and the United States were firmly engaged in rebuilding Italy's international position. France was negotiating with Italy for an alliance and a customs union. The United States, with French help, was putting pressure on a reluctant England to accept Italian membership in the European Recovery Program (the Marshall Plan).

Italy had remained officially neutral in the Cold War for the duration of the peace-treaty negotiations. It could not afford to antagonize any of the powerful victors. Unofficially, of course, most Italians sympathized with the West (except for the extreme left), although there was considerable resentment at the hard British position. And Italy was fundamentally dependent on American good will.

The peace treaty was accepted with considerable bitterness by Italian anti-Fascists. They felt that they had staked not only their personal futures but, more importantly, the political future of the country on collaboration with the Allies, who had then let them down. When the treaty was presented to the Italian Government for signature, there were voices raised against signing it. The United States, however, warned the government that economic aid would be cut off if it did not sign. When it was presented to the Constituent Assembly for ratification, distinguished anti-Fascists—such as the philosopher Benedetto Croce and the pre-Fascist Prime Minister Francesco S. Nitti—denounced its harshness. But Italy had no choice. It ratified, protesting that the treaty was unduly harsh, that it did not take into account the anti-Fascist resurgence of the Italian people or their contributions to the final struggle against Germany. It ratified, to enable it to be present at the Marshall Plan Conference of July, 1947, to bring an end to the occupation, to finish off a dark chapter in the history of modern Italy.

3

Political and Economic Revival

Political parties suppressed by Fascism had been gradually re-forming, and new ones developing, even before the overthrow of Mussolini. Although they were still illegal in the summer of 1943, the Badoglio government of technicians had made no effort to suppress them. On the contrary, it had maintained informal contacts with the principal party leaders and had released political prisoners of Fascism. After September 8, 1943, the parties in central and northern Italy were forced again into the underground. Behind the Anglo-American lines in the south, however, although still technically illegal, they were actually in open operation and engaged in recruitment and discussions, held congresses, and formed ranks. The top leadership was composed of older men who had been active in the pre-Fascist period. Beneath them was a group of younger men, products of the Italian universities of the 1930's and 1940's who threw themselves into the struggle to build a new and better world.

Although no elections were held, it was apparent, even in this early period, that the principal postwar parties would be the Christian Democratic, Communist, and Socialist parties. The Action Party had a brilliant intellectual leadership, but no mass base. The Liberal Party mainly comprised the old notables of pre-Fascist days. The southern Liberals in particular had long since been cut off from contact with the emerging world of workers and peasants who were indifferent to upper-class nineteenth-century paternal benevolence. Thus the party, again especially in the south, became an elite party representing the powerful landowners and the respectable practitioners of the free professions.

The Socialist and Popular parties had been the two largest parties in the final years of the pre-Fascist period. Fascism hurt the Socialists badly; they had neither the skills and techniques to survive in the underground nor the protection of the Vatican. As the earliest of the mass parties, however, they had a long, solid tradition on which they could hope to build in the post-Fascist future.

The Communist Party, founded in 1921 as an extreme left-wing splinter of the Socialists, had only a few years to develop before the Fascists outlawed all competing parties. It was able to survive by going underground, nevertheless, and in spite of some splits among its leaders inside Italy and in exile, it emerged in 1943 with a small but very tight base in the industrial cities and in the countryside of central and northern Italy. From about 10,000 adherents in 1943, it grew to a membership of 400,000 card-carrying Communists by the beginning of 1945. Skillfully organized and adequately financed, the Party rapidly established an elaborate system of sections and cells throughout the whole country. Within a few years, this communications network made the Italian Communist Party the largest Communist Party in the Western world.

The Christian Democratic Party emerged after the fall of Fascism as the successor to the old Popular Party, which had been founded in 1919 by the Sicilian priest Don Luigi Sturzo. During the 1920's, the Vatican had sacrificed both the party and Don Sturzo in order to come to terms with Fascism. Some of the leaders, Don Sturzo included, went into exile. Others found asylum and protection in the Vatican, where Alcide De Gasperi, for example, worked as a librarian. A small core of Christian Democrats continued to exist in Italy under Church patronage, in case the situation changed and there might be a role for them once more. A younger group found opportunities for organizational experience in the youth and adult groups of the Italian Catholic Action Society, a lay organization under Church direction. When Fascism fell, these men were ready to step into the political world, and would, in fact, furnish a large share of the party's cadres.

Even in its early years, the Popular Party had been a collection of disparate groups with widely differing orientations. Only a common confessional bond and Catholic Church discipline held them together, and schism even then was potentially present. But under Don Sturzo's direction, the Popular Party had a predominantly progressive and reformist policy and had succeeded in bringing large numbers of Catholic rural and village men into the Italian political arena, from which they had been excluded in the past both by the Liberals' upper-class disdain and by Vatican prohibitions. It is true that, like the Socialists, the Populists brought their masses into the political arena only as voters, not as activists, for politics then, as now, was a game for a "ruling class" that manipulated the large masses.

After 1943, the Christian Democrats retained this disparate agglomeration of supporters who ranged from left to right, from radical workers to conservative landowners and industrialists. The conservative elements, however, were far more prominent, for the fear of postwar left-wing extremism had led the formerly laic and liberal middle and upper classes to turn to the Church and to the party identified with it as their best defense. The Church, like the monarchy, symbolized authority, order, and stability, all seriously menaced; but the Church, unlike the monarchy, was not too incriminated in the Fascist catastrophe, and was, moreover, in a far better position to survive it. So the Christian Democratic Party had not only a large popular base demanding postwar progress and substantial reform but also important lay and clerical influences, fearful of radical innovation and concerned mainly with stabilization and restoration. In addition the party was weak in organization and communications; it would have to depend on the network of Catholic parishes spread throughout Italy to reach its electorate, and upon the efforts of the parish priests and diocesan bishops to mobilize money, activists, and voters.

A simplified description of Italy at the end of hostilities would therefore seem to be that of a country caught in a struggle between the forces of revolution and those of restoration. In May and June of 1945, superficial appearances indicated the victory of revolution. The liberation of the Po Valley unleashed upon the country the "wind from the north," and the wind appeared to be blowing from the far left. The danger of direct revolutionary action having been minimized, the question became: Could the forces of revolution gain their ends through party and political maneuvers and economic seizures?

Partisan bands had taken over many of the factories and plants in the north, Italy's major industrial area. In numerous cases the management was expelled on grounds of collaboration with the Nazi occupiers and Il Duce's Fascist Social Republic. Factory councils were set up to operate the firms. This was a *de facto* purge, but one conducted with relative restraint. Managers and owners with clean records were members of the councils and active in plant administration. Nevertheless, the threat to private property and capitalistic ownership was evident.[1]

The threat was further magnified by the financial purge attempted by the central government to punish those who had profited from Fascism. All of Italian big business was potentially vulnerable, for large firms had been a principal beneficiary of Fascist economic policy. In addition, in November, 1945, the government drew up a new economic plan that called for a capital levy and a discriminatory allocation of raw materials, both of which favored small firms rather than the large trusts. The purge, the levy, and the allocations were part of a twofold objective: economic reconstruction and the redistribution of wealth.

Resistance to these economic operations was both internal and external. Right-wing Liberals and conservative Christian Democrats considered them an attack on the economic structure of society. Allied occupation officials (the Allied Military Government was still in control in the north) considered them in the same light, and also as a substantial hindrance to the rehabilitation of the economy. The Economic Section of the Allied Commission threatened to withhold coal and other raw materials unless they were used efficiently. The argument of efficiency was used to break the factory councils and restore former managers. Allied

---

[1] Riccardo Levi, "L'azione economica e sociale dei CLN dell' alta Italia," *Il Ponte,* November–December, 1947, pp. 994–1000.

officers protested against the capital levy and the allocation policy that were aimed at redistributing the wealth.[2]

The government in power at the time was led by Ferruccio Parri, Action Party leader and partisan hero. He had become Prime Minister in June, 1945, not because of his party's strength, but as a compromise between the competing candidacies of Alcide De Gasperi and Pietro Nenni, leader of the Socialist Party. Nenni represented the wing of his party advocating close unity of action with the Communists.[3] He believed that divisions among the left had been responsible for the past victories of Fascism and Nazism and that the workers could not afford to be divided in the future if the triumph of reaction were to be prevented. This outlook, however sincere, would make the Socialists vulnerable to Communist strategy. Naturally, neither the Allies nor the conservative forces in the Italian Government could look to a Nenni victory with equanimity. The Christian Democrats imposed an effective veto, but failing to get the prime ministry for their own candidate, they consented to the Parri compromise. All six parties of the Committee of National Liberation participated in Parri's cabinet.

The Allied Military Government blocked the CLN committees in northern Italy from taking over provincial and communal governments. Local officials were appointed by Allied Commissioners. Many of them were CLN leaders, but their authority came from the Allied occupation officials, not from the CLN committees. Thus the northern attempt for a degree of autonomy and independence from domination by Rome was thwarted.

The negotiations to form the Parri cabinet had taken so long that the spirit of revolt attendant on the liberation of the north was quickly diluted. In the autumn of 1945, a miasma of doubt, hesitation, and disillusion settled over the country. The conferences for a peace settlement were going badly, and Italian political leaders were being made aware of what was in store for the country. Economic reconstruction, dependent on always insufficient external supplies, was limping along. Inflation was rampant.

---

[2] *Economist* (London), November 24, 1945, p. 752.

[3] The party's full name was the Italian Socialist Party of Proletarian Unity.

Food was in short supply. The parties and the government seemed to be bogged down in conflicts and maneuvers which had little relevance to the needs of the vast majority of the population. Law and order were difficult to enforce. Fear and hostility were widespread.

In this atmosphere, it was not surprising that there emerged political movements of a turbid and negative nature. Separatist organizations had begun to operate in Sardinia and especially Sicily after the liberation of these two major islands of Italy. Conservative and reactionary forces feared that radicals would take over the central government on the mainland. The more substantial landowners believed they could better protect their holdings by separation. Although in 1944 the Americans and British had both repudiated the separatists' claims of Allied support,[4] the agitation nevertheless continued. Its peak was reached in the immediate postwar period.

Another development of concern was the ambiguous movement called Uomo Qualunque (Any Man), led by the journalist Guglielmo Giannini. It was a party that attacked all parties, a reaction against the complications, hesitations, compromises, and problems of a struggling party system. Its point of view was, "Down with politicians—Down with talk," and it was able to find support in the difficult postwar years when everything appeared to be going wrong.

A major issue to be resolved was the disposition of the monarchy, or, as the Italians called it, the Institutional Question. The truce established in April, 1944, had provided that King Victor Emmanuel III would nominate his son, Humbert, as Lieutenant-General of the Realm, retiring then to private life, and that at the end of the war, the people would have the opportunity to decide their form of political organization, monarchy or republic. When the Allies occupied Rome in 1944, the American Government had insisted that Victor Emmanuel live up to his pledge before returning to his capital. Humbert had, in subsequent months,

---

4 Alleged British complicity with the separatist movements was based on an assumption that the British policy of keeping Italy weak and of dominating the Mediterranean would be advanced through creating new states tied to England by treaties and, perhaps, the granting of bases.

played a formally correct role, but had tried to use the various crises of the CLN to insert conservative forces and personages outside that group into the political arena.

The end of the war had brought a tremendous surge of republican enthusiasm, especially in the north, where the King's flight from Rome was bitterly remembered. As time passed, however, and all the troubles and difficulties had wrought their influence on the evolution of opinion, monarchist sentiment revived. The parties committed to republicanism, mainly on the left, wanted to settle the issue as quickly as possible, while the public mood was still in their favor. The monarchists, conversely, wanted to delay the decision, hoping that the passage of time would work to their benefit and that the influence of authority and tradition would increase as the shock of the war receded into the background.

Within the cabinet, the Christian Democratic and Liberal leaders represented divided parties, containing both monarchists and republicans in their ranks. The Action, Socialist, and Communist parties were decisively republican, although the Communists would have had no hesitation in supporting a king, as long as he might be useful to their game. During the war, in fact, Palmiro Togliatti had backed both Victor Emmanuel and Marshal Badoglio. Prime Minister Parri's drive to get a constituent assembly elected to settle the issue and to draft a new constitution, in combination with the economic plan of November, 1945, led to an open attack on the government by conservative Liberal leaders of the south. The Liberal cabinet ministers resigned. Although northern Liberals came to Parri's defense, the Christian Democrats saw their opportunity to get the prime ministry they had wanted the previous May. Then the Communists, interested in making a deal with the Catholics (both the Church and the Christian Democratic Party), shifted their support. Parri's government fell.

In December, 1945, a new six-party cabinet was formed with Alcide De Gasperi as Prime Minister. But the internal equilibrium of the cabinet had definitely shifted to the right. De Gasperi was not personally a conservative, but powerful pressures from within his own party and from the Church forced him to move in that direction. The British and the Americans, concerned over the power of the extreme left, were eager to reinforce his position. The day after the new cabinet was formed, they announced that at the end of December, the north—still under Allied Military Government supervision—would be turned back to the control of the Italian Government. Exclusion from the north had been one of the weaknesses in the position of De Gasperi's predecessor.

A few days later, De Gasperi announced that officials such as career prefects and police chiefs would replace CLN appointees as of January 1, 1946. At the same time, he proclaimed that the High Commission for Sanctions Against Fascism would be dissolved not later than March 31, 1946. Its functions would be turned over to the courts, and these were manned by judges who, for the most part, had been in office during the period of Fascism. The speed with which a restoration was accomplished was remarkable.

It must be remembered, however, that it was not a simple restoration of Fascism. If it is true that most of the business leaders, military and civil bureaucrats, professors, and journalists who regained or maintained their posts had worked or made careers under Fascism, it is also true that most of them were hardly dyed-in-the-wool Fascists. Many were half-Fascists, opportunists who held party cards to get ahead, or ordinary professionals who had to take out party cards in order to keep their positions. A number of them had always remained anti-Fascist; others saved their honor by their contributions to the overthrow of the regime and to the resistance movement. The catastrophe which Fascism brought on Italy shook many of them to the core. All of them, however, whether true converts or opportunists, could thank the Christian Democrats for saving them from a purge, and De Gasperi's party was the principal beneficiary of their gratitude.

Not the only one, however. The extreme left was also willing to accept former Fascists. As Minister of Justice, Togliatti would later be responsible for promoting a widespread amnesty for political prisoners, and the Communist Party would have some success in attracting ex-Fascists, intellectuals, and trade-unionists. Except for the top-ranking Fascist hierarchs, most of those who had made careers under Fascism found that there was still a future for them.

The new De Gasperi government also made dispositions to settle the problem of the monarchy. The decisions reflected the predominance of conservative influence. The Liberals had not been the only party working for delay. Leaders of both the Christian Democratic and the Labor Democratic parties (the Labor Democrats were nonexistent in the north and minimal in the south) played the monarchist game. They proposed that local elections be held first, to postpone settlement of the Institutional Question. Officially, the Allies were neutral, unofficially they supported the monarchy, the British more strongly than the Americans.[5] Administrative (communal and provincial) elections were scheduled for the spring of 1946, while the political election was postponed to June 2, 1946. The final choice was to be left to the people in the form of a referendum, to be held at the same time that the Constituent Assembly would be elected to draft a new constitution for either a republic or a monarchy. The left-wing parties had wanted the Constituent Assembly to make the decision. Women would be voting for the first time in the history of Italy, and the parties of the left feared the traditionalist outlook of Italian women, almost always attracted to the panoply and social snobbery of monarchy and aristocracy, and generally susceptible to the influence of the priests. And it was becoming ever more obvious that the Church was in large part promonarchist.

In another decision, the cabinet decreed that since the negotiations for a peace settlement were in progress, the Constituent Assembly would be restricted to drafting a constitution, elaborating election laws, and ratifying treaties. The left-wing parties had wanted the Assembly to function as a parliament also, establishing and supporting a government, passing laws, appropriating funds, and carrying on all the functions of a legislature. If such a body had a left-wing majority, major reforms could be enacted before a constitution came into effect. But in a multiparty cabinet not dependent on a parliamentary majority and ruling instead by

---

[5] De Gasperi claimed that the United States wanted the local elections to be held first to insure the establishment of democracy in the towns and villages.

decree, the conservatives could, in effect, defeat any attempt at reform.

The administrative election returns showed the Christian Democratic, Communist, and Socialist parties to be the three largest, as had been suspected all along. The last two were definitely republican. A poll of Christian Democratic Party cardholders in April, 1946, found 73 per cent to be republican. This poll represented a sample of party activists—the most politically conscious party workers—not the large masses of Christian Democratic voters who held no party cards, were rural, female, or generally apolitical. Nevertheless, the reviving monarchist forces were panic-stricken. They bombarded the Allied Commission with pleas to postpone the referendum. The Allied Commission refused: it had not set the date, the cabinet had. The monarchists persuaded King Victor Emmanuel III to abdicate on May 10, 1946, in favor of his son, who became Humbert II. The left charged that the Institutional truce that had established the Lieutenancy in 1944 was thus violated. It, too, appealed to the Allied Commission, which refused to intervene.

The Church was openly enlisted in the monarchist cause. The Vatican remained neutral, but the Italian clergy intervened, which they had a right to do as citizens, but not as priests. The issue was shifted from Monarchy *vs.* Republic to Monarchy *vs.* Communism, to Christianity *vs.* Communism. On June 1, 1946, the day before the referendum, Pope Pius XII himself addressed the Italian people. Without mentioning republic or monarchy, he called on the voters to choose between materialism and Christianity, between the supporters and the enemies of Christian civilization.[6] Given the context of the campaign, it would be difficult to misunderstand the plea.

The following day, the referendum and elections revealed the wide divisions in the population. The republic was endorsed by a ratio of 54 per cent to 46 per cent, 12,717,923 votes to 10,719,284, but the south had given its strong support to the monarchist cause, and only in the center and north had the republic gained substantial backing. For a few days, Humbert appeared ready to

---

[6] The English translation of the text appears in the *New York Times,* June 2, 1946.

plunge the country into a crisis of the first order by claiming
procedural irregularities in the voting. But he could get no support from the Allied Commission, and Prime Minister De Gasperi told him to go. The threat collapsed and Humbert, King for
three weeks, left for exile in Portugal. Thus the House of Savoy
paid for the errors committed by Victor Emmanuel III between
1922 and 1946.

The big monarchist vote did not mean that large masses of the
population were true legitimists. Any possibility of a restoration
of the House of Savoy quickly disappeared, and within a few
years, except to nostalgic members of the upper class and impres-
sionable middle-class women, the idea of a return to monarchy
seemed extremely remote. A monarchist party would run candidates for office with substantial success in Naples, and it would
even expand its voting base in the early 1950's, but the foundation of the party's strength was a combination of the corruption
of the poverty-stricken southern subproletariat and the retaliatory
bitterness against the center and north. It became, in part, another protest party, and to some degree a calculating seller of support to the Christian Democrats in return for patronage and
favors.

The election of members to the Constituent Assembly verified
the previous electoral indications. The Christian Democrats received 35.1 per cent of the vote, the Socialists 20.7 per cent, and the
Communists 18.9 per cent. None of the others received as much
as 10 per cent. The Liberals, who had a long pre-Fascist tradition
of rule, were reduced to 6.8 per cent of the vote. The Action
Party, which had played a noble role in the resistance, was again
shown to have no mass base. It had suffered a preliminary split in
February, and a short time after the election it dissolved, its
members entering other parties of the center and left. Uomo
Qualunque, fundamentally Fascist in tone, attained minor representation, receiving a small but visible 5.3 per cent of the vote.

Thus was the Institutional Question resolved. The trend toward restoration that was operative in Italian society had not
saved the monarchy. The Fascist inheritance was not so much
the political organization that would be re-created to glorify
Fascism's tarnished image as it was the mentality of autocratic

disdain for equalitarian principles, the contempt for parliamentary institutions, and the subservience to hierarchy that was still prevalent among large parts of the populace who did not vote for Uomo Qualunque. But these persistent attitudes derived from centuries-old traditions that even the liberalizing movements of the Risorgimento had failed to destroy.

The Constituent Assembly was racked by the varying pressures for economic and social reform and the strong resistance offered by powerful forces of moderation and conservation. The Constitution it produced, reflecting these countervailing forces, contained a mixture of Marxist, Catholic, and Liberal doctrines. It went into effect on January 1, 1948, with its bundle of compromises.[7] Obeisance was made to the principle of private property and, at the same time, to the principle of social and political controls over the economy. In effect, the document sanctioned the mixed economy actually in existence in the country. Along with articles guaranteeing the basic freedoms of thought, speech, and writing were articles permitting censorship. An article guaranteeing freedom of religion was juxtaposed with the famous Article 7, in which the Lateran Pacts of 1929 were, in effect, written into the Constitution. These pacts gave the Roman Catholic Church a privileged position in the life of the country, the state, and public education. Communist votes were crucial in getting Article 7 through the Constituent Assembly. While provisions were made for the maintenance of the centralized Italian state, other provisions aimed at creating a decentralized system of considerable regional autonomy.

Some of the articles of the Constitution were normative; they would become legally binding automatically. Others were programmatic, expressing hopes for the future. An example is Article 4, which proclaimed, in face of mass unemployment (that would continue for a decade), the right of all citizens to work. Many of the articles could be made effective only by implemental legislation, which was often long delayed. Some fundamental organs of the state that were created by the Constitution took years to become established. The Constitutional Court did not come into

---

[7] An English translation can be found in Norman Kogan, *The Government of Italy* (New York: Thomas Y. Crowell Co., 1962), pp. 188–215.

existence until 1955, and the Superior Council of the Judiciary not until 1958. In 1965, the regular regions had yet to be created,[8] and the legislation to establish procedures for holding referenda had yet to be passed.

That a constitution was drafted at all was due to the fact that the second and third largest groups in the Constituent Assembly, the Socialists and the Communists, took a relatively moderate position on crucial economic and religious issues. Neither of them pushed for a socialized economy. Pietro Nenni argued merely for social control of economic activity, to be exercised in a democratic, decentralized, and efficient manner. Togliatti's position was that "the Constitution is not a Socialist constitution but represents a transition period in which there exists a struggle for an economic regime in which there exist economic forces that tend to spill over into each other."[9] In spite of a powerful left in the Constituent Assembly, including part of the Christian Democratic Party itself, the Constitution was not even a very reformist document. What can be said is that it did not prevent reform in the future. A judgment of the work of the Constituent Assembly was expressed by the ideological leader of the left-wing Christian Democrats, Giuseppe Dossetti:[10] "In just a few short months, the propulsion toward reform was contained. And in a few years, progressively compressed up to the point of being practically wiped out for now."[11]

De Gasperi was primarily concerned with re-creating the political institutions of democracy, halting the drastic inflation, and reviving, not changing, the economy. This meant reviving existing businesses and economic organizations. Power over the key industries was concentrated in the hands of a few powerful individuals and groups, whether ownership was public or private. To accomplish revival, foreign help was indispensable, and this was mainly available from the United States, which itself had no

---

[8] Special regions to accommodate linguistic minorities or separatist movements were established early. Trentino–Alto Adige, Val d'Aosta, Sicily, and Sardinia.

[9] Quoted in Joseph LaPalombara, "The Politics of Economic Planning in Italy" (mimeographed essay, 1964), p. 25.

[10] He later abandoned politics for the priesthood.

[11] Quoted in LaPalombara, *op. cit.*, pp. 25–26.

fondness for left-wing economic doctrines. At the end of hostilities in Italy, a joint Allied-Italian program had been drafted. Relief supplies were provided by the Allied forces as a military responsibility while the war against Japan was still in progress. These were cut off after the Japanese surrender in September, 1945, but the American Government granted a substitute credit of $100 million for the acquisition of food and other relief supplies from the United States. Rehabilitation of the economy was to be borne initially by the Italian Government with dollars acquired from the lire spent by American troops in Italy, from emigrants' remittances, and from the small amount of exports Italy could send to the United States. The restoration of the communications and transportation systems had been partly achieved by the Allies during the war; afterward, Italy was able to get the Allied war surplus located on its soil, principally port machinery and railroad equipment. In June, 1945, Italy received permission to trade with Allied and neutral countries. This consent was meaningless until the end of the year, when the Allies gave up control of the north, the principal commercial and trading area.

Financial claims were settled between Italy and the British and American governments in the following years. In October, 1946, the United States granted a credit for the lire spent by American governmental agencies in the purchase of supplies in Italy, and waived charges for the supplies it had brought in during the war to keep the population alive. In January, 1947, De Gasperi came to America and arranged for a major loan. In April, 1947, the United Kingdom credited to Italy the value of lire spent by British forces in the peninsula after June 1, 1946, and of all services and supplies furnished by Italy to British forces after that date. Italy paid for British military equipment transferred to its forces and for the war surplus that the British had left in the course of their war operations. All in all, between 1943 and 1947, foreign aid totaled approximately $2 billion, of which almost $1.75 billion came from the United States.[12]

In spite of the weakness of the Italian Government and its dis-

---

12 Bruno Foa, *Monetary Reconstruction in Italy* (New York: King's Crown Press, 1949), p. 35.

integrated public administration, certain kinds of rehabilitation were handled very quickly and effectively. Within a few months after the end of hostilities, essential services had been restored throughout the country. Italian hard work and Allied equipment got roads, bridges, harbors, railroads, and utilities into operating order, and by the end of 1945, it was again possible to move by rail and road from one end of the peninsula to the other. Railroad rolling stock, trucks, and merchant marine were badly wrecked and would take much longer to replace. In contrast to transportation and communications facilities, the Italian industrial plant survived the war without extensive damage. The textile industries were among those to get back into full action most quickly, while heavier industries—dependent on large-scale imports of foreign coal and other raw materials—took longer.

Revival of the economy was left essentially to the operations of a system of laissez faire. This was congenial to the outlook of the postwar Minister of the Treasury Epicarmo Corbino, a Liberal in politics and economics. Nor did the left-wing Marxist parties make any serious demands for a reconstruction based on controls and allocations, such as the Labor government was executing in England. They limited their drive for drastic reforms to the verbal level. They used their positions in the government to gain some concessions, such as sliding wage scales designed to help workers keep up with the declining value of the lira. They obtained the freezing of industrial employment. This latter policy, which was in essence a way of hiding the real unemployment in the country, had the consequence of making production costs very high. Another high-cost factor—the obsolescence and expensiveness of many traditionally protected machine industries—further reduced Italy's competitiveness in foreign markets. In effect, agreement was reached on a practical, if not openly stated, compromise that gave Italy a period of relative social peace.

The laissez faire policy actually pursued, which imitated American postwar decontrol measures, aggravated an already drastic inflation. The lira had been declining throughout the war, and fell even faster after hostilities ended. No real attempts were made to reintroduce rationing except for some basic foodstuffs, such as bread, sugar, and olive oil. A black market was in widespread operation, and the rationing system was progressively slackened to the point of losing almost all effectiveness.

Fundamentally, the wartime and postwar inflation was due to the drastic drop in production. In 1945, industrial production was 23 per cent of the last prewar year, 1938. Agricultural production was dislocated. Fertilizers and machinery were lacking. The wheat harvest in 1945/46 was only half of the normal requirement, and extensive hoarding and maldistribution aggravated the shortage. The people in the cities suffered terribly. But inflation was due also to the huge amount of currency in circulation, much of it the lire of the Allied Military Government. Even though the United States eventually gave the Italians credit for American expenditures of such lire, the fundamental solution to inflation was, of course, to increase the supply of goods and services and to reduce the supply of money in circulation. "By the midsummer of 1947, the extreme shortages of coal and other key materials had, to a large extent, disappeared and all-around recovery of production was well on its way."[13] But the currency and credit crises were coming to a peak.

The official exchange rate of 100 lire to the dollar and 400 to the pound sterling, established at the end of the war, had long since become obsolete. In early 1946, the government was permitting exporters and importers to use a special rate of 225 lire to the dollar. While limited, this permission drove the official rate out of effective use by the end of 1946. Black-market rates for foreign currencies were even higher, because of demand by importers capable of making exorbitant profits and because of a capital flight caused by wealthy businessmen who were fearful of possible radical socialization at home. The government, however, declined to practice open devaluation for fear of psychological and political repercussions. In 1946, exporters were permitted to use 50 per cent of the foreign exchange they acquired on the free market instead of turning all their foreign currencies over to the exchange-control authorities. This further reduced the unofficial value of the lira. By early 1947, Italian prices had become so high on the international market that the remarkable recovery of the

---

[13] *Ibid.*, pp. 46–47.

export trade came to an end. Furthermore, the sterling crisis of August, 1947, tied up Italian sterling balances and depressed international purchasing power. Since a good share of Italian exports went to the sterling market, the repercussions in Italy were sizable.

The amount of money in circulation inside Italy (and probably also its turnover) had been increasing throughout the last half of 1946 and the first half of 1947, so that the revival of production did not bring about a decline in prices. On the contrary, prices kept rising rapidly, forcing another round of wage increases based on the cost-of-living sliding scales. While union labor in the large plants was thus able to protect its real income to a certain degree, the numerous artisans, workers in family-sized firms, and white-collar employees suffered enormous decreases in real income. The currency inflation was a consequence of extensive deficit financing by the government, inevitable considering the many burdens of relief and rehabilitation—of subsidies and social welfare payments—it had to bear. Its ability to collect taxes and elicit hoarded savings was limited. The Bank of Italy made banknotes available to the government to finance public operations. Commercial banks were advancing credit to the government (which owned the biggest of the banks already), and also to private business to cover payrolls expanded by inflationary wage increases and by reviving production. By the middle of 1947, coincident with the foreign-exchange crisis, the policy of laissez faire and the absence of effective controls brought fiscal difficulties to a head.

At this point, Professor Luigi Einaudi was made Deputy Prime Minister, as well as Minister of the Budget. An outstanding economist of the classical school, he became the "dictator" of the country's financial policies. His strategy was the powerful application of credit control. Reserve requirements of the Bank of Italy were raised. Bank loans were cut back ruthlessly. The stock market boom collapsed. Prices fell, and the value of the lira rose on foreign exchanges. Exchange controls were relaxed to permit more imports, further reducing prices. The announcement of the Marshall Plan in the summer of 1947 gave a psychological impetus toward promoting financial stability. In November, 1947, the official exchange rate was abolished as being meaningless. From that time, the rates in the market reflected a realistic evaluation of the lira's international position. The wild inflation was over.

The merits of Einaudi's tight credit policy were undoubted; its demerits should be mentioned also. It brought about a substantial recession. Unemployment increased somewhat, although the freeze on firings and layoffs was still in effect. Businessmen were caught with large payrolls and dropping prices; the government had to extend its areas of intervention to come to their rescue. Interest rates, always high in Italy, became even higher. The reconstruction of the Italian economy was brought to a halt and production actually declined. Production revived the following year, however, after the April, 1948, election victory of the Christian Democrats and the coming into effect of the European Recovery Program. By 1949, Italian productivity, as a whole, regained prewar levels and in some sectors rose far beyond them.

Since the major gainers were the large monopolies, which had flourished under Fascism, it can be argued that a more austere and equitable method of reviving the Italian economy could and should have been pursued, one that did not depend so much on the greed, speculation, and unabashed self-interest that the system of laissez faire permitted, one that would have been fairer to the masses of the population. By 1949, the economy was restored, but the national averages could only superficially conceal the vast discrepancies in wealth, the extreme poverty of large parts of the population being made all the more irksome by the lack of self-denial and the conspicuous consumption of the fortunate minority. New and old wealth was visibly on display; sharp operators had made killings in all kinds of markets—black, gray, and white. The Italian people had worked very hard, but only a small number of them had been substantial beneficiaries of the revival.

Yet it must be admitted that the cabinets of the period were too weak to have been able to manage successfully a system of priorities and controls. They had too little command over their own bureaucracy, to say nothing of their command over the people as a whole. And the people had too little faith in, or respect for, their own government to have collaborated with a rationing system. But these deficiencies and attitudes of the government and the people in the immediate postwar period were only extreme manifestations of more deep-rooted and fundamental problems. Even in "normal" times, both before and after the war, the governments of Italy have lacked the support and consensus of the people, who themselves have lacked the social solidarity necessary to accept common sacrifices for common goals.

The inflation during the war and immediate postwar periods had made a strong impact on the behavior of the masses and the political class. The "defense of the lira" became a political slogan to be reckoned with. Fear of even a slight inflation provided ammunition for political parties to use against reforms and reformers. In the early 1950's, new production was held back on the grounds that it would cause the price level to rise. The implementation of the Constitution was opposed with the argument that the economy could not afford the budget deficits that implementation might bring.

Since the Constituent Assembly was not a full-fledged legislative body, the cabinets continued to govern essentially by decree, as they had been doing ever since the Fascist period. The composition of the cabinet was changed, however, to reflect the results of the 1946 election. De Gasperi no longer felt obliged to include the representatives of parties that had practically ceased to exist, i.e., the Action Party and the Labor Democratic Party. The Liberals were unwilling to collaborate, so De Gasperi constructed a four-party government that included representatives from the three largest parties—Christian Democrats, Socialists, and Communists—and from the small Republican Party, which had obtained 4.4 per cent of the vote. The Republicans, the inheritors of the nineteenth-century traditions of the democratic radicals Giuseppe Mazzini and Carlo Cattaneo, had refused to participate in any government under a monarchy. With the establishment of a republic, this obstacle was removed and they entered the cabinet. Their most prestigious leader was Count Carlo Sforza, who would soon become Foreign Minister.

The Constituent Assembly met on June 25, 1946. Two days later it elected Enrico De Nicola, the eminent Neapolitan jurist and politician, as Provisional President of the Republic, thus replacing a displaced king with an outstanding monarchist, a man ready, nevertheless, to support the fledgling republic loyally. This was a wise move to conciliate the monarchist south. His presence as provisional head of the state was, in its limited way, an attempt to reunite a badly divided people.

The Italians were disunited in many ways, and the poverty-stricken masses were susceptible to Communist-Socialist manipulation. The frightened middle and upper classes thus demanded more police protection and the enforcement of order. They took out their resentments against the Christian Democrats (who were in a cabinet with Communists and Socialists) and the workers by voting for Uomo Qualunque in a number of local elections in the fall of 1946, especially in provinces from Rome southward.

The electoral losses to the extreme right made the Christian Democrats more restive about the government coalition with the extreme left. The growing intensity of the Cold War at the international level brought American pressures to bear against the continuation of the cabinet. (It has been claimed that an American condition for the loan granted to Italy during De Gasperi's visit to Washington in January, 1947, was the ejection of the Communists and Socialists from the government.) The same month, those Socialists who opposed continued unity of action with the Communists (they were led by Giuseppe Saragat) walked out of the Socialist Party.[14] The Socialist schism widened the gap between the Christian Democrats and their left-wing allies. The combination of pressures and circumstances made it only a question of a short time before a pretext was found that would topple the government. In May, 1947, the pretext was created and De Gasperi resigned as Prime Minister. In the negotiations for the succeeding cabinet, the Communists and Socialists were dropped.

While a substantial percentage of Socialist parliamentarians had followed Saragat in the schism, a far smaller percentage among the rank and file had done so. In subsequent months, other splits from Socialist ranks would occur, but it took several

---

14 After the split, the remaining Socialists resumed their historic name, the Italian Socialist Party.

years before the various schismatic groups could unite in what finally became the Italian Social Democratic Party.

Until May, 1947, the Communists and Socialists approved of the economic aid received from the West. Their attitude changed after their expulsion from the government. When in the summer of 1947 the Marshall Plan Conference was called to establish a European-wide organization for reconstruction, and after the Soviet Union rejected the American invitation to participate, the extreme left began a campaign against American aid, charging that it was a tool of American economic imperialism. Political strikes were called, in the autumn of 1947, to protest against the Marshall Plan and to prevent supplies from being delivered. The atmosphere of the country was one of intense excitement, but the strikes were only sporadic successes economically, and failures politically. For they showed that the Italian worker was reluctant to demonstrate over issues which were not directly concerned with immediate, tangible objectives, and that Communist manipulation of the working class and its organizations had its limitations. That the strikes were even occasionally successful was due to the Communist domination of the united labor movement. This domination was crucial to the Communist displacement of the Socialists after 1946 as the principal party of the extreme left. The splintering of the Socialists and the break between the Christian Democrats and the far left had, among the trade unions, repercussions that the political strikes called by the Communists served to magnify.

Politically oriented, Italian unionism before the advent of the Fascist regime had been divided among Socialist, Catholic, and Anarchist union federations (plus independents). Under Fascism, the party and the regime had taken control of the entire union movement. During the war, Allied officials in southern Italy encouraged the creation of one nonpolitical trade-union confederation, and in Rome—behind the German lines—Communist, Socialist, and Christian Democratic labor leaders were also thinking of unity. They had all paid a bitter price for the divisions of the working class in the past. On June 4, 1944, one day before the Allies entered the capital, a pact had been signed that created the

Italian General Confederation of Labor (CGIL). While claiming to be independent of all political parties, and proclaiming that workers of differing faiths and ideologies could collaborate for common goals, the CGIL established three secretaries-general (a premature troika?): Communist, Socialist, and Christian Democratic. From the very beginning, it was not, therefore, an apolitical organization. This tripartite division of offices was carried all the way down to the provincial and local levels.

The Communists rather quickly established their domination of the CGIL. They had organizational experience and personal leadership that the others could not match. The principal Communist trade-union leader, Giuseppe Di Vittorio, was undoubtedly an outstandingly dynamic and charismatic leader and a true son of the masses. By 1945, when the north was brought into the CGIL, the Communists were definitely the strongest group.

At the end of 1945, the Christian Democratic labor leaders were beginning to react against Communist exploitation of the CGIL for their own ends. As the strains in the political coalition increased, these were transferred to the trade-union movement. By 1947, the Christian Democrats were engaged in open polemics against the domination of the other two parties, and the Cold War was being increasingly injected into the Italian labor scene. With the calling of political strikes against the Marshall Plan, the conflicts were further increased. The CGIL was a member of the World Federation of Trade Unions, and its behavior was strongly influenced by this Soviet-controlled body. If it could control Italian labor effectively, the chances for the Marshall Plan to succeed in Italy would be considerably reduced. But these strikes turned into political failures. The final straw came, however, when the CGIL called a general strike to protest the attempted assassination of Palmiro Togliatti in July, 1948. Some of the rank-and-file Communist workers were under the mistaken impression that the Party was a revolutionary party, and in some central and northern provinces they actually seized control of local governments and key communications points. The Party quickly brought them under control and dampened whatever revolutionary fervor they might have had. As a reaction to the strike, the leaders of the Christian Democratic and Catholic Action workers announced that a new, nonpolitical labor confederation would be created. It was formally set up in October, bearing the cumbersome title, Free Italian General Confederation of Labor (LCGIL).

The Communists claim that the American Government, the Vatican, and the Christian Democratic Party forced the split, and therefore bear the responsibility for dividing and weakening the Italian labor movement. There cannot be much doubt that all three welcomed the split. The Christian Democratic Party and the Americans unquestionably helped to finance the new confederation, which, however, did not acquire any reputation for nonpolitical identification. Republican and Social Democratic labor leaders and workers were, on the whole, reluctant to join what had every appearance of an organization sponsored by Catholics and Christian Democrats. They remained in the CGIL a while longer. By May, 1949, however, they too withdrew, and on June 4, 1949, they created a new federation, the Italian Federation of Labor (FIL). The new organization was under substantial American and Italian pressure to merge with the LCGIL, and in fact, at a FIL conference in Naples, some of the FIL leaders succeeded in forcing a vote on fusion with the LCGIL. The vast majority of the rank and file refused to go along, however, and in March, 1950, created still another federation, the Italian Union of Labor (UIL). Several weeks later, the formal fusion of the LCGIL and the remnants of the FIL took place. The new organization was given the title of Italian Confederation of Workers' Unions (CISL). Supposedly free of any party or ideological domination, it was recognized in fact as a Catholic labor federation, and it operated as a faction in the faction-ridden Christian Democratic Party. With very few exceptions, its leadership was drawn from Christian Democratic Labor elements or from the Christian Associations of Italian Workers (ACLI), a branch of Catholic Action.

By 1950, consequently, the three major labor confederations were formed. The CGIL was still the largest and still under Communist and Socialist leadership, with the Communists dominant; the CISL was next in size and clearly Catholic; while the UIL was the smallest and clearly Social Democratic and Republican.[15] This splitting seriously weakened the effective economic and political power of the union movement. The maneuvering and jockeying for position of trade union leaders antagonized many of the rank and file, for all sorts of personal animosities and rivalries were involved—as well as questions of domestic and international politics—and none of it appeared to have anything to do with the immediate, daily problems of the ordinary workingman. In disgust, many of them left organized labor completely, thus weakening its position still further.

The first election of a parliament under the new Constitution was scheduled for April 18, 1948. The preceding winter had been bitter. The 1947 split in the Socialist Party had left it more firmly in the hands of those committed to unity of action with the Communists. The two parties agreed to present a common list for the election, and this aggravated the fears of the other parties.[16] In the early spring of 1948, tension mounted. The single event that brought it to its peak, however, occurred outside the country: the February, 1948, *coup d'état* in Prague, which led to the Communist takeover of Czechoslovakia. The Italian election campaign was immediately turned into a struggle of apocalyptic proportions, and the vote was depicted as a telling climax in the battle between Christ and Antichrist, between Rome and Moscow.

The United States mobilized its economic and political weapons to stem the apparent red tide. On March 15, 1948, the State Department announced that all economic aid would be cut off if the Communist-Socialist slate won.[17] The U.S. persuaded the French and British governments to join in a tripartite declaration favoring the return to Italy of the entire Free Territory of Trieste, including both Zones A and B. Americans of Italian origin or extraction were encouraged to bombard their relatives in Italy with letters urging them to vote for the government parties. In

---

[15] A neo-Fascist federation, CISNAL, would be formed in 1952, and there are also many independent unions. CISNAL has never amounted to much.

[16] The election system was a list system of proportional representation, modified by the right of the voter to choose his preferences within the party list.

[17] Text in the *New York Times*, March 16, 1948.

American Catholic churches, priests encouraged their parishioners to write to any Italian friends or connections. In Italy, various cardinals and bishops were ordering their priests not to administer sacraments to anyone voting for the pro-Soviet slate.

The danger was exaggerated, although many honest and serious people were convinced by its reality. It served, however, on the international level, to commit more American resources to Italy. When the election was over and the returns were in, the percentage of the vote received by the Marxist parties was slightly less than their vote in the election of 1946. Adding the Social Democratic vote (which did not exist in 1946) to the Communist-Socialist vote makes this result readily evident. The election returns are shown in Table 1.

TABLE 1
ELECTION RESULTS, 1946 AND 1948

Parties	1946		1948	
	Popular Vote (Per Cent)	Assembly Seats	Popular Vote (Per Cent)	Chamber Seats
Uomo Qualunque	5.3	30	2.0	6
Monarchist	2.8	16	2.8	14
Liberal	6.8	41	3.8	19
Christian Democratic	35.2	207	48.5	305
South Tyrol Populist			0.5	3
Republican	4.4	23	2.5	9
Social Democratic			7.1	33
Socialist	20.7	115 }	31.0	183
Communist	19.0	104 }		
Other	5.8	20	1.8	2
Total	*100.0*	*556*	*100.0*	*574*

Source: Italia, Istituto Centrale di Statistica.

Internally, the scare drew large numbers of conservative and moderate voters into the Christian Democratic Party, which they thought was the most effective bulwark against an apparent Communist seizure. The campaign had weakened, not the left, but the smaller parties of the center and right. The influx of right-wing elements was so marked that on the morrow of the election De

Gasperi found it necessary to affirm that the Christian Democratic Party was and remained a democratic party with progressive social goals.

Although the Christian Democratic Party had received less than half the popular vote, it had an absolute majority of the seats in Parliament. The Vatican put tremendous pressure on De Gasperi to form a one-party Catholic government. This he resolutely refused to do, deeply fearing the consequences of a sharp Catholic-secularist division. He had no desire to revive the bitter clerical-anticlerical splits of the late nineteenth century. Instead he re-formed a coalition government of four parties, taking parties to the left and to the right as allies, but all formally committed to principles of democratic parliamentary government. Joining the coalition were the Liberal, Republican, and Social Democratic parties, and this center coalition, as it came to be called, was the basis of future governments for seven years.

De Gasperi was also subject to tremendous pressure, this time from America as well, to outlaw the Communist and Socialist parties. He refused to countenance such an action, thereby demonstrating an independence from American pressure in crucial areas of domestic political choice.

In foreign affairs, however, there gradually evolved a close relationship between the two countries. During the negotiation of the peace settlement, Italy had refrained from overtly siding with the West in the growing split between the Soviet and non-Soviet worlds. It could not afford to antagonize one of the principal victors and thereby provoke a further hardening of attitude toward the defeated state. Even after the peace treaty was signed, the Italians were slow to side politically with the Western victors for several reasons. The government sought to avoid further aggravation of domestic antagonism. The British, who were still uncertain as to their commitment to Italy, displayed a distinct coolness toward it. And, finally, Italians hoped that their country, singly or with France, might play a mediating or conciliatory role in the sharpening rivalry between the superpowers. This conception of a "third force" between East and West was felt to be consistent with full Italian participation in the Marshall Plan. Count Carlo

Sforza, the Foreign Minister, made no hesitation in arguing their compatibility.[18]

Then, in late 1948 and early 1949, under the impact of the Berlin air-lift crisis, the United States evolved the idea of a Western military alliance in the form of the North Atlantic Treaty Organization. The U.S. wanted Italian membership in NATO and exerted pressure to get it. Resistance, however, was encountered both inside and outside Italy. Outside, the British raised objections to Italian participation. Inside, the extreme left and extreme right opposed such participation. This internal opposition was based on historical, and relatively logical, grounds. The neo-Fascists opposed NATO because they considered the British and the Americans to be enemies of Italy. They were especially Anglophobic, for they blamed on the British the loss of their colonies and of Trieste. On the left, the Communists opposed NATO simply because it was anti-Soviet. The Socialist position was more complicated. Socialists had a historic aversion to balance-of-power politics, which they regarded as the major cause of war. They disliked a world divided into blocs. They had a tradition of neutralism and anti-imperialism and were too easily and superficially persuaded by their Communist allies that NATO was an imperialist alliance. So Nenni justified Socialist opposition to Italian membership in NATO on the grounds that his party was applying the policy of its predecessors, who had opposed Italian membership in the Triple Alliance and later in the Triple Entente.

Both extremes were in the opposition, however, and the government had a solid majority in Parliament. It was not the opposition that made the government hold back, but uncertainty within the governing coalition. Sforza's hopes that Italy could play a third-force role gradually evaporated under the combined influence of a deteriorating international situation and the repeated warnings from his ambassador in Washington, Alberto Tarchiani, that the American Congress could not be expected to finance Italian economic recovery and receive in return nothing more than neutralism. In 1949, this was a fair argument, although the late

---

18 See Carlo Sforza, "Italy, the Marshall Plan, and the 'Third Force.'" *Foreign Affairs*, April, 1948, p. 455.

1950's would show that Asian and African states could exchange nonalignment for American dollars very nicely. After Sforza's conversion, it was still necessary to convince De Gasperi, whose reservations reflected a variety of opinions in his party. Many Christian Democrats felt that Italy, as the home of the Catholic Church, should stay out of the East-West political conflict in order to protect the Church, a universal body not tied to any blocs, cultures, or economic or political systems. Other left-wing Christian Democrats identified NATO as the foreign counterpart of domestic conservatism, an instrument for blocking domestic social reform and freezing the internal, as well as the international, status quo.

De Gasperi was finally convinced by Sforza that Italy could not afford to remain isolated from the other nations of the West. De Gasperi however, when confronted by strong opposition within both his party and the ecclesiastical circles, brought himself around to doing something to which he was opposed in principle: to call on the Church for help. He took Sforza to see Pope Pius XII to explain the case for NATO. Sforza convinced the Pope and the Catholic opposition collapsed.

In the spring of 1949, the NATO treaty was submitted to Parliament. In his arguments, De Gasperi rejected the idea that NATO was necessary to halt potential Soviet military aggression. He publicly doubted that war was likely or even conceivable in Western Europe. He argued instead that Italy had to join NATO to guarantee continued economic aid and to assure the continued possibility for Italians to emigrate. He assured Parliament that such participation would be no hindrance to trading with the states of the Soviet bloc and announced that he was sending an economic mission to Moscow to negotiate a new trade agreement.[19] Parliament ratified the treaty and Italy was a member of NATO.

The year 1949 may be said to have marked the end of a period in postwar Italian life. In that year was completed the liquidation of the most obvious political and economic consequences of the war. The economy was restored to prewar levels. The country was again an active participant in the international community, a member of all the organizations existing in Western international

---

19 *Atti parlamentari, 1948–1949,* Senato della Repubblica (Italy), 1st Legislature, pp. 6534–44.

life, with the exception of the United Nations.[20] The domestic
political system appeared relatively stable, with a four-party coalition commanding a clear majority in Parliament. The dangers
and fears of the immediate postwar period seemed to have been
successfully overcome.

---

[20] Italy was prevented, by successive Soviet vetoes, from joining the United
Nations until 1955. The Russian Government announced that it had no objection to Italian membership but would block it as long as the United States
and its friends opposed the admission of Communist states of Eastern Europe.
Italy supported the "package deal" of 1955, by which a large number of Communist and non-Communist states gained admission to the United Nations.

4

Economic Innovations

The revival of the economy to prewar levels was hardly a goal to satisfy either the people or their political leaders. In fact, the contrary happened: relief from the most, abject misery stimulated further demands. This was particularly true in agriculture, where low productivity, in general, and backward forms of landholding, especially in the south, became a focus of renewed agitation on the part of a dissatisfied peasantry. Stimulated by political movements and sincerely interested in alleviating centuries-old poverty as well as in using peasant unrest as a political weapon against the economic and political status quo, propertyless southern peasants were seizing unused lands that were part of the vast holdings, the latifundia, of southern aristocratic owners. Often these were absentee landlords living in metropolitan areas while their local agents exploited a helpless mass of farm laborers who at best might not have more than 100 or 150 days of work per year.

Concern over the economic and social disabilities of the south had been expressed by both southerners (Giustino Fortunato, Gaetano Salvemini, Francesco Nitti) and northerners (Sidney Sonnino, Umberto Zanotti-Bianco) since the last decades of the nineteenth century. The governments of both pre-Fascist and Fascist Italy had attempted sporadically and inconclusively to rehabilitate southern agriculture and social life through land-reclamation projects, mosquito control, reforestation, and other means. None of these efforts had been serious enough or sustained enough to change agricultural and social patterns fundamentally. Mussolini had drained the Pontine Marshes south of Rome to use as a show piece of Fascist achievement, but then he became diverted to policies of imperialistic aggrandizement. The post-Fascist governments after 1944 seized some of the landed properties of prominent Fascists as part of the financial purge of those who had profited from Fascism. This was a first step in expropriating land, but it could not furnish the basis for more general agricultural reform.

In 1949, farm laborers went on strike under CGIL leadership. The hue and cry that resulted, the tensions raised, not only in rural areas but in political headquarters in Rome, forced the government to take some alleviatory action. American pressure, expressed through Marshall Plan administrators located in Rome, added to the growing feeling that something had to be done. De Gasperi and his Minister of Agriculture, Antonio Segni, a Sardinian landholder and university professor, prepared legislation for the breakup of large, backward landed estates. (Modern agricultural operators using advanced techniques were excluded from the legislation, no matter how large their holdings.) In April, 1949, De Gasperi proposed the redistribution of 3.7 million acres of neglected farmland. The bill went into an interministerial committee for examination. Confagricoltura (Confederation of Agriculture), the agricultural organization of the large landowners, put such pressure on the ministers that the bill was stalled in committee. In the fall of 1949 and spring of 1950, landless peasants in Calabria and Apulia, and later in the Roman *campagna,* stimulated by Communist agitators for the most part, seized unworked tracts of land. These seizures produced further political agitation and finally prodded the government into action.

De Gasperi's bill had been moderate. It would have left the landowners with substantial holdings, and the government would have compensated them for their losses partly in cash and partly in government securities. In turn, the peasants were to pay the government for the land they received, in installments over thirty years. Nevertheless, delay in Parliament induced the government to compromise—and to split up—its proposals. In May, 1950, a special bill for the Sila area of Calabria, where the peasant outbreaks had been particularly sharp, was pushed through Parliament. The *stralcio* ("pruning") law, intended as an advance installment of the main act, was passed in October of the same year. This covered certain areas of the Po Delta, the Tuscan Maremma, Sardinia, and various sections of the southern mainland. (Sicily was excluded; its land reform was placed under the aegis of the new Sicilian regional government.) Then the cabinet quietly proceeded to abandon the main law, so that only one-third to one-half of the land originally scheduled for distribution ever went to the peasants.

The government's responsibilities did not end with the partition of the land. Administrative agencies set up in each land-reform area not only were responsible for the reassignment of holdings but were also involved in supplying animals, constructing houses and barns, educating the new holders, and doing other kinds of social welfare work. In some cases they became paternalistic, treating the peasants like incapable children who would be in need of constant tutelage.

Some weaknesses of the reform were apparent immediately. The landowners kept their best land and got rid of their marginal or useless holdings by giving it to the reform agencies. Much of the land turned over to the peasants was not suitable for intensive farming. Other weaknesses became apparent later. Under pressure to provide land and incapable of conceiving of a situation other than permanent rural overpopulation, administrators allocated tiny plots to too many families; even under the best of circumstances, farming them would involve a bitter struggle to make a bare living. After 1959, when a rural exodus of substantial proportions would take place, the fallacious assumption of permanent rural overpopulation would be exposed, and the worst land abandoned. Another weakness was that the beneficiaries were picked by lot, rather than by presumed potential ability to run a farm, and some of them proved to be absolutely incapable. Although it was charged that favoritism and influence were used in making the allotments, there seems to be little evidence that voting Christian Democratic helped anyone obtain land. There is plenty of evidence, however, that the reform agencies themselves were instruments of Christian Democratic patronage.

The land reform was an economic revolution in the areas where it took effect, but appeared in the following years to have been of little political consequence. Whatever hopes might have been held that the creation of a large number of new peasant proprietors would break the influence of the extreme left on the beneficiaries were not borne out by subsequent elections. The Christian Democratic Party did not gain many votes in the reform areas. On the other hand, the party earned the enmity of landowners and conservative middle and upper classes, especially in the south, who threw their political support to the reviving Monarchists and to the neo-Fascists. At this time, the latter were organized in the Italian Social Movement (Movimento Sociale Italiano, MSI), which had been created in 1949 out of some sections of the disintegrating Uomo Qualunque.

Redistribution of land was by itself not enough to convert the impoverished and retarded south into a modern society. Development of nonagricultural resources was also required, and in 1950 the government introduced a bill for the creation of a development agency, the Cassa per il Mezzogiorno (Southern Italy Fund). It was to spend 1,200 billion lire over ten years (later prolonged several times with more funds) for the purpose of creating the prerequisites for a developing economy. Half of the original appropriation came from counterpart funds of the European Recovery Program. The Fund was related to agricultural reform in its concern with dams, aqueducts, roads, irrigation, and other elements of economic development that together are generally classified as infrastructure. But it was hoped that this infrastructure would provide a basis for industrial and commercial, as well as agricultural, development. It was anticipated that private initiative would step in to take advantage of the public investment. To stimulate private investment, a whole series of special credit facilities were established to make loans at exceptionally low interest rates. In addition, special tax waivers were authorized.

The operations of the Southern Italy Fund provided much material for controversial discussion. Enemies charged that it lost considerable effectiveness because of graft and corruption. These are difficult charges to prove, and most Italians take graft and corruption for granted, assuming them to exist even when they do not. Some things are fairly clear, however. The selection of sites and projects were often influenced by political considerations. The central government was subjected to tremendous pressure by local political organizations to locate a project here rather than there, to support the political ambitions of candidate or faction X rather than Y, to reward the commune or province that provided a nice majority and to punish the one that supported the opposition. As public works and the jobs resulting therefrom were (and are) important electoral factors—especially in the south, where clientelism remains strong—these practices were perhaps inevitable. They are not peculiar to Italy, but they did reduce the effectiveness of the programs.

An additional cause of ineffectiveness lay in the behavior and reaction of the traditional government departments. Some of them tried to get their hands on the Fund to aid in the building of departmental empires, but the Fund had been created outside the old-line departments precisely because of the low opinion of their ability to operate a strikingly new project. The departments then reduced their own regular spending in the zones where the Fund was operating, so that what was conceived as an extraordinary supplement to government investments became, to a certain degree, a substitute. In 1951, public works constructed in the south by the regular government departments represented 45.8 per cent of the national total. Five years later, the percentage had declined to 41.5 per cent. By 1959, it was down to 29.7 per cent; in 1961, it rose slightly to 31.7 per cent.

Another unquestioned result of the institution of the Southern Italy Fund was the impetus it gave to northern industry. Especially in the Fund's initial stages, the north gained perhaps more than the south. While unskilled southern peasants could be used on road building, dam building, and other projects, the heavy equipment, the earth-moving and road-grading machinery, was of necessity manufactured in northern plants. Tractors and other farm machinery purchased to modernize agriculture came from the same source. It is not surprising, consequently, that the Southern Italy Fund helped to contribute to northern industrial expansion.

In the early 1950's, hopes for a rapid expansion of private industry in the south were not realized to any significant extent.

The south appeared to lack substantial entrepreneurial tradition. The land, rather than industry, had been the traditional focus of southerners with savings to invest, for land was the established source of prestige and social status. Existing favorable tax laws encouraged speculation in real estate, and it remained more attractive than unfamiliar industrial development, in spite of the special incentives offered. The unusual credit facilities made available by the creation of new governmental loan agencies for the southern mainland, Sicily, and Sardinia (separate ones were created for each of these areas) did not have powerful capacities for attraction. In the mid-1950's, the large northern and central industrial firms, capable of self-financing out of their own profits, did not need to borrow extensively for expansion. Consequently, hopes that northern industrialists would locate plants in the south in large numbers went unfulfilled. Some of them certainly did—Olivetti, for example, constructed an office-machine factory in the Naples area—but most were cautious. They had doubts about southern markets for their products and about the capacities of southern labor. The national wage contracts negotiated by the unions provided for lower wages in the south, but these were not sufficiently lower to offset the many attractions of the north. The result was that the expansion of Italian industry remained concentrated in the north.

In spite of the difficulties and drawbacks, the land reforms and Fund programs are still among the most striking developments in postwar—or even modern—Italian history. Progress was made in attacking a whole pattern of living, shaking up age-old habits and customs, in order to permit the unification of the country economically, socially, and culturally. This move toward unity was slow in starting and remains far from complete.

Marshall Plan aid had been geared originally to promote economic recovery, which was essentially accomplished by 1949. The aid was not halted at that time but was continued until 1952, when the European Recovery Program was declared completed. Substantial portions of the counterpart funds accumulated under Marshall Plan operations had been used to help finance the Southern Italy Fund. The question now was whether northern business would be stimulated to continue the general economic expansion. This was not necessarily to be taken for granted.

Italian business was traditionally based on small and protected markets. Both public and private business enterprises had been operated with a mentality oriented toward securing an agreed slice of a small pie, rather than toward competing for a larger share of a bigger pie. Pre-Fascist and Fascist regimes had encouraged protection, controls, and cartel arrangements, and had discouraged competition. Italy had been, and still was, so poor a country that it was difficult to conceive of the nation providing a growing and vital market. There was no certainty these habits of long standing could be shaken.

They were, but it was not easy. It required a political leadership determined to engage in a program of development. It required a good dose of fear of the consequences of the failure to develop. The fear was, and is, present. All Italian society, all social classes, are pervaded with fear: the poor fear misery, unemployment, and abuse of power by those above them; the middle classes fear for their social and economic status; the rich fear loss of their wealth and privileges. Fear was nothing new in Italian history, but in the atmosphere of the Cold War of the early 1950's, with large and active Communist and Socialist parties spurring the disinherited to advance more and more claims on society, the only answer was to enlarge the pie. Determined men in the government pushed the hesitant private industrialists along.

One impetus was the realization by private industry that its failure to expand would threaten it with seizure by the government. Not that extreme Marxist parties of the left would come to power by revolution—certainly after 1948 they were recognized as being of little direct danger—but there was little moral or ideological commitment to private enterprise throughout most of Italian society. During the first half of the twentieth century, the Italian state had acquired major economic assets, such as railroads, insurance firms, coal mines, mechanical enterprises, and banks. In the 1930's, in its attempt to bail out many firms and banks grievously hurt by the great depression, Mussolini's government had ended up by acquiring a controlling stock interest in substantial parts of the economy. Many of these firms were grouped by Mussolini into a large holding company, the Institute for Industrial Reconstruction (IRI), which the republic inherited. Many groups described as center in Italian politics, inside and outside the Christian Democratic Party, would always be ready to demand that the state step in wherever and whenever private enterprise showed unwillingness to exercise dynamic initiative.

It was assumed not only that the domestic market was expandable but also that foreign markets could be made available through political cooperation. Count Carlo Sforza, the Foreign Minister between 1947 and 1951, when he retired because of ill health, was a Europeanist of long standing. While he avoided wrestling with the hard issues of regional integration and preferred to talk in generalities and aphorisms (one of his favorite was: "Boundaries must be written in pencil, not ink!"), he stimulated the at first uninterested and later reluctant De Gasperi to realize the advantages to Italy of European unity.

Sforza had begun his program with a failure. He negotiated, in 1948, a customs-union agreement with France behind the backs of unsuspecting Italian businessmen, who only later awoke to the fact that they might have to face French competition. Sforza had foreign-policy, as well as economic, goals in mind and thought that Franco-Italian unity would increase the political power of the two countries throughout the world, thus enabling them to play better the third-force role he then had in mind. The Italian business community was saved by the more alert French business, agricultural, and labor interests—equally protectionist in mentality—who proceeded to exercise enough pressure on the French Parliament to prevent ratification of the treaty.

The next opportunity came in 1951 and 1952, when the French Government, through Maurice Schumann, proposed the establishment of the Coal and Steel Community. Italy's coal industry is minor and in the hands of the government. Its resources of iron ore are insignificant. Its steel industry had been developed in the latter part of the nineteenth century under the protection of governments determined to make Italy a great power. Without this protection it never could have met the competition of Western

European producers, for it was dependent on imports of its basic raw materials. During the 1930's, many steel firms failed and were taken over by the Fascist government through the mechanism of the IRI. At the beginning of the 1950's, they were technologically backward, compared to foreign competitors, and would have been unable to withstand the strain of an unprotected situation.

For these reasons, the private steel producers opposed Italian participation in the Coal and Steel Community. Their objections would have carried more weight if they had been dominant in the industry, but they were not. The major steel producers were government-owned, but the government could not ignore the consequences of unrestricted foreign competition either, for it could not afford to add to the already existing mass of unemployed. It was committed to operating all of its enterprises at a loss in order to keep men at work. Desirous of participating in the initiation of a new economic community, it found, with the toleration of the other European members, a compromise path. Italy was permitted to join with a five-year period of grace before its steel industry would be exposed to the full effects of foreign competition. During those five years, it would have to modernize its plant to prepare for the day of reckoning. In an earlier period, the Italians would not have prepared, but would have drifted along and then requested an extension of the special exemption. That this was not done points up the difference in the atmosphere and attitudes of the 1950's. Under the dynamic and driving leadership of the engineer Oscar Sinigaglia, the Italian steel industry was converted in five years into a modern and efficient producer, capable of competing with the best in the world. Its production expanded dramatically, and when the grace period expired, instead of collapsing it surged on to further advances.

The performance of the steel industry was imitated by the other branches of industry in which large-scale firms were the order, such as the mechanical, chemical, and petroleum plants. In the five years between 1950 and 1955, the Italian gross national product increased at an average annual rate of between 5 and 6 per cent. The increase was actually fluctuating from year to year, as the figures in Table 2 indicate. The main reason for the fluctuations was the varying harvests in agriculture, which still employed

TABLE 2
GROWTH RATE OF GROSS NATIONAL PRODUCT, 1951–55
(*In Per Cents*)

Year	Increase
1951	5.9
1952	2.9
1953	7.3
1954	4.4
1955	7.5

Source: Bank of Italy, *Relazione 1958*, p. 197.

close to 40 per cent of the labor force. Industrial output increased on an average of nearly 10 per cent per year during this period. The early discovery of large reserves of natural gas in the Po Valley, and of smaller reserves of petroleum, created a major new source of the energy in which Italy was traditionally deficient. Located near the principal centers of industry, these discoveries provided a further stimulus to economic expansion. They had been made by the state-owned petroleum company, AGIP (Italian General Petroleum Agency), which was incorporated in 1952 into the newly created National Hydrocarbons Trust, the ENI. Under the leadership of the dynamic left-wing Christian Democrat Enrico Mattei, the ENI was created to unify the state-controlled properties in the petroleum industry. It became a major public holding company, comparable to the IRI.

The dramatic increases in productivity in the advanced parts of the economy were due primarily to technological improvements and modernization of the existing plant. In these years, Italian industry caught up with the rest of the world. In addition, the Italians brought into full productivity the existing surplus plant and labor. The ending of quantitative controls and the liberalization of imports, carried through after 1949 by the Minister of Foreign Trade, Ugo La Malfa, gave Italian industry access to the most modern foreign machinery and equipment, from which it had previously been cut off by the operation of exchange controls and quotas. The increases in efficiency due to modernization, coupled with the low wages due to the divisions within the labor movement and the debilitating effects of mass unemployment, led to declines in labor costs that served to make Italian prices competitive in foreign markets and to a substantial expansion of exports. The economic recovery and development of the other advanced countries of the Western world not only increased the demand for Italian products but provided the basis for the beginnings of a mass tourism from which Italy would profit greatly in subsequent years.

This happy picture was not the total portrait, however. It applied only to the part of the economy more or less advanced and ready for still further evolution. Whole sectors of Italian economic life were outside this zone, in a state of underdevelopment. Agriculture, which was still the largest area of manpower absorption, struggled along in its efforts to improve, with only marginal success. The numerous tiny artisan and retail enterprises, employing the members of one family, or perhaps one or two outside assistants, had no dramatic increases in efficiency or in profits. The increased wealth resulting from development and modernization was poured back into more investment or into the increased consumption of the business and commercial circles of the increasingly prosperous cities. The workers in the advanced industries enjoyed increases in real wages, although not comparable to the increases in productivity and profits. The result was that during the 1950's the gap between the two Italys was enlarged, rather than diminished.

The absence of a significant increase in employment was striking. Increased efficiency was the principal goal. The surplus labor kept on the payrolls in the late 1940's because of legal requirements could now be fully used. While there was some increase in nonagricultural employment, more of it probably went into the low-paid, small-scale artisan and distribution sectors than into industry. There was, in addition, a small exodus from agriculture. It has been estimated that between 1950 and 1959, larger industry absorbed only about 120,000 workers, while construction and transportation accounted for 400,000 to 500,000 more. At the same time, new elements—youths reaching working age and housewives seeking to enlarge the family income—were entering the labor market.[1] Thus, neither unemployment nor underemployment diminished substantially.

In the first half of the 1950's, unemployment was actually increasing. While Italian unemployment figures are debatable from both statistical and political standpoints, they are the only ones we have, and the broad picture they present is dramatic enough. The statistics of Table 3 are revealing. It can be seen that 1954

TABLE 3
UNEMPLOYED REGISTERED AT LABOR EXCHANGES, 1950–55

Year	Number of Registrants
1950	1,860,100
1951	1,938,300
1952	2,073,400
1953	2,181,300
1954	2,197,300
1955	2,161,000

Source: Italian Ministry of Labor.[2]

was the worst year for unemployment—and the figures do not show the underemployment, which is difficult to measure. Considering that the total labor force of that period was approximately 20 million persons, they indicate that roughly 10 per cent of the working population was unemployed during the first half of the 1950's.

That the figures were not worse was due to the vigorous emigration policy followed by the government. After the war, the Foreign Office invested a tremendous amount of time and energy in promoting arrangements for both permanent and temporary emigration. Its success was limited. Italian emigrants had to compete with millions of racial, religious, and political refugees fleeing from various types of persecution. Immigrant quota systems, such as those of the United States, were discriminatory. Many receiving countries were selective on the basis of skills (including literacy) that were in short supply in Italy. Failure of adjustment

[1] Vera Lutz, *Italy: A Study in Economic Development* (London: Oxford University Press, 1962), p. 75.

[2] *Ibid.*, p. 64.

abroad, or the completion of contracts when the emigration was temporary, meant a steady stream of returners. The result was a net emigration over these years of about 150,000 per annum.

The failure to make greater inroads on poverty and unemployment led to demands both inside and outside Italy that the government take steps to push the rate of development even faster. In 1952, Parliament established an investigating commission named for its chairman, the Social Democrat Roberto Tremelloni, to make a thorough investigation of unemployment. Officials of the American aid program urged the government to ease the tight monetary and credit policies in order to expand production and employment. The memory of the inflation of 1946/47 was so sharp, however, and the "defense of the lira" was so imbedded in the political mythology of the dominant economic ministers, mainly right-wing Liberals or Christian Democrats, that the hard-money policies were continued.

Political unrest was the consequence, and the voting power of the two extremes actually increased. The pressures generated led to strains within the ruling coalition, with demands by important groups for a revision of political alliances.

5

The Difficulties of Centrism

The political and economic strains of the years after 1948 made the life of the four-party coalition difficult. The unrest generated by increasing unemployment and peasant seizures of the land led to frightened demands by middle- and upper-class spokesmen for stern repressive action. Under the instructions of the Christian Democratic Minister of the Interior, Mario Scelba, mobile flying squads (*celeri*) of national police, often recruited from ex-Fascist elements, were generous in their use of such weapons as rubber truncheons and wooden clubs. Although the extreme left was manipulating the unrest, the moderate left was genuinely disturbed by the brutality. In addition, the Social Democrats felt that the reform measures enacted were too compromised by concessions to the conservatives, especially as represented by the Liberal Party.[1]

On the opposite side, however, the conservatives felt that the Christian Democrats had not been firm enough in handling the unrest. They resented De Gasperi's refusal to outlaw the Communist and Socialist parties. They resented the agricultural reforms that had been instituted, in spite of their limited nature. They considered the reforms a symbolic attack on their whole

---

[1] In later years, Giuseppe Saragat admitted that "in the years of centrism, the Italian Social Democratic Party had to sacrifice part of its program because of the social blindness of the Liberals." *Corriere della sera* (Milan), November 2, 1964.

structure of prestige, status, and economic power, for their absolute right to their own possessions was thereby contested. They felt that the government was ineffective in challenging American and British inaction on the Trieste problem, and resented Italy's close link to the Atlantic alliance and to the United States.

A good part of De Gasperi's time and effort was involved in trying to maintain a balance between progressive and conservative elements inside his own party and within the coalition. He had less and less success in these efforts, so that by 1951 both the Social Democrats and the Liberals had left the government, although they continued generally to support it in Parliament. Since the Christian Democrats in any case had a majority by themselves (the 48.5 per cent of the votes received in 1948 had given them by law over 53 per cent of the seats in the Chamber of Deputies), the votes of the minor parties were not absolutely necessary, but were welcome when forthcoming.

An additional source of friction was the manipulation of patronage by the Christian Democrats at the expense of their small coalition partners. Almost all of the government-controlled corporations were put into the hands of Christian Democratic executives. The various appointments to public and semipublic agencies were also monopolized by the dominant party. Even academic appointments became subject to political manipulation.

The Catholic Church and its principal lay organ, the Italian Catholic Action Society, became increasingly aggressive in public life. Recommendations by high clerics, whether on personnel or on policy, not only brought about increasing resentment from the lay parties but frequently caused embarrassment to the Christian Democrats. De Gasperi had a very strong sense of the independence of the state from the Church, and he fought a hard battle against the clericalization of Italian life. When he retired from the political scene, his successors were in a much weaker position, and Church intervention in lay affairs expanded rapidly. To a considerable degree, this was the fault of the party itself. De Gasperi had never built up a strong party organization at the local level. The party depended on the clergy to support it at election time and to tell the voters for whom to vote. Parish churches were often converted into political headquarters. The Civic Commit-

tees, established by the Catholic Action Society, supplied the campaign workers and election agents. If priests and Catholic Action
leaders were crucial to success, it is not surprising that they demanded their say after the elections were over. Naturally, they
did not all speak with one voice, but in the early 1950's the predominant voice of the Church was conservative, if not reactionary. This was a further strain on Christian Democratic relations
with the lay allies, especially the Republicans and the Social
Democrats.

The combination of factors leading to discontent with the
Christian Democrats was revealed in the results of the administrative elections held in 1951 and 1952. The Christian Democrats
lost over 4 million votes (compared to the parliamentary election
of April, 1948), a drop from 48.5 per cent to 35.1 per cent. While
some of these votes were lost to the left, the Socialists having
made some gains, most were lost to the right, to the rising Monarchist and neo-Fascist (MSI) parties. These two parties practically tripled their vote, gaining especially from Rome southward.
The elections demonstrated that the Christian Democrats had
never been as strong as the 1948 election had indicated them to
be, but had merely been able to exploit a temporary situation—
the *coup d'état* in Czechoslovakia—that was no longer repeatable.

The 1952 election had been especially crucial in Rome itself.
The city had a strong neo-Fascist core, but was surrounded by a
belt of poverty-stricken slum areas that were strongholds of the
extreme left. It was doubtful that the Christian Democrats and
their minor centrist allies would get enough votes to acquire a
majority in the communal government of the capital. In this
situation, Luigi Gedda, autocratic president of the Civic Committees of Catholic Action, precipitated a political crisis by demanding of De Gasperi that the Christian Democrats ally with
the Monarchists and the MSI in Rome and further south, to stave
off the possibility of a left-wing victory. Gedda threatened to
organize an "outright Catholic party" pledged to carry out a program of "authoritative democracy" if De Gasperi refused.[2] In

---

2 The Christian Democrats are not formally a "confessional" party and reject any attribution that they are the representatives of the Church in political life. The effort to promote a center-right coalition in Rome was known as

addition, the Civic Committee of Rome advocated to the Christian Democrats the detachment of the peripheral areas of the commune from the central city, with the "red belt" to be made into a number of subcommunes. This latter proposal, designed to guarantee right-wing control of the city itself, was rejected by the party.

De Gasperi put up a bitter battle against allying with the extreme right. He knew that a center-right government in Rome, the capital, would become the basis for similar demands at the national level. He felt that the only long-run solution to Italy's problems was for the party of Christian Democracy, like the British Labour Party, to be progressively oriented with a strong social commitment. He had already described his party as a "center party looking toward the left." He had to fight not only Catholic Action but also the whole right wing of his party and a substantial body of opinion in the Vatican led by Pope Pius XII, who threatened to publish, in the Vatican paper, *L'Osservatore romano*, an endorsement of a separate list of Catholic candidates. In May, 1952, De Gasperi's position prevailed, the Pope retreated, and the coalition for Rome was composed of Christian Democrats, Social Democrats, Republicans, and Liberals. But to many conservative Catholic voters, it was obvious that the Church had no prejudices against the Monarchists and the MSI, both claiming to be good Catholic parties, and the increase in their vote has already been noted.

In Italy it is commonly believed that De Gasperi was supported by Monsignor Giovanni Battista Montini, then a Prosecretary of State and later Pope Paul VI. It should not be inferred that all members of Catholic Action shared Gedda's views or supported his demand for an opening to the right. Especially in the youth

---

the "Sturzo Operation." Don Luigi Sturzo, the founder of the Popular Party in 1919, had returned to Italy after the war and was made a senator for life. He had become rather conservative in his old age, but he was a republican and democrat always. How his name got attached to the affair is unclear, but it is hard to conceive of him advocating an alliance with Monarchists and Fascists. In the summer of 1965, Giulio Andreotti, one of De Gasperi's principal aides, wrote that Pope Pius XII was directly involved in the "Sturzo Operation." See Andreotti's journal, *Concretezza*, August 14, 1965, as reported in the *New York Herald Tribune* (Paris Edition), August 16, 1965.

organization, he met considerable resistance, which, however, was crushed. After the failure of Gedda's offensive against De Gasperi, the leaders of the Catholic Action youth group faced a purge at the hands of the Church conservatives. Carlo Carretto, president of the youth organization, left for Africa as a missionary on the basis of "authoritative suggestions." Don Arturo Paoli, who had warned Pius XII of the Fascist danger in the south, left Italy as a chaplain to emigrants. Mario Rossi, Carretto's successor, was purged two years later as a "left-wing deviationist."

Although the Christian Democrats suffered large over-all losses, together with the centrist parties they were able to hold and to gain control of a number of major cities in the center and north, including Rome itself. This success was due to changes in the election laws for the 1951/52 elections. In communes of over 10,000 in population, a premium of two-thirds of the seats in the communal council was given to the alliance obtaining a plurality of the votes. For the provincial councils, a prize of two-thirds of the seats was given to the alliance list that elected a simple majority of the council. It was by these devices that the center parties gained control in a number of formerly left-controlled cities, such as Florence and Turin.

The rise of the Monarchists and neo-Fascists had been particularly noticeable from Rome southward. Both of these parties had grown after the disintegration of the Uomo Qualunque, which had received its death blow in the election of 1948. The Monarchists were led by two southerners, Alfredo Covelli, of Benevento, and Achille Lauro, a wealthy shipowner of Naples. The formal goal of the party was the restoration of the monarchy. Since Article 139 of the Constitution states that the republican form of government is not subject to constitutional amendment, the party's goal could be achieved only through revolution. In fact, it was not a revolutionary party, but rather a conservative or reactionary one. Its appeal was to nostalgic members of the upper class and to those of all classes who spend their time reading magazines filled with gossip of princesses, aristocrats, and movie stars. This audience could never give it many votes; however, it was able to gather the votes of a mass of poverty-stricken southern subproletarians. Its greatest success was in Naples, where it was

able to demonstrate the effectiveness of personality (Lauro's), corruption, and a feudal and absolutist past on the sensibilities of a
semiliterate, miserable population. The party's conception of
social consciousness was the distribution of a paternalistic largess
to the unfortunate.

The MSI, the Italian Social Movement, is generally called neo-
Fascist, but the prefix "neo" is inappropriate because the MSI
was composed mainly of relics of the immediate past. Its leadership came from secondary levels of Mussolini's National Fascist
Party, which was outlawed by the republican Constitution. In its
early years, the intransigent elements who had remained loyal to
Mussolini's Fascist Social Republic, the Republic of Salò, anti-
monarchist and anticapitalist, had controlled the MSI. Later, after a number of violent internal wrangles, these groups were
superseded by the more moderate elements from the south, who
favored collaboration with the Monarchists, conservative Liberals,
and Christian Democrats. It attracted some of the youth, especially secondary-school students, who had had no direct experience with Fascism. They were available to carry out destructive
raids on meeting halls and section headquarters of the left-wing
opposition and to beat up Communists and Socialists who were
caught out alone (for the *Missini* were always careful to outnum-
ber their opponents). Like the Monarchists, the MSI employed
nationalist and anti-Communist themes, combined with pious
displays of devotion to the Church. The party held its first national congress in 1952.

Like the extreme left, the Monarchists and Fascists represented
a protest against the conditions of Italian society. The Fascist
protest was the more ideological and uncompromising, however,
and was able to resist the erosion that would eventually sap Monarchist strength in the late 1950's. But in the meantime, these two
right-wing parties were flourishing in their southern strongholds,
available to join with Christian Democrats and Liberals to form
majorities in southern communal and provincial governments.
They demanded their price, a share in the *sottogoverno*—the
corruption and patronage.

The election results of 1951/52 were a warning of what might
be expected in the parliamentary election scheduled for 1953. A

stable government based on a solid majority possessed by the center parties appeared highly unlikely. This unfavorable forecast
led to the desperate decision to tamper with the election laws.
A combination of proportional representation and a special
premium was to be substituted for the existing proportional representation system of election to the Chamber of Deputies. Specifically, any alliance of parties that received one vote more than
50 per ·cent of the votes in the nation would gain two-thirds of
the seats in the Chamber. The law would convert a nominal majority among the people into a powerful one in Parliament. That
it was a very undemocratic device was disregarded by its proponents. That it resembled the Acerbo Law of 1923, by which
Mussolini had achieved his first Fascist majority in the Chamber,
was obvious to everyone with any knowledge of Italian history.[3]
Yet it was put forward by men who had been personal victims of
the results of the Fascist juggling of election laws.

The introduction of the bill created an uproar in Parliament.
The Communists immediately baptized it the "swindle law." The
three small allies of the Christian Democrats—Liberals, Social
Democrats, and Republicans—reluctantly supported the changes,
fearful that their failure to do so would mean an alliance between
the Christian Democrats and the extreme right after the election,
yet knowing that if the juggling succeeded, the Christian Democrats would again gain an absolute majority in the Chamber and
could then proceed to govern with or without them at will. Individual members of the three parties refused to go along, however. They formed a new group, Unità Popolare, led by such
men as former Prime Minister Ferruccio Parri and the distinguished lawyer Piero Calamandrei, a former rector of the University of Florence, but the group did not attract enough members
to prevent the stormy passage of the bill.

The election campaign was fought out on two major issues:
the "swindle law" and the land reform. A minor issue was the
still-open Trieste dispute. The United States again intervened

---

[3] The Acerbo Law provided that the party receiving 25 per cent of the
votes would receive two-thirds of the seats. It was through the use of this law,
plus threats and other means of "persuasion," that Mussolini got his parliamentary majority from the 1924 election.

through its ambassador, Clare Boothe Luce, who publicly warned of the unfavorable consequences for Italy—in terms of American support—if the center coalition lost. A reaction to this foreign intervention, stimulated by nationalistic resentments, caused the statement by Mrs. Luce to be widely criticized, and her words probably did De Gasperi more harm than good. The Church again repeated its warnings, and the Civic Committees again launched their campaigns.

On June 7, 1953, the election was held for both houses.[4] The vote for the Chamber, shown in Table 4, gives the important re-

TABLE 4
VOTE FOR THE CHAMBER OF DEPUTIES, JUNE 7, 1953

Parties	Popular Votes	Seats Won
Christian Democratic	10,834,466	261
Liberal	815,929	14
Republican	438,149	5
Social Democratic	1,222,957	19
Communist	6,120,709	143
Socialist	3,441,014	75
Monarchist	1,854,850	40
Fascist (MSI)	1,579,880	29
Other	693,505	4

Source: Italia, Istituto Centrale di Statistica.

sults. The four center parties received 49.85 per cent of the votes, 57,000 short of the 50 per cent plus one vote required to earn the extra premium.[5] The defection of Unità Popolare, which did not win any seats but gained 171,099 votes, had cost the center coalition its prize. The Christian Democrats, while gaining from their low point in the 1951/52 local elections, received 40 per cent of the vote, much less than their 1948 sweep. Their three small allies suffered serious losses also, far more than the votes picked up by the Unità Popolare. The big gainers were the extremes, the

---

[4] Although the Senate then had a six-year maximum term, it was dissolved at the same time as the Chamber. In 1962, the Constitution was amended to give the Senate a five-year maximum term coincident with that of the Chamber.

[5] The "swindle law" was abolished the following year, and the election to the Chamber was again based on proportional representation.

Communists and Socialists on the left, the Monarchists and Fascists on the right. The latter two improved on their performance in the administrative elections of the previous year. The Communists made major gains in the south, as that part of the country gradually became politicized.

The election of 1953 marked the end of De Gasperi's political career. Although the four center parties had a slight margin in Parliament (proportional representation is never perfect), De Gasperi's efforts to form a new four-party government broke down. The Social Democrats were smarting from their losses. The left wing within the party reproached it for having gone along with the "swindle law" and having, in general, covered the center, which had moved more and more to the right. De Gasperi then tried to put forward a one-party minority government but failed to get the support of Parliament. He retired from politics and died a year later.

It was during this time that a new alignment was proposed. Pietro Nenni suggested during the Chamber debate that his party was available for an "opening to the left," that is, a coalition extending from the Christian Democrats through the Socialists. The suggestion evidenced the beginnings of the separation of the Socialists from Communist tutelage. (In the 1953 campaign, the Socialists had run their own slate, rather than combine with the Communists as in 1948.) De Gasperi had considered Nenni's proposal and then shelved it as premature. But there were left-wing Christian Democrats and Social Democrats who were interested, and the idea would grow until it became the dominant issue at the end of the decade.

This account has been centered on the policies, actions, and maneuvers of the political elite, the "ruling class," as Italian scholars and journalists define it. In the life of the "popular masses"—again an Italian phrase—the hue and cry over the "swindle law," American intervention, capitalism, socialism, and legality made hardly a ripple. In the medium-sized and small towns, in the villages and rural areas, the debates of the politicians and intellectuals were ignored, although the Trieste issue appears to have made a small impact. A study made by International Research Associates in communes in which substantial shifts of votes had occurred in 1953 from the Christian Democrats to the Communists, or vice versa, showed that local economic issues, local jobs, local public works, favors, improvements, and clientelism were the important influences on voting behavior, not the big national issues and ideological rivalries.

6

The Decline of Centrism

De Gasperi's failure to organize a government reflected the troubled nature of the second legislature from 1953 to 1958. The reformist urge that had marked the early years of the preceding legislature was further diluted by the energy absorbed in finding majorities that would then collapse and have to be re-created. In many cases, the cabinets of the next five years were minority governments dependent on the abstention of the right-wing parties or the occasional support of the left wing on determinate issues. The tendency was to postpone solutions to major issues, such as the revision of the principal legal codes inherited from Fascism and the establishment of a regulatory system for the development of atomic power.[1] Postponement was due to the succession of cabinet crises and to the dependence of the Christian Democrats on right-wing support on various issues, the price paid being one of delay. The second legislature has therefore often been described as the "legislature of immobilism."

---

[1] The Civil Law Code, the Criminal Law Code, the Codes of Civil and Criminal Procedure, were all Fascist in origin. At the beginning of 1965, commissions established by the third legislature had not yet completed the drafting of new codes.

As Italy is deficient in coal and petroleum and had practically exhausted the available sources of water power, atomic power was commercially feasible earlier in Italy than elsewhere. Regulation was delayed, however, by the bitter battle over public *vs.* private control of atomic plants. Not until 1962, when the electric-power industry was nationalized, was the issue settled.

This generalization is valid for the major questions of domestic politics; it is invalid for foreign affairs and for business development. Economic production continued to expand at a good rate, and after 1954 the level of unemployment declined slightly, as the growth of employment began to be greater than the growth of the labor force.

It was in the area of foreign affairs, however, that the most dramatic events took place. Here, first attention must be given to the Trieste problem, an issue left unresolved by the peace settlement. It will be recalled that the peace treaty had assigned most of Venezia Giulia and the Istrian Peninsula to Yugoslavia. The area around the city of Trieste was detached from Italy and made into the independent Free Territory of Trieste. The peace treaty provided that the Security Council of the United Nations would select a governor to supervise—in the name of the international community—an elected government of the Free Territory. Until the governor was chosen, the Free Territory would remain under the occupation of the victorious Allies. The growth of the Cold War in the late 1940's made it impossible for the Security Council to agree on a governor, so the military occupation continued.

The Free Territory had been divided into two occupation zones, A and B. Zone A was under Anglo-American military administration, Zone B under the Yugoslavs. The city of Trieste and a stretch of territory west of the city were included in Zone A. The population, totaling over 300,000 people, was overwhelmingly Italian in ethnic origin, with a small Slovenian minority. Although Zone B extended over more than twice the territory of Zone A, it had only about 75,000 inhabitants, most of whom were Slovenians. The Italian population in the coastal villages of Zone B had left their homes in the early years of the Yugoslav occupation. The Communist government of Marshal Tito had in effect integrated the area into the Yugoslav federation.[2]

It will be remembered that the United States, France, and the United Kingdom, to help De Gasperi in the 1948 election campaign, had issued a public declaration that called for the return of the Free Territory, including both zones, to Italy. This declara-

---

2 Zone A was Italianized to some degree also, in currency and administrative systems, but it was not integrated into Italy.

tion immediately became the minimum basis for all Italian claims to the area. A few months later, however, the dramatic split between Stalin and Tito occurred. To support Tito's independence and to widen the first rift in the unity of the Soviet bloc, the Western Allies dropped their pressure for a Trieste solution, and the divided occupation continued. Italian nationalists became more and more bitter at the Allies for sacrificing Italian interests to larger considerations of power politics. In subsequent years, riots occurred in Zone A, as well as in Italy proper, and were encouraged by right-wing elements condemning the Italian Government for its subservience to its Western allies. Since a British general commanded and British troops were in the majority in the occupation of Zone A, the already existing undercurrent of anti-English feeling was aggravated by the measures used by the occupation forces to restore order.[3]

Again to aid the Christian Democrats in the electoral campaign of 1953, the United States proposed to De Gasperi that Italy accept a solution to the Trieste dispute on the basis of a partition of the Free Territory along the lines of the two zones, with some slight modifications of the border in favor of Yugoslavia. The United States pledged to use all of its considerable influence on Marshal Tito to get him to accept the partition. Although there was strong support in the Italian Foreign Office for this solution as the best available, De Gasperi, at that time both Prime Minister and Foreign Minister, rejected the American offer.

After De Gasperi's failure to form a new government in the summer of 1953, the Christian Democrats turned in desperation to other men, but none had any more success. As the country had now been without a government for several months, the party conceived the idea of a provisional nonpolitical, or "administrative," cabinet to tide the country over until a new majority in Parliament could be negotiated. This administrative cabinet was formed by Giuseppe Pella, a right-wing Christian Democrat with no

---

[3] Anti-English sentiment had been built up by Fascist propaganda from the time of the Ethiopian War and the sanctions imposed against Italy by the League of Nations under British urging. The hard line taken by Britain after World War II, especially against the restoration of the pre-Fascist colonies to Italy, had caused more bitterness.

strong following in the party, but with close ties to northern business and financial circles. His cabinet was composed of Christian Democrats and a few independent technicians. In presenting his government to Parliament, he emphasized its provisional and limited nature, although the tone of his remarks on foreign policy indicated a somewhat independent attitude toward Italy's allies. This was calculated to get right-wing support and it worked, for only the Communists and Socialists voted against him a few days later when he received his vote of confidence. The Social Democrats and MSI abstained.

Pella now sensed his opportunity to convert his administrative and temporary government into a political one, and seized the Trieste issue as his vehicle to real power. Adopting a nationalist and belligerent tone in a speech on September 13, 1953, he proposed that a plebiscite be held in the whole Free Territory. At the same time, he indicated that Italy's ratification of the European Defense Community Treaty might depend on satisfaction received on Trieste.

The creation of the Coal and Steel Community in 1952 had stimulated further efforts toward European integration. In the political sphere, the Europeanists worked to draft a constitution for a European federation, but their effort made slow progress. The idea of adding West Germany's weight to the defense of Europe—while avoiding the creation of a new German army—led at this time to the evolution of the concept of a European army. The United States threw its influence behind the scheme, and in due course the principal countries of Western Europe signed a treaty creating a European Defense Community. In both France and Italy, there were considerable reservations, however, and not only among those of the extreme left. In both countries, doubt existed as to whether the treaty would be ratified by their respective parliaments. Pella was now claiming compensation on Trieste as the price of Italy's participation in the EDC.

England and America responded to Italian pressure by offering to let Italy replace them in the administration of Zone A. The Italian press was enthusiastic and Pella's reputation increased strikingly. But Tito reacted violently, and on October 10, 1953, he warned that Yugoslavia would consider Italian entry into

Trieste an act of aggression. The tension increased on both sides and the British and the Americans backed down. Demonstrations took place in subsequent weeks in both contending countries and in Trieste itself. On November 6, local police forces under Allied Administration fired upon demonstrators in that port city; six people were killed and many more wounded. This led to hostile demonstrations in Italy against its two allies, especially against the British Embassy in Rome. Pella wanted to go to Trieste to be present at the funeral of the victims. It would have been magnificent politics, but the Allies refused permission. His presence would have stirred up another demonstration. At this point, Pella sent two Italian divisions to the border area near Gorizia. The Yugoslavs countered immediately. The situation was less serious than it appeared, for Pella—and probably Tito—was bluffing. The British and the Americans proposed a conference, which Tito rejected because Pella stipulated that the tripartite declaration of 1948 had to be the minimum basis for discussion. A few days later, both sides withdrew their troops from the border area and the tension was reduced, but the issue was left unresolved.

Pella's behavior had alarmed Christian Democratic leaders, who were aware of his domestic political motivations. De Gasperi criticized him more and more openly, as did Scelba. By January, 1954, Pella was running into trouble with the party secretariat, which was gradually moving to the left. Amintore Fanfani, an economic historian by profession who had been associated in the late 1940's with Giuseppe Dossetti in the Catholic intellectual group around the magazine *Cronache sociali,* had organized a new current within the Christian Democratic Party, the Iniziativa Democratica. Less extreme than the *Cronache sociali* group in its leftist social and economic principles, and less integralist in its Catholic philosophy,[4] the Iniziativa Democratica proclaimed a progressive pro-

---

[4] Catholic integralism may be described briefly as a movement aiming to have all human activities, especially political and social activities, impregnated by a Catholic inspiration. It seeks to achieve a Catholic social order that would minimize and, in the long run, eliminate all social and political movements based on different inspirations, such as Marxism, liberalism, secular humanism. It is antipluralist in its ultimate objectives, although it can collaborate with groups of non-Catholic inspiration for pragmatic political objectives. Integralists may be right or left wing in their economic

gram aimed at the popular masses, rather than at the upper classes. Fanfani, the most practical politician of the old *Cronache sociali* group, was building up the Iniziativa Democratica influence within the party secretariat. Thus attacked from a number of sides, Pella was forced to resign as Prime Minister.

For two weeks, Fanfani tried to form a single-party (*monocolore*) government. He was looked upon with considerable suspicion both inside and outside his party. The right wing, within and without Christian Democracy, distrusted his anticapitalism. The democratic lay parties of the left had reservations because of his background of associations with corporatism and integralism. Having finally put a Christian Democratic cabinet together, Fanfani saw it defeated by Parliament. It was one of the very few times in the history of postwar Italy that a government was overthrown in a formal vote of no confidence. Fanfani's defeat led him to concentrate on building up the position of his faction within his party. Here, he had more success. At the Christian Democratic Party congress held in the summer of 1954, the Iniziativa Democratica emerged as the principal current. Fanfani was elected Secretary-General of the party.

After Fanfani's failure to form a government in January, 1954, the Christian Democrats decided to return to the earlier center coalition. Their negotiations with their former allies were difficult, but were finally concluded successfully by means of contradictory promises. To the Social Democrats, they promised a series of social reforms; to the Liberals, the Ministry of Industry and Commerce, in order to reassure private business that the reforms would not amount to much in practice. The Republicans remained outside the cabinet but promised to support it in Parliament. On this basis, Mario Scelba, former Minister of the Interior, hated by the left parties for his mobile police squads and strongarm tactics, succeeded in forming a government.

Scelba was plagued from the beginning by scandals, in which he had no direct part. The most crucial of these was the Wilma Montesi affair, which got the government involved in a sordid

---

orientations. The *Cronache sociali* integralists were left wing, and enamored of corporatist ideas. Luigi Gedda would be a right-wing integralist.

intrigue of rivalries. Foreign Minister Attilio Piccioni, a Christian Democrat, learned that his son was implicated in the scandal. Piccioni was forced to resign, his career ruined.[5] Factions of the Christian Democratic party used the scandal to embarrass and undercut other factions. The Carabinieri were rivals of the national police (the Pubblica Sicurezza of the Ministry of the Interior). Scelba was also the Minister of the Interior. The whole business revealed a web of collusion, corruption, and rivalry among colleagues, and threw the public administration and the government into the worst possible position.

Heir to the unresolved Trieste issue, Scelba also tried to use the EDC treaty as a means of resolving it. He knew that the EDC was unpopular with some groups within his own party and among his allied Social Democrats, who feared even indirect German rearmament. He might have pushed EDC through Parliament if he were able to tie it in with a diplomatic success on Trieste; otherwise, he was doubtful of the effects on his own majority of a parliamentary debate. The French Parliament resolved the EDC issue by voting it down, thereby eliminating the necessity for the Italians to act upon it.

Scelba did succeed in settling the Trieste question independently. Through the insistence of President Einaudi, Piccioni had been replaced at the Foreign Ministry by a man who would be willing to accept the partition of the Free Territory, Gaetano Martino of the Liberal Party. In the autumn of 1954, England and America revived the earlier scheme of dividing the Free Territory between Zones A and B. They proposed the same boundary rectifications in favor of Yugoslavia that De Gasperi had turned down in the spring of 1953. In the fall of that year, Pella had reasserted the claim to the whole Free Territory. One year later the Italians accepted the Anglo-American proposal, and the rectifications in favor of Yugoslavia were even greater than those rejected by De Gasperi. This time, Tito was more tractable and agreement was reached in October, 1954. Technically, Italy merely replaced the British and the Americans in the administration of Zone A; thus, the Italians could assert that their claim to Zone B was not

---

[5] Piccioni had been considered De Gasperi's political heir. Three years later, the courts found his son to be completely innocent.

renounced. Actually, everyone knew it was a partition of the Free Territory, and in fact Trieste was incorporated into Italy in subsequent years.

This solution was a bitter pill for the Italians to swallow, and the government did not feel equal to presenting the agreement to Parliament for consent to presidential ratification of it as a treaty. Instead, the government called the accord a "memorandum of understanding," taking the position that since it was an interim measure, not a definitive treaty, parliamentary approval for ratification was unnecessary. Scelba announced to the Senate, however, that President Einaudi had already given his approval of the memorandum. In fact, Einaudi had done more than give approval; he had actively backed it behind the scenes. Scelba then asked for, and received from both houses, resolutions endorsing the work of his government. The problem of treaty ratification was thus side-stepped.

Resolution of the Trieste problem led to the expansion of economic relations between the two claimants to the territory, so that in future years Italy became Yugoslavia's most important foreign supplier and best customer. In addition, a weapon that had been used with some success to poison internal politics was removed from the hands of Italian nationalists. One negative consequence of the years of agitation over Trieste was the stimulation of Austro-German agitation over the South Tyrol. If Italians were outraged that their compatriots were forcibly deprived of their irredentist rights, the South Tyrolese in the Alto Adige and the North Tyrolese in Innsbruck were similarly outraged. The Italians refused to recognize the similarity between the two agitations, but from the mid-1950's onward, the South Tyrol problem would grow to create another difficulty in foreign affairs.

It is evident that the Trieste issue, no matter how sincerely felt, had been manipulated to build up domestic political positions and to appeal to nationalistic and right-wing sentiments. These were the years of reaction and obscurantism in Italian public life. Anti-Fascists were called saboteurs of Italian national honor. The resistance movement was denigrated; partisans were characterized as bandits, murderers, and even Communists. The Communists had been trying to take all the credit for the resistance, but now the opposite extremists just granted them the credit as a favor.

Interest in ideas and in political action had drastically declined. Compared to the heated and tense atmosphere of the immediate postwar years, this decline might be interpreted as a growing acceptance by the general public of the institutions of the new republic, and of the political system. This would be an incorrect inference, however. The decline of political commitment was no indication of any such consensus, rather it marked a privatization of personal and family life, signifying an exclusive concern with immediate, materialistic goals. The phenomenon was apparent in the universities, historic home of the militant and committed youth of Italy. In the mid-1950's, the youth, in their preoccupation with private careers, seemed to have forgotten all about the struggle for a better world. The gradually widening market for professional skills created by a developing economy provided opportunities for young men as long as they avoided any identification as political extremists.

On the whole, the business community had always been naturally conservative, but a combination of fear and opportunism had led it to meet, with a policy of compromise, both the social demands of the times and the social commitments of the Christian Democratic Party. As insurance against left-wing political victories, business firms had even found it useful to collaborate with the CGIL and to provide some financing for the Socialist and Communist parties. The principal organization of the business community, Confindustria (Confederation of Industry), led by the Genoese Angelo Costa, had followed this cautious and moderate line throughout the late 1940's and early 1950's.

By 1954, business attitudes were hardening. Encouraged by the political expansion of the right-wing parties in the previous year, by the Republican victory in the United States, by the atmosphere emerging in Italy, Confindustria decided on an aggressive campaign against both the left and the center. Under the stimulation of the large electrical corporations located in Milan, Angelo Costa was replaced by Alighiero De Micheli, president of Assolombardo (Lombard Business Association). Instead of giving most of their support to the Christian Democrats, they put more and more money into the Liberal Party.

In the spring of 1954, Giovanni Malagodi became Secretary-General of the Liberal Party. An able and dynamic man, he was openly identified with the large industries of the north. His party had been divided between conservative and progressive wings. The progressive wing did not identify liberalism with unrestrained free enterprise and rugged nineteenth-century laissez faire capitalism. Reformist in the American New Deal sense, the progressives felt that the party had not been sufficiently firm in defending the principle of the separation of Church and state from the increasing pressure of Catholic confessionalism and the Church on their major ally, the Christian Democratic Party.

Under Malagodi's leadership, the Liberal Party became more and more openly the spokesman for big business and the opponent of any economic reformism or public intervention in the market place. The success in capturing the Liberal Party further encouraged the "economic right" in their attacks on the center coalition. The progressive wing of the party attempted to counter these trends without much success, and after a year and a half, finally split off to found the Radical Party, in the fall of 1955.

The Radical Party had a numerically weak base, and in its short life (it was practically defunct by 1962), it never elected any candidates to Parliament, although it was able to elect some members to local and provincial councils. It had an influence, however, far beyond its membership. Two weeklies identified with the Radical point of view, *Il Mondo* and *L'Espresso,* had a circulation and impact among intellectual and political leaders far beyond the confines of the party, and the various study groups, research congresses, and debates promoted by these organs of opinion provided a stimulus to political thought that contributed to the activity of the democratic left. For the Radicals became ardent exponents of the replacement of centrism by a coalition of parties from the Christian Democrats to and including the Socialists.

But the opening to the left could not become a reality in the atmosphere then prevailing. It has already been noted that Confindustria's position was hardening to the right.[6] It launched an ever more aggressive attack on the divided labor movement. Workers were becoming more cynical and less disposed to back their union leaders. Membership was declining. Those workers in the elite group—the employees of the large and expanding firms—were benefiting from higher salaries and improved real incomes. Under the influence of this combination of pressures and benefits, the most exposed of the labor federations, the CGIL, was in trouble: still the largest of the federations, it was now to be openly besieged by the American Government. American labor advisers, as part of the policy of weakening Communist influence, had supported the schisms in the CGIL that had occurred in the late 1940's. They had favored the CISL and had discouraged the UIL in subsequent years. In 1955, Mrs. Luce, the American ambassador in Rome, promoted a new policy to undermine the CGIL still further. The United States Department of Defense used to award "off-shore" contracts to European manufacturers for the production of military equipment that the United States Government was furnishing its allies. Mrs. Luce succeeded in having the Defense Department proclaim that no further contracts would be awarded to Italian firms in which the CGIL candidates won over 50 per cent of the votes in the election to the internal commissions.[7] Since these contracts were important to several major industries, the profits and jobs of a large number of people were at stake.

The test of the new American policy came in the plant elections of the Fiat Company in April, 1955. Fiat, the largest private business in Italy and the major producer of automotive vehicles and other heavy equipment, had a substantial number of off-shore contracts. In 1954, the CGIL had received 60 per cent of the votes for the internal commission; now, in 1955, it dropped to 38 per cent. Comparable results occurred in other large firms. The American policy appeared to be successful. Appearances can be deceptive, however. Many workers, often encouraged by their CGIL

---

[6] Confindustria does not control all of Italian industry, and a number of firms are not guided by its policies.

[7] The internal commission represents the workers in a plant in all dealings with the management regarding the application of work rules, etc.

leaders, voted for the other labor federations but remained basically Communist or Socialist in their orientation. They were voting for their jobs, not for a different union. In later political elections, the Communist and Socialist vote increased. The CISL was only a temporary beneficiary of the American pressure. Italian employers used the situation to erode all the unions, not only the CGIL. In 1958, the CISL was split wide open in the Fiat plant by the appearance of a splinter union, led by dissident CISL leaders, that was suspected of having company support. The consequence was that the democratic, as well as the Marxist, labor movement suffered substantial setbacks.

Other setbacks were suffered by the forces of democratic liberalism during this same period. The Catholic Church appeared to be enduring a period of reaction, and this had some influence on the domestic scene. The political eclipse of De Gasperi removed a barrier to clerical and integralist forces within Catholic circles. After 1952, Pope Pius XII was a sick man. During this time, a group of conservative Curia cardinals, of whom Alfredo Cardinal Ottaviani was the most voluble, if not the most important, appeared to get the upper hand in the Vatican and to use it heavily in Italy and France.[8] Under Cardinal Ottaviani's direction, the Holy Office smashed the worker-priest movement in France. In Italy, young Catholic Action intellectuals were careful not to get caught when reading the works of such French Catholic thinkers as Teilhard de Chardin, Jacques Maritain, or Emmanuel Mounier.

Under Church pressure, censorship became more vexatious. Article 21 of the Constitution prohibits publications and entertainments "contrary to good morals." While some constitutionalists insisted that only post-censorship was permissible under this article, in fact pre-censorship of moving-picture scenarios, stage plays, and radio and television scripts was exercised by a bureau in the executive office of the Prime Minister. (In later years, after the creation of the Ministry of Tourism and Spectacles, the bureau was transferred to this ministry.) The censorship was exer-

---

8 Carlo Falconi, an Italian expert on Vatican affairs, called this group *Il Pentagono* ("The Pentagon").

cised so arbitrarily that while many salacious films got through, scripts of social and political criticism were blocked.

Freedom of religion, although guaranteed by Article 8 of the Constitution, was under fire. Protestant evangelical denominations, especially the Church of Christ, found that the police harried all their activities, closed their meeting halls on a variety of pretexts, and generally made life difficult. The Fascist law of public security of 1931 was still in effect and was used to ban a wide variety of different activities.[9]

A further oppression of the period was the restraint on freedom of movement. A gradual exodus from the countryside was taking place, for peasants were going to the cities in search of jobs. Article 16 of the Constitution guarantees freedom of movement, but still in effect was an old Fascist law that prohibited anyone from moving to another locality unless he had the guarantee of a job; on the other hand, jobs could be offered only to individuals officially registered as residents of the locality. The law was not enforced effectively, and the peasants continued their influx into the urban slums. Since they were illegal residents, however, they could not register to vote or register in the unemployment exchanges. They could not even demand rights and social welfare payments from their employers, for they could not afford to expose themselves. They were the helpless victims of abuse and exploitation. The Constitutional Court finally denounced the Fascist law as unconstitutional, but it was not until February 18, 1961, that the old decree was superseded by new legislation. The indifferent enforcement of this Fascist decree indicates some of the saving graces in Italian life during this period of reaction. Through inefficiency, whether natural or deliberate, and through a certain sense of human compassion, some of the more vexatious aspects of the period were softened and made more tolerable.

Some of the reformist zeal still present at the end of 1954 had led to the passage of a law extending pensions to peasant farmers. Motives other than reform were behind its passage: it was an instrument for consolidating the control of the Christian Democratic

---

[9] A full discussion of many of these cases was provided by the outstanding civil rights lawyer Piero Calamandrei. See *Dieci anni dopo* (Bari: Laterza, 1955).

farm federation, the Coltivatori Diretti, over peasant proprietors. It was a measure welcome to all concerned, no matter what political motives were behind it.

Another positive act was the passage of the Vanoni Plan in 1955, formally entitled, "Ten-Year Plan for the Development of Employment and Income." It was introduced and fought for by the Christian Democratic Budget Minister, Ezio Vanoni, supported by the left wing of his own party and the other parties of the left. There were six fundamental goals: (1) an increase of annual investments to 25 per cent of gross national product; (2) a growth rate averaging 5 per cent per year in gross national income; (3) a moderate increase in consumption, but not enough to deprive the economy of increased savings for investment; (4) a balance in Italy's international payments to maintain adequate foreign exchange reserves and reasonable price stability; (5) elimination of structural unemployment over ten years; and (6) a reduction in the wide gaps in levels of income between north and south, industry and agriculture, upper- and lower-income groups.

The motivations behind the Vanoni Plan were revealed by the evidence that the economic growth of the previous years had made little appreciable impact on unemployment or on poverty in those areas of the country that were traditionally backward. The pressure of right-wing interests inside and outside the government, while insufficient to block passage of the bill in Parliament, was adequate to undermine the "planning" aspects of the project. Scelba was Prime Minister when the Vanoni Plan was put through Parliament, but he and his successors, Segni and Zoli, reduced the plan until it was nothing more than a series of projections of future economic developments. Both private and public firms went ahead their own way, making decisions based on their calculations of their own best interests, without any commitments or obligations to accede to broad goals laid down by a national agency.

As a set of projections, the Vanoni Plan appeared audacious. Yet events proved that some of these forecasts were actually conservative. The growth of gross national income in the following years of the 1950's was closer to 6 than to 5 per cent per annum, one of the highest growth rates in the Western world. Italy's balance of international payments became very favorable indeed, due to the expansion of exports and of the tourist industry, so that the lira became a hard currency and Italy accumulated a substantial gold and foreign-exchange reserve. Price rises were kept moderate until the early 1960's and thus the real incomes of those who were working and making profits did increase substantially.

On the other hand, unemployment did not decline significantly until the end of the decade. The economic gap between contrasting sectors of Italian society widened rather than narrowed, with the north advancing more rapidly than the south, industry more rapidly than agriculture, profits and wages more rapidly in the modernized large-scale sector than in the traditionally artisan, handicraft, and small-scale merchant sectors.

It is not surprising, therefore, that political tensions thrived as they had in the past, and became even more acute. At the Christian Democratic congress of 1954, the center-left section of the party—the Iniziativa Democratica—had won control of the party organization, and Amintore Fanfani was elected Secretary-General. Fanfani was actually more conservative than his reputation, but he appeared as a dangerous symbol to the right wing of Italian society. His election had been one of the factors disenchanting Confindustria with the Christian Democrats and inducing that business organization to concentrate even more of its hopes on the Liberals.

Fanfani was more interested in power than policy, at least in the short run, and his first efforts were directed toward building up his party as an organization. Under De Gasperi, the party had had little in the way of an effective grass-roots organization and had depended on related Catholic groups—such as the Civic Committees of Catholic Action, the Coltivatori Diretti, the CISL and the Church network of parishes—to carry out the election campaigns and round up the voters. Fanfani now engaged in an effort to create a wide and strong party base that would leave his party somewhat more independent of these related organizations. He even made an effort to establish a network of party cells in the factories. Since a large number of politicians, inside as well as outside the party, had a strong stake in preventing the rise of a more integrated Christian Democratic Party, Fanfani had only partial success. Undoubtedly, the party as such was developed considerably in the following four years, and the influence of the *partitocrazia*, the party bureaucracy, rose, as it did in all other parties except the Communist, where it had always been dominant. But Fanfani was never able to make his organization dominant, and at best it became one more faction in the shifting league of interests which composed the Christian Democratic Party.

A transition of a different nature was at work inside the Socialist Party. Ever since the electoral defeat of 1948, there had been Socialists who questioned the pact of unity of action with the Communists. They recognized that they could accomplish little for their supporters, mainly workers, if they did nothing but protest the inequities of Italian life from outside the governing coalition. They recognized that neither the conditions of life nor the line followed by the Communists provided opportunity for successful revolution. Reluctance to undermine the "unity of the working class" had retarded the development of this point of view, and in the intervening years, the Socialists had suffered heavily through internal schisms and the loss of their electorate. By the early 1950's, at least two identifiable currents were apparent in the party: the "autonomists," led by Giovanni Pieraccini and Riccardo Lombardi, called for more independence of action, while the *carristi* defended the line of close cooperation with the Communists. The *carristi* were particularly strong among the Socialists in the CGIL, who were in close working contact with the dominant Communist leadership of the labor federation.

In the 1951 and 1952 local elections and in the 1953 parliamentary election, the Socialists had already run independent tickets wherever proportional representation was used. During the parliamentary election, Nenni, who was straddling the factional differences among his followers, had enunciated publicly for the first time the concept of the opening to the left. This was, in effect, the assertion of a reformist, rather than maximalist, position; it was also the recognition of Socialist willingness to collaborate with bourgeois parties within the political framework of the democratic republic if a common program of social benefits and economic reforms could be agreed upon.

Foreign policy had ceased to be a divisive issue. Although the

Socialists had originally opposed Italy's entry into NATO, by
1955 they were ready to accept the alliance—provided that it was
used for defensive purposes only (they had originally condemned
it as aggressive in intent) and provided that the emphasis in the
alliance shifted from military to economic and political cooperation. Since the Christian Democrats were also primarily concerned
with NATO as a means of aiding Italian economic development,
the two parties were not too far apart. As the intensity of the Cold
War spirit was moderated by a growing atmosphere of *détente,*
which finally led to the 1955 Geneva understanding between the
United States and Russia, the Socialist reconciliation with Atlan-
ticism in the "spirit of Geneva" was promoted. The Socialists
were now willing to accept the Western alliance if it followed a
policy of rapprochement with the Soviet bloc.

At the Turin congress of the Socialist Party in the spring of
1955, Nenni made it clear that he was repeating his offer of an
opening to the left and that his party was ready to test the possibility of collaboration with the Christian Democrats. This renewed
offer, combined with the growing conservatism of the Liberals and
the shift to the left among the Christian Democrats, made the
center coalition of Prime Minister Scelba ever more precarious.

President Luigi Einaudi's term of office had come to an end,
and his advanced age led him to refuse to run for a second term.
The two houses of Parliament elect the president in joint session.
For the first three ballots, a two-thirds majority is required; after
the third ballot, a simple majority is sufficient. The Christian
Democrats not only did not have the necessary majority, but as it
turned out, could not keep control over their own parliamentarians. The official candidate of the party organization and of the
cabinet, Cesare Merzagora, President of the Senate, was a rather
conservative man, and a small left-wing group of Christian Democrats put forward the name of Giovanni Gronchi, President of the
Chamber of Deputies, in competition. Fanfani tried to hold his
party in line for its official candidate, but a group of right-wing
Christian Democrats led by Guido Gonnella undercut Fanfani
and threw their support to Gronchi. It was obvious that they were
less interested in the person of Gronchi than in the opportunity

to set Fanfani back in his efforts to build up a disciplined, integrated party.

At this point, Nenni saw the opportunity to insert the Socialists into the struggle. Gronchi was known to be sympathetic to the idea of collaboration between Christian Democrats and Socialists. He was known to have a more elastic conception of the Atlantic alliance than the official government position—involving less subservience to the United States than Gaetano Martino's conception —although Gronchi was not a neutralist, as his enemies claimed. There were so many rumors to the effect that Mrs. Luce opposed Gronchi that Prime Minister Scelba was obliged to announce publicly that the United States was not exerting pressure for or against anyone. In fact, the rumors aided Gronchi by bringing to him the backing of nationalists of the right. Once Nenni was able to mobilize his own party's support behind Gronchi and to negotiate with right-wing Christian Democrats and other conservatives, the battle was won. The Communists swung over, and the Christian Democratic government leaders, faced with the prospect of having a president from their own party elected by the extreme left and the extreme right against the center, released their supporters, who all voted for Gronchi and made his election overwhelming.

The presidential election had produced strains on the government and on the parties, especially the Christian Democratic Party. Nenni's skillful maneuvering had enabled him to insert an opposition party, considered beyond the pale, in all respectable circles, into the victorious presidential majority. Fanfani's failure to hold the Christian Democrats together in support of the party's candidate had exacerbated differences among various factional leaders. Scelba had been a vigorous opponent of Gronchi's election to the presidency of the republic. It is not surprising, consequently, that when the Prime Minister submitted his government's routine resignation to the new President, Gronchi did not invite him to form a new government. Instead, the head of the state called upon Antonio Segni. This action was the first indication that an enlarged conception of the presidency was to emerge in the Italian political system.

From the very beginning of his seven-year term of office, Gronchi made it clear that he did not conceive of his role as that of a mere ceremonial figurehead who wrote and spoke only at his government's dictation. He had his own ideas about policy and personnel, and about the broad goals of Italian political evolution. In his inaugural address to Parliament, he condemned a social order that left large sections of the population estranged from it, referring to "those working masses and middle classes whom universal suffrage has conducted to the doorstep of the state's edifice without introducing them effectively to where political direction is exercised." And he defined the goal of government policy to be "the reconciliation of the people with the state about which we dream and toward which we work."[10]

Dreams and work are both necessary, but in the Italy of 1955, there was still a long way to go before that reconciliation dreamed of by Gronchi could be realized. The government was so bogged down in contradictions that it was practically impossible for it to move in any direction, right or left. It was in fact stalemated. Outside of Italy, events were occurring, however, which would have an additional impact on the country's internal political alliances.

---

[10] Giovanni Gronchi, *Discorsi d'America* (Milan: Garzanti, 1956), pp. 39, 99.

7

Stirrings of Revisionism

The explosion that rocked the Italian left in the spring of 1956 was Nikita Khrushchev's report to the Twentieth Congress of the Communist Party of the Soviet Union, *The Crimes of the Stalin Era*. The "secret" report, once it was translated and published by the American State Department and thereby exposed to the rest of the world, aggravated all the stresses and strains inherent in the evolution of the Communist and Socialist parties in Italy. 138838

Within the Communist Party, stirrings for a revision of policies and attitudes were confined to the intellectual elite and the leadership. The defense of all the past policies of the Soviet Union seemed hardly justified now that Russian leaders were themselves openly condemning them. Khrushchev's attack on the "cult of personality" threatened Palmiro Togliatti's position among his own colleagues. Togliatti maneuvered skillfully, however, and was able to isolate his critics effectively by using a combination of ideological concessions and toleration of criticism, while at the same time rallying all the personal interests of his followers to preserve the party's unity as the condition of political effectiveness. Administrative elections were due in June, 1956, and all Communist leaders who had positions in communal or provincial governments had a stake in their posts and in maintaining the unity of the Party organization.

To soften the impact of Khrushchev's exposures, Togliatti openly adopted a position of criticism of his Soviet comrades. While endorsing the elimination of the cult of personality, he questioned the past behavior of some of the current Russian leaders and demanded to know what they had failed to do to prevent some of the crimes of the Stalin era. Most importantly, however, Togliatti seized upon Khrushchev's assertion of the legitimacy of "various paths to Socialism" as an endorsement of the actual policy of the Italian Communists, who were claiming their own "Italian way to Socialism." Their submission to Soviet policy had been limited to international affairs; inside Italy, from the very beginning of the post-Mussolini era, they had always determined their own strategy and tactics.[1] Togliatti now openly asserted the doctrine that the Soviet Union and the Soviet Party were no longer the "guiding state" and "guiding Party" for the world Communist movement. Every Party was free to follow its own course; there were a number of centers of power and policy; "polycentrism" was the term he used. The following year, before a meeting of his own Central Committee, he asserted that the unity of the international Communist movement was based on the "common goals and ideals" of the several national parties, not on a system of hierarchical discipline, and he re-emphasized that each Party was completely independent in the formulation of its own Party line.

By these verbal measures and concessions, Togliatti succeeded in keeping the internal unrest minimal, and his position was reinforced by the results of the administrative elections held that summer. While the Communists suffered some losses in the major northern cities of Genoa, Turin, and Milan, they continued to make small but steady gains in the country as a whole, and especially in the south and the islands. The elections confirmed once again that the overwhelming majority of Italians who voted Communist did so because of the conditions of their personal daily lives, not because of dogmatic issues or events occurring thousands of miles away.

---

[1] For example, Stalin had opposed the Italian Party's policy of opening ranks to anyone, whether or not he was a knowledgeable and believing Communist. The Party had done so in spite of Stalin's objections, and this rejection of any ideological qualification for membership can be found in the Party's Constitution.

The effect of Khrushchev's exposures on the Italian Socialists was far greater. All their past sacrifices on the altar of "proletarian unity" seemed hardly justified by the abuses now revealed. The autonomist wing of the party received major reinforcement from these events, and the policy of seeking a reinsertion into the Italian constitutional political game was buttressed. The open affirmation that the sacrifice of political democracy was too high a price to pay for socialism, and that the one was not to be subordinated to the other under any circumstances, would not be long in coming. Within a few months of the Twentieth Congress of the CPSU, Pietro Nenni wrote in one of the Socialist Party's journals that the defects revealed by Khrushchev were not the results of the errors of one man, but were due to the degeneration of the Soviet political and legal system. It was the method of dictatorship that had to be abandoned; the mere replacement of one man by some others was not enough.

Logically, the Socialist reaction further encouraged their assertion of electoral independence from the Communists. In the 1956 administrative elections, therefore, the Socialists, along with the Social Democrats and Republicans, successfully urged a return to the method of proportional representation for electing councilmen in all communes over 10,000 in population.[2] This enabled the smaller parties to run their own independent slates; the Socialists separately from the Communists, the Republicans and Social Democrats separately from the Christian Democrats. The Socialist slates made a number of electoral gains that furthered their autonomy.

Growing Socialist autonomy laid the logical premises for reunification of the two Socialist parties. In August, 1956, Pietro Nenni and Giuseppe Saragat met at the resort town of Pralognan to discuss the issue. There is little information yet available as to what was said, but the conclusion was negative and the two political parties continued to go their independent ways.[3] Strong fac-

---

[2] Success in getting the election law revised was due to the Social Democrats and Republicans, who threatened the Christian Democrats with a government crisis at the national level if the changes were not made.

[3] Nenni has hinted that Saragat was the one who was unready for reunification, but until more is known any judgment is premature.

tions within each, however, would make the reunification issue an important question of policy from that time.

The shocks reserved for the Italian left in the year 1956 were not yet over. Even more dramatic than Khrushchev's revelations in the spring were the Polish and Hungarian uprisings of the following October. The Hungarian revolt was the real blow, especially to the Italian Communist Party. The Party's leadership abandoned any attempt to give a unified explanation of events. The official Party paper, *Unità,* lamely called the Hungarian uprising a counter-revolution organized by foreign and domestic reactionaries, while the interpretation published in other pro-Communist papers was notably different. The Communist leadership of the CGIL openly sided with the Hungarian insurrectionists, and Communist intellectuals signed manifestoes of protest against the Party leadership.

But discipline was slowly restored and the Party ranks were reunited. The Anglo-French-Israeli attack on Egypt helped divert attention from Hungary and enabled the leadership to launch an attack on Western imperialism. The efforts of the government of Imre Nagy to detach Hungary from the Soviet bloc were used to justify the Russian intervention. Even some dissident Communists could accept the necessity for the Soviet Union to guard its defenses and prevent disintegration of its East European alliance, and could thus overlook any mistakes the former Stalinist-type Hungarian leadership had made in handling Hungarian workers.

Nevertheless, the Communist losses were not negligible. It has been estimated that approximately 300,000 members left the Italian Communist Party at that time, and among them were some important political and intellectual leaders whose prestige would be missed. The Party's capacity to attract new intellectual leadership from among Italian youth declined considerably. Events appeared to confirm the benefits that ambitious young men might derive by avoiding political identification and commitment. The Communist youth federations, Party schools, training programs, all had to be scaled down in view of the reduced number of new recruits. The curious phenomenon of a declining Party membership coupled with an increasing voting support would characterize the Communist Party's future, for the 1958 and subsequent elections demonstrated that the Party could still function efficiently as an electoral machine.

The effects of the Hungarian uprising were dramatic among the Socialists. Nenni denounced the circumstances and conditions that had caused the Hungarian revolt, insisting again in public and in private that they represented the failure of a system, not of a man.[4] The Socialist Party, rejecting the Russian interpretation of the uprising as a counter-revolutionary plot, asserted the rights of the Hungarian workers and condemned the Soviet intervention. Nenni returned the Stalin Peace Prize he had received in an earlier year.

A few months later, in February, 1957, a Socialist Party congress met at Venice to assess party policy. Angelo Roncalli, the Archbishop of Venice, later Pope John XXIII, wished the Socialists a successful congress. Nenni's speech and the confirming resolutions later adopted by the delegates reasserted the interpretation given to the events of the previous year: Stalinist degeneration was inherent in the system and in the political and legal institutions of the Soviet Union more than in the man. The values of democracy and of liberty were as important as socialization of the means of production. The Socialists accepted the practices of parliamentary democracy, including the multiplicity of parties, and free elections, not only as means to social justice but as ends in themselves. The unity-of-action pact, which, in fact, had been moribund at the national level for a number of years, was practically, if not formally, finished.

But the results of the Socialist congress were not so clear-cut. Alongside these verbal statements and unanimously adopted resolutions was the contradictory fact that a substantial number of the incoming party directorate elected by the congress came from the extreme left-wing faction, the *carristi*, who favored continued collaboration with the Communists. In the election of

---

4 In an exchange of letters with Mikhail Suslov, who had written in August, 1956, to complain about Nenni's condemnation of the Soviet system rather than one man, Nenni reiterated in October that the Hungarian events proved that the defects were due to the system. The letters were published in *Avanti,* October 25, 1964, after the defenestration of Khrushchev.

delegates, carried out in the party sections preparatory to the national congress, the secretariat had maneuvered the voting in such a way as to produce delegations suspicious of, if not antagonistic to, Nenni's thesis.[5] They voted for his resolutions, and then they elected to the principal party organs a number of men who were loath to carry them out. Thus, Nenni was obliged to work with many men who were not yet ready to follow his leadership. While the *carristi* were in an over-all numerical minority, they held key positions in the party, the CGIL, and the cooperatives. Some of them were accused of being on the Communist payroll, an accusation difficult to prove.

In every respect, the Socialist position remained ambiguous, and the ambiguity was exploited by the right wing of the Italian political spectrum. The continued association of Socialists and Communists in local governments and in the CGIL led these right-wing forces to assert that the proclamations of Socialist autonomy were all fraudulent, nothing more than a Marxist scheme to achieve power by a different tactic. This line of attack made life more difficult for those Social Democrats, Republicans, and left-wing Christian Democrats who were arguing that Socialist cooperation was necessary to achieve stable and progressive government. The evolution of the Socialist position could not be rapid. It had to overcome many years of past association with the Communists and to disregard the tempting hope that the Italian Communists were not unrecoverable for a progressive democracy. It had to fight its way against all the obstacles raised by external conservative forces who preferred to keep the Socialists in a position of sterile protest outside the effective centers of political power, rather than have them join and reinforce the democratic left.

The outcome of the Socialist congress revived a variety of attacks on the political parties, attacks that had persisted with various degrees of intensity throughout the postwar period. Uomo

---

[5] In the elections of the delegates to the party congresses held in the various sections, there was often little participation by the mass of party cardholders. In many cases only an insignificant minority of members came to section meetings, thereby making it easy for the local secretaries to get their own friends elected.

Qualunque, flourishing temporarily in the early years, had been one type of attack against party politics. Another type had taken the form of criticism of party control over parliamentarians. It was charged that the party organizations outside the chambers made policy and determined the voting positions of their parliamentary delegations, but since almost all national party leaders were also parliamentarians, the lines of influence were not that simple. Yet there was no question that the most influential parliamentary leaders derived their positions from the roles they played in their national party organizations. In the search for a means of breaking external party control, some critics advocated, without effect, the abandonment of proportional representation and its replacement by single-member districts.

A different line of attack was leveled at the full-time party bureaucrats, the *partitocrazia*. They were accused of manipulating parties to build their own power and fortunes, thus undermining —when they did not falsify—the wishes of the rank-and-file party members. They were charged with being the enemies of freedom, the crushers of internal party debate, the stultifying and rigid opponents of the evolution of new ideas. The results of the Socialist congress had appeared to verify these criticisms.

The critics came from many positions within the political spectrum and advanced their charges from a variety of motives. Some critics, such as the novelist Ignazio Silone, were sincere democrats anxious to improve the operations of the parties and to strengthen internal party democracy. Others used their attacks on party organizations as a decoy for assaults on political parties as such and, more fundamentally, on parliamentary democracy itself. The defense of permanent party organizers came from one who was himself a leading member of a *partitocrazia*, Giovanni Malagodi, Secretary-General of the Liberal Party. He argued, in Silone's own review, *Tempo presente,* that politics in the middle of the twentieth century was a full-time job, that all aspects of life were becoming bureaucratized, that the old world of the local notables was dying. In a world of many nationwide mass organizations that are, in reality, nationally organized interest groups, he argued, only a nationally organized party can stand up to them and mediate among the entrenched interests—only the party organization, structured at a national level, has some kind of vision of the national interest.[6]

In fact, the party bureaucrats were not so powerful as their critics maintained. Even the most formidable of the *partitocrazie,* that of the Communist Party, could not successfully suppress all internal debate and discussion all of the time, nor could it block the evolution of ideas nor avoid the challenging impact of external events. As for the most important of Italian parties, the Christian Democratic, it was so torn by factions, so pressured by extraparty confessional and economic interests—such as the Church hierarchy, the Catholic Action Society, and the Coltivatori Diretti —that the party secretariat at best was just one more competitor for power within the party. There was no dictatorial leadership; on the contrary, Italy, lacking effective leadership, was forced to muddle through a number of difficult economic and political issues.

One of the most controversial of the economic problems of the period was the disposition of exploration rights for petroleum and natural gas in the Po Valley. A dynamic left-wing Christian Democratic politician, Enrico Mattei, had built up a small government-owned oil corporation, AGIP, inherited by the republic from Fascism, into the large and aggressive National Hydrocarbons Trust (*Ente Nazionale Idrocarburi,* commonly known as ENI). The four-party Segni cabinet, which succeeded Scelba's government in the latter months of 1955, inherited a running dispute (dating back to 1949) between AGIP and the foreign international oil corporations. The ENI wanted exclusive exploration rights in the Po Valley, while the foreign corporations wanted private enterprise to participate in the search for additional sources of methane gas and petroleum. Mattei had tried to break into the international oil consortium in the past, but had been rebuffed, and he was now reacting vigorously. He could mobilize the left wing of his own party—and other parties of a Socialist orientation—to support the principle of state control of fundamental sources of energy. Behind the foreign corporations stood domestic Italian business interests, conservative Christian

    [6] Giovanni Malagodi, "Il segretario e gli 'apparati,' " *Tempo presente,* February, 1959, pp. 137–41.

Democratic, Monarchist, and Liberal politicians, and the American and British governments. The American ambassador, Mrs. Luce, was particularly aggressive in fighting the ENI's effort to get exclusive control, and her attempt probably boomeranged by stimulating the Italian's nationalist feelings. The final political battle lasted for over a year, and in the end Mattei won. Parliament passed legislation giving exclusive exploration rights to the ENI.[7]

This was only one of the battles lost by Italian business interests during the time of the Segni cabinet. Another one involved the reorganization and coordination of all government-owned businesses. Attempts to get the government at least partly out of business failed: no private firms wanted to buy the weak, inefficient government companies, and the strong, dynamic ones were not for sale. These latter had many powerful friends and interests behind them. The Ministry of State Participations was created in January, 1956, to supervise the many existing publicly owned firms, coordinate their plans, and develop their possibilities. Confindustria fought its creation violently, but the fears of this business organization that the new ministry would prove to be the rallying point for a widespread attack on private enterprise turned out to be groundless. The ministry's powers were limited by law, and even more so by the facts of their existence. The many public corporations were, in reality, private empires with their own vested interests and political and economic connections. The Italian Government was too weak to control effectively its own creatures, who carried out their own commercial policies, sometimes in collaboration with, and sometimes in opposition to, private enterprises.

Two additional battles lost by Confindustria involved its control over its public member firms and influence over development

---

[7] It must be emphasized that the ENI monopoly was limited to the Po Valley and to exploration and production rights. It was given no monopoly on production in the rest of Italy. The Gulf Oil Company is producing oil from concessions in Sicily. In addition, other foreign firms, such as Shell, Esso, and British Petroleum, distribute Middle Eastern petroleum products throughout the country. The ENI's marketing subsidiary, AGIP, distributes supplies obtained from foreign, as well as domestic, sources. A major foreign source has been the Soviet Union.

policies in the south. The publicly owned firms, which came under the vast IRI complex, were regular dues-paying members of Confindustria, and it, of course, was dominated by the large private industrialists. Confindustria, in bargaining with labor organizations, reached nationwide agreements binding on all its members, including the state-owned businesses. Thus, a private-interest group controlled many policies of public firms. In addition, the funds collected by Confindustria from its members were used to attack the government and the principle of government ownership of productive enterprise.

The parties of Socialist orientation had always objected to this situation, claiming that public ownership was thus stripped of all social content and that the IRI firms, in acting for purely selfish purposes, behaved like the private monopolists. As early as 1954, De Gasperi had come around to this point of view. In the fall of 1954, a resolution calling for the withdrawal of all publicly controlled firms from Confindustria was introduced by Giulio Pastore, left-wing Christian Democratic Deputy and president of the CISL, and passed by Parliament. This was merely a resolution, not a law, and three more years of legislative battle were required before it was implemented by legislation. The final detachment of the public firms came in 1957, and was related to the creation of the Ministry of State Participations, which would presumably replace Confindustria in speaking for public enterprise. The detachment (*sganciamento*), however, did not have the awful consequences feared by private-business groups. The administrators of the public firms maintained their old contacts with their private counterparts, even though the public firms no longer paid dues to Confindustria or were bound by its contracts. Eventually, a new association of publicly owned companies was created, Intersind, to represent public management and to negotiate labor contracts in behalf of public firms.

A more significant struggle raged over the evolution of governmental policies for the development of the south. Originally, the program had restricted the government's role to agricultural reform and—through the instrument of the Cassa per il Mezzogiorno—to the provision of the fundamental infrastructure to lay the foundations for subsequent industrialization. It was left to private business, encouraged by special credit benefits and tax concessions, to carry out the actual industrialization. As it turned out, private industry, both southern and northern, moved very slowly to take advantage of the supposed opportunities. Industrialization was lagging behind seriously. Under the circumstances, there was more and more agitation by economic planners and southern interests for the Fund (Cassa) to engage in direct industrial investment and for the state-owned firms to expand their southern operations. Confindustria fought this pressure bitterly, arguing that the public sector should be restricted to infrastructure and that industrialization should be left to private business. This battle it also lost. In 1957, legislation was passed that required all firms owned or dominated by the state to locate 60 per cent of their new investments in the south and to work toward the eventual goal of having 40 per cent of their total investments located in that area. But legislation is one thing and performance is another. Although, in subsequent years, the ENI reached the percentages required by the 1957 legislation, many of the IRI corporations did not.

Through its principal spokesman, Confindustria, private business lost a number of legislative battles in the years following 1955: detachment of the public firms, the Ministry of State Participations, southern industrialization, the Po Valley petroleum monopoly. The defeats were due to a variety of reasons. In the legislature, it was obvious that important factions in the Christian Democratic Party were becoming less responsive to the pressures of big business. In addition, the business community itself was not unified; many firms failed to follow the Confindustria position when they had no direct stake in the issues involved. In the fight over the legislation for southern industrialization, there were wholesale desertions by southern business and commercial interests from the Confindustria line laid down by northern industrialists. The Neapolitan and Sicilian Chambers of Commerce and industrial groups welcomed more money flowing into their areas and had no ideological preconceptions concerning the source of the money, public or private. Their views were reflected in the voting behavior of southern Christian Democratic legislators.

Another factor in the Confindustria defeats was the growing injection of new money into politics. Enrico Mattei was actively bracing his position by buying and supporting newspapers and financing various parties, especially the left wing of the Christian Democratic Party. As Confindustria became more embittered at Christian Democratic progressives and shifted more support to the Liberals, the contributions from public firms to Christian Democrats would compensate for the reduction of private money. Both private and public contributors tended to give their funds, not to any party as a whole, but to the factions and individuals within the parties who best supported their interests. This was especially true of the Christian Democrats, and a consequence was a further undermining of Fanfani's efforts to gain organizational control over his party.

Before the 1956 administrative elections, Confindustria had approached the Confederation of Agriculture (Confagricoltura) and the Confederation of Merchants (Confcommercio) with a proposal for joint and open support of those candidates and parties that would defend the interests of private enterprise. They created a new political group, Confintesa, to finance and endorse publicly individual candidates ready to accept such backing. The effort failed magnificently. The public endorsement by Confintesa was practically valueless for collecting votes. Almost all of the endorsed candidates were defeated in 1956. In 1958, businessmen would return to working behind the scenes through factional party leaders and governmental bureaucracies for the protection of their interests.

A major success for big business was the establishment of the European Common Market. The French defeat of the European Defense Community in 1953 had brought the movement for European integration to a temporary halt. Efforts to revive the integration process were launched in 1956 and crowned with victory with the Treaty of Rome in March, 1957, the final act of the expiring Segni government. For the large-scale modern businesses of Italy, penetration into the markets of the advanced countries of northwestern Europe was a much more attractive prospect than penetration of the backward and underdeveloped Italian south. Rationalization and modernization of their operations, plus low wage costs, made many of them effective competitors in European markets. Since the reduction of tariffs contemplated by the Common Market treaty was to be gradual and subject to brakes in case of necessity, the representatives of Italian big business felt that the dangers of opening their domestic market to foreign competitors could be minimized. And, since the underlying economic principles of the European Economic Community emphasized a market economy and private enterprise, they hoped that Italy's membership in this community would protect them from socializers and planners in their own country.[8] It was anticipated that the Common Market would provide an alternative to a too rapid expansion of the domestic market, for the latter would result in a social and economic upgrading of the most poverty-stricken people, causing them to increase their political claims, and would thus bring instability.[9] The Common Market, like the policy of promoting emigration abroad, could function as a partial escape from facing some harsh realities at home.

These calculations were not, of course, the only reasons for Italian interest in the European Economic Community. A minority of the intellectuals were true Europeanists who looked upon the Common Market as a step toward the political and cultural integration of the continent. Others saw in such unification the means to a revival of the international power position of Italy and of Europe. There were Italian supporters of the Gaullist third-force concept. Still others opposed the third force but looked upon economic unification as a means of increasing Europe's relative weight within the Atlantic alliance, which they considered dominated by American power. Some emphasized the common moral and spiritual patrimony of the Western European

---

[8] Since the prospects for socialization and government planning would be increased if the Socialists were brought into the governing coalition, the Common Market could be used as an argument against this danger. Thus, Gaetano Martino of the Liberal Party argued during the election campaign of 1958 that the Christian Democrats were not free to choose an opening-to-the-left policy because the Common Market treaties prohibited policies of government direction and control over the economy. See *Il Corriere lombardo* (Milan), April 28, 1958.

[9] In Italy, as elsewhere, the initial effects of economic development were increased political radicalism and an expansion of the electoral strength of the extreme left.

countries. But unquestionably crucial was the hope and expectation that a Common Market could help to protect Italy from the internal dangers of an aggressive and growing left.

In the autumn of 1957, Parliament authorized ratification of the treaties to establish the European Community. Not surprisingly, the Communists voted against authorization. The Socialists voted in favor of the establishment of Euratom and abstained on the Common Market. They emphasized, in their publications, that they did not oppose European federalism in principle: they were suspicious of the role and influence of large cartels and capitalistic interests in the projected economic community, but they thought that vital Socialist movements in the Common Market countries might effectively counter them. One of their principal leaders, Riccardo Lombardi, wrote that the Common Market could do Italy positive good if it forced those Italian firms that were backward and inefficient to modernize as the price of survival.

The Common Market not only divided the Socialists from the Communists but temporarily divided the Communist Party internally. The trade-union wing of the Communist Party, with Giuseppe Di Vittorio of the CGIL taking the lead, saw in the European Economic Community an institution of potential benefit to the Italian worker. Socialist influence within the labor confederation was having some impact on the Communist comrades in this respect. For a short time, Di Vittorio led a battle to change the minds of his Party colleagues. Party discipline prevailed, and Di Vittorio and other Communist trade-union leaders were brought back into line. In subsequent years, however, the regional community would have its effect on Communist thinking, and in 1963 the Communists would openly endorse the Common Market.

During this whole period, Italy was experiencing contradictory demands in international affairs. Men working for greater Italian integration into the Western system were countered by other men working for more independence. President Gronchi felt that Italy was far too subservient to, and underrated by, its allies, especially the United States, and argued that a more direct pursuit of Italy's national interests was compatible with loyalty to the Atlantic alliance. The Socialists, who disliked military blocs, made known that they would be more interested in the Atlantic orientation if its military aspects could be de-emphasized in favor of economic and political aid. The troubles of European colonial empires in Africa and the Near East opened up prospects for Italian business and political penetration at the expense of Great Britain and France.

The policy of a more independent stance by Italy received the name "neo-Atlanticism." The title was first used in 1955 by Foreign Minister Giuseppe Pella, in connection with the launching of a more active policy among the Arab and North African states, and quickly got confused with the idea of a "Mediterranean Vocation." Both of these policies were denounced: some proclaimed them to constitute disloyalty to Italy's allies; others ridiculed the idea that economically and militarily poor Italy could have much influence in new states, which mainly wanted guns and money. Their supporters argued that Italy could represent the Western world better than England, France, and the United States, since these countries, for a variety of reasons, were looked upon with suspicion and in some cases hatred in the "emerging countries."[10]

The Mediterranean Vocation idea was later taken up by left-wing Christian Democrats, Social Democrats, Socialists, and others who advocated cultivation of the countries of the "third world." It was also compatible with the thaw in Soviet-Western relations after the Geneva Conference of 1955, which reduced the pressures on the Western countries to maintain absolute solidarity. It corresponded to a drive by Enrico Mattei and the ENI to break into the Middle Eastern oil markets. Mattei cared nothing for Italy's official foreign policy or for the Ministry of Foreign Affairs. He negotiated his own agreements and dealt directly with foreign governments. In the autumn of 1957, his first major break-through in the Middle East was announced: a concession agreement with

---

10 There was no doubt that the great majority of Italians had looked upon the defeat of England and France in the Suez Crisis at the end of 1956 with bitter pleasure. England had run Italy out of Africa, and now its turn had come. Since these two Italian allies had also been opposed by the United States and most of the members of the United Nations at the time of the crisis, it was a safe position for Italy to take. But these underlying attitudes were hardly compatible with the spirit of Europeanism.

the government of Iran that was based on the formula of 75%: 25%, with the larger return going to the host country. This upset the 50% : 50% policy employed by the international oil concerns in their Middle Eastern contracts and antagonized Italy's important allies—the United States, Great Britain, and France. The agreement with Iran was followed by others in the Middle East and in North and Central Africa, often made with the new governments of former British and French colonies.

The policy of Italian penetration of the Near East and Africa won the endorsement of the left-wing parties. It was another point of contact between the Socialists, on the one hand, and the Christian Democrats and Social Democrats, on the other. It was another possible basis of unification between the two Socialist parties, or of bringing the Socialists out of the opposition into collaboration with the government. As a consequence, the issue of neo-Atlanticism lost its exclusively foreign-policy associations and became involved in the whole problem of domestic realignments. Pella, who had originated the policy and the phrase in 1955, dropped it when the debate between Atlanticists and neo-Atlanticists was converted into a conflict between the opponents and proponents of the opening to the left.

The interest in expanded trade relations with the countries of the Soviet bloc and the third world was not confined to the ENI or to other publicly controlled businesses. Private firms were just as anxious to pursue increased opportunities for profit. In this pursuit, they were not bothered by political or ideological preclusions. They would buy from, and sell to, any variety of regime: Communist, Fascist—no matter the country or the political system. This had been the policy of all Italian governments in the entire postwar period, but the thaw in international politics after 1955 and the decline of colonial empires with their protected markets opened new opportunities to Italian trade. In 1957 and 1958, Confindustria was pressuring the government to use all its influence with its allies to eliminate, or drastically reduce, the NATO embargo lists of items forbidden for export to the Soviet bloc. Conservative politicians and businessmen, such as Baron Raffaele Guariglia, the Monarchist Senator, or Teresio Guglielmone, the Christian Democratic Senator, were heading private economic missions to Moscow and Peking. Out of consideration for its ally—the United States—Italy did not recognize Communist China, but did not let nonrecognition stand in the way of business.[11]

---

[11] An agreement between Italy and Communist China, reached at the end of 1964, led to the opening of commercial offices by the two countries (in Rome and Peking, beginning in January, 1965). At the time of the agreement, Foreign Minister Giuseppe Saragat announced in Parliament that the Italian Government favored recognition of Communist China but would take action only in accordance with its allies, not unilaterally, as France had done.

8

Constitutional and Political Evolution

The republican Constitution of 1948 provided for the creation of a number of new regional, judicial, and economic institutions. With the intention of limiting the exclusive power of a centralized and hierarchical political system, it was planned that the new institutions should be set up as independent centers of authority, protected from the domination of the cabinet and Parliament. In the late 1940's, the extreme left had opposed this constitutional trend on the grounds that it would limit the sovereignty of the people as expressed through the supremacy of Parliament. In plain words, as long as the Communists had some hope of capturing the central government, they did not want any limitations on that government's authority. The Christian Democrats, on the other hand, had a political tradition, extending back to the years before Fascism, that favored decentralization and federalism.

With the coming into effect of the Constitution, the positions of the principal parties became reversed. After the April, 1948 election, the Christian Democrats had an absolute majority in Parliament and dominated the cabinet. They postponed the implementation of those constitutional provisions that would have set up relatively independent judicial institutions and regional governments. Only the special regional governments were created —in those peripheral areas of the country where independence movements or linguistic minorities were present and where temporary autonomy had already been granted. These were Sicily, Sardinia, the Val d'Aosta (French-speaking), and Trentino–Alto Adige (with a German-speaking majority in the Alto Adige).[1] The Christian Democrats simply neglected to create governments for the rest of the regions.

The Communists and Socialists, on the other hand, became supporters of regionalism and judicial independence. Cut off from the government, in opposition to, and excluded from, all positions of power in Rome, they controlled 20 to 25 per cent of the local and provincial governments throughout Italy. Since they were especially strong in the central regions—Tuscany, Emilia-Romagna, Umbria—there was a good possibility they would win electoral control over regional governments in those areas if the regular regions were created. So the Christian Democrats and their allies continued to ignore the Constitution, and in precisely those parts of the country where the left opposition was strongest, strengthened and reinforced the powers of the Ministry of the Interior and the prefects.

For a number of years, the implementation of judicial reform was likewise postponed. Legislation to supplant the Fascist legal codes under which the country was still living was pigeonholed. Civil codes, criminal codes, and security laws that dated from the time of Mussolini were still in force. Two new judicial institutions provided for by the Constitution—the Constitutional Court and the Superior Council of the Judiciary—remained unimplemented.

In the 1950's, pressures from the professional associations and law schools, as well as from the democratic parties within the cabinet and the opposition, led the government to undertake, reluctantly and slowly, the establishment of these judicial institutions. The Constitutional Court was perhaps the most revolutionary in its implications. The Constitution of prerepublican Italy, the *Statuto albertino,* inherited from the Kingdom of Sardinia upon unification of the country in the nineteenth century, was an open constitution. Any act of Parliament passed by a simple majority was legal. Once Mussolini had obtained control over

---

[1] In 1963, a fifth special region, Friuli–Venezia Giulia, was created, with its capital at Trieste.

Parliament, he was able to put through any bill he wanted without constitutional obstacles. To prevent a repetition of this situation, insofar as a dictatorship can be prevented by legalistic devices, the framers of the 1948 Constitution had created a special amending process, and a Constitutional Court to pass on the constitutionality of legislation and decrees having the force of law. Failure to appoint the judges had been a way of avoiding the establishment of the Court.

In 1953, De Gasperi had finally decided to take action, but the creation of the Court was delayed for two more years by disputes over the filling of its positions. Article 135, paragraph 1, of the Constitution provided for a fifteen-judge Court, five nominated by the President of the Republic, five elected by the two houses of Parliament in joint session, five elected by the members of the highest regular and administrative courts (the Court of Cassation, the Court of Accounts, and the Council of State). President Einaudi insisted that the Constitution assigned to him the exclusive right to name the first group of five judges; the cabinet, controlled by Christian Democrats, claimed that the President must accept the five nominees suggested to him by the Council of Ministers. Einaudi finally won his battle, and his nominees were his own choices. But the delay was not yet over. Implemental legislation already passed required that the five judges to be elected by Parliament receive a three-fifths majority. After the 1953 parliamentary election, the Christian Democrats and their allies had no such majority. To elect the judges required logrolling with the opposition. The Communists held out for a fair share, one out of the five. It took until the end of 1955 for the Court to be constituted. It began functioning in April, 1956. Under the Constitution, the Court elects its presiding officers from among its own members; the judges chose Enrico De Nicola, the former Provisional President of Italy, as the first President of the Constitutional Court.

In the interim, a debate had raged over the limits of the Court's jurisdiction. Minimalist legal thinkers maintained that the Court was limited to judging the constitutionality of legislation and decrees enacted only after April, 1956, not of pre-existing law. This thesis would have preserved a whole body of Fascist law, as well as laws and decrees put into force in the years after Mussolini's downfall. The Court disposed of the argument in its very first decision, asserting that prior laws were subject to judicial review, and could be nullified if found contrary to the preceptive norms of the Constitution. With this decision, the Court did not automatically throw out the Fascist legal codes and legislative inheritance. They remained in effect until replaced by new codes, legislation, and decrees, or until the Court modified or destroyed them in whole or in part as particular cases on particular issues came before it for decision.[2] As of 1965, the major Fascist codes of criminal and civil law had not been superseded by new codes and were still in effect. A few of their articles had been replaced by subsequent legislation and a few others had been thrown out by the Constitutional Court. The behavior of the Court has been cautious, rather than daring.

In two broad areas of constitutional interest—civil rights and centralization—the Court soon had many cases to hear. Generally, it defended the important personal freedoms of speech, the press, and religion. Also it usually upheld the central government in controversies with the special regions, especially with the Sicilian regional government.

The problem of enforceability of the Court's decisions was a difficult one. As mentioned earlier, the Italian executive branch, historically, had not been accustomed to being checked. The result was that a number of Court decisions were ignored by administrative and political officials. Enrico De Nicola resigned in protest when a cabinet minister refused to adhere to the Court's decisions. His successor, Gaetano Azzariti, would also complain of the same problem.

If an independent Constitutional Court bothered executive officials, a really independent regular magistracy was potentially a greater source of concern. In the long run, the ordinary courts, handling the routine daily judging of litigation, would have more impact on the social system than the courts at the apex of the

---

2 A case comes to the Constitutional Court when the judges of the regular courts conclude that a constitutional issue is in controversy in a case they are hearing. Only they can transfer the case to the Constitutional Court.

judicial hierarchy. The doctrine of the independence of the magistracy had roots going back to the nineteenth century. Even before Fascism, however, the courts were often held to be subservient to the government in practice. Under Fascism, of course, the situation degenerated, although the judges fought a losing battle to maintain their professional standards.

The judiciary in Italy was (and is) a career service into which a young man entered after finishing law school and passing the competitive examination. (Not until 1964 did a woman enter the judiciary branch in Italy.) Assignments and promotions had traditionally depended on the Ministry of Justice, and the knowledge that a magistrate's career was at the mercy of a political minister, and of the higher judges who could influence the minister, had undermined the backbone of many magistrates in the past. The framers of the Constitution, aware of these historic conditions, had attempted to reinforce the doctrine of judicial independence by taking control of the magistracy away from the Ministry of Justice and vesting it in a new institution, the Superior Council of the Judiciary. Article 105 of the Constitution gave the Superior Council the following powers over judges: appointment, assignment and transfer, promotion, and discipline.

For eight years, the successive governments, and Parliament, had withheld the necessary enabling legislation to implement this part of the Constitution. In the middle of the 1950's, agitation was building up, especially among the younger magistrates themselves. In 1956, inside the National Association of Magistrates, the younger judges began to organize, and within two years took control of the association from the older senior judges who had dominated it. Their pressure on Parliament, together with that of the political parties and of the bar associations, finally led to the establishment of the Superior Council of the Judiciary in 1958.

The 1958 act was subject to vigorous criticism by the magistrates' association. The Constitution provides that two-thirds of the Superior Council be elected by the Judges from among their own members, one-third by Parliament in joint session from among law professors and practicing lawyers. The 1958 enabling act divided the judges, of whom there were then about 5,300, into three categories for the purpose of electing the judicial members of the Superior Council. As a consequence, the judges on the Superior Council that represented about 300 of the highest-ranking magistrates equaled those that represented the remaining 5,000. In addition, the 1958 act assigned disciplinary functions to a Superior Council committee that was to be composed almost exclusively of the representatives elected by the high-ranking magistrates. The younger judges protested, citing the constitutional dictum: "Judges differ only in diversity of function [Article 107, paragraph 3]." The 1958 act also continued the traditional method of setting higher salaries for the judges of the higher courts. The magistrates' association argued that Article 107 was thus violated and that salaries should be equal regardless of the type of judgeship, with increments based on seniority alone. In the opinion of the younger judges, the legislature's implementation of the Constitution on this question was defective. It left the judges open to fear of their superiors and to the temptations of economic careerism, both factors being capable of undermining judicial independence. They continued to protest, through their magistrates' association, but without avail. In 1960, the small minority of high-court judges split off to form their own association, from which the younger judges were excluded. The struggle was a conflict of generations, as well as a conflict of hierarchy, with the postwar generation of the lower courts arraigned against some of the holdovers of the Fascist period.

Another controversy, one that finally brought about the collapse of political centrism, was the debate over the agrarian pacts. The land reform of the early 1950's had created a number of new peasant proprietors, but had done little or nothing about the problem of sharecropping—*mezzadria*. Sharecropping was particularly prevalent in central Italy—in Tuscany, Emilia, and Umbria—and the sharecroppers provided a major source of voting power for the Communist Party in those areas. The struggles over constitutional reform, over detachment of the public firms, over public investments in southern industry, had been eroding the Segni cabinet between 1955 and 1957. During these two years, Segni, whose reputation as a moderate leftist was based on the fact that he was Minister of Agriculture at the time of the passage of the land-reform legislation (1950), was moving steadily to the right.

Moderate revision of the legislation concerning the *mezzadria* had been undertaken during the war and the immediate postwar period. The share of the income to go to the sharecroppers was increased, and they had been given greater security against eviction. Their situation was still an extremely difficult one, which explained the Communist gains, and the left parties and the left wing of the Christian Democratic Party were now negotiating for further improvements. Meanwhile, through the influence of the landowners on the Liberals and on the moderate and conservative factions of the Christian Democrats, a bill was introduced in early 1957 to increase the number of "just causes" available to a landowner to justify eviction, thus weakening the peasant's power to bargain with the landowner.

On February 28, 1957, the Republican Party, in protest, withdrew from the majority. With the support of the Monarchists and neo-Fascists (MSI), the cabinet was able to continue in existence for two months, but was reduced to routine administration. The situation became increasingly embarrassing for the Social Democrats. In May, 1957, Giuseppe Saragat publicly attacked the government, of which his party was a member, and Segni presented the cabinet's resignation to the President of the Republic. The bill to reform the agrarian pacts was discussed for another year, straining the discipline within the Christian Democratic Party. In a rare display of rebellion in Parliament, the trade-union Christian Democrats openly voted against the bill in the spring of 1958, when it came up again. It was finally dropped and the whole problem was postponed for five years more.

Segni's cabinet was followed by a one-party (*monocolore*) minority government of Christian Democrats that was headed by the Tuscan anti-Fascist Adone Zoli. It had no agreed majority in Parliament and was intended to function as an interim cabinet until the parliamentary elections scheduled for 1958. The Monarchists and neo-Fascists decided to support Zoli, certain that his government would not do anything in the way of reforms. These votes were extremely embarrassing. Zoli decided to accept the

Monarchist votes, but rejected the neo-Fascist support as "neither necessary nor desirable." The day following the vote of confidence, however, a recount showed that the MSI votes were necessary for a majority. Zoli handed in his resignation. Before accepting it, President Gronchi surveyed the situation with the political leaders. The only alternative was an opening to the left. But *L'Osservatore romano* editorialized clearly against such an alternative. Gronchi then refused to accept Zoli's resignation; the Prime Minister swallowed his objection to the Fascist support and the cabinet received a new vote of confidence. In view of the coming elections, the Christian Democrats were anxious not to be identified with Fascism. Zoli was a weak man and the party and government were being run by Fanfani, the Secretary-General of the party. The cabinet's position was strengthened by the general knowledge that if it were overthrown, the only remaining choice would be for the President to dissolve Parliament and call for immediate elections. And the parties did not want the election—for which they were as yet unprepared—pushed forward in time.

During Zoli's government, there were a few accomplishments of minor importance. The government completed its absorption of the national telephone system, over which the state already had majority stock control through the IRI. Legislation for the Cassa per il Mezzogiorno was extended. The final touches to the controversial bill establishing the Superior Council of the Judiciary were added. The Common Market treaties, negotiated by the preceding cabinet, were routinely ratified. Fanfani broke Communist-Socialist control over the Republic of San Marino.

Most attention was concentrated on the coming election, and to prepare for it the Christian Democrats who were under Fanfani chose to emphasize their relatively progressive tendencies. Their attacks against the Liberals on their right became stronger and were reciprocated. In February, 1958, the Minister of the Interior, Fernando Tambroni, dissolved the Monarchist government of the city of Naples, charging it with corruption. Some thought this was a tactical mistake that would make a martyr of Achille Lauro, the Monarchist leader and Neapolitan mayor. At the same time, the Christian Democrats continued to reassure their supporters of their own moderation by carrying on an anti-Communist barrage, reinforced by Catholic Action posters showing Russian tanks in the streets of Budapest and Communist and Socialist parties manacled together indissolubly.

Relations between Church and state became a major election issue, especially in Tuscany. The Bishop of Prato, an industrial city north of Florence, had publicly declared and written that a young couple of his diocese were "sinners" and "public concubines" for having been married in a civil, rather than religious, ceremony. The couple sued the Bishop for slander and defamation, and the court in Florence accepted jurisdiction of the suit. On March 1, 1958, it found the Bishop guilty and assessed a small fine. The Vatican reacted violently: for the first time since 1929, a bishop had been tried in an Italian court. The next day, in protest, Pope Pius XII canceled a forthcoming celebration of the nineteenth anniversary of his ascension to the papacy. The day after this, the Vatican announced the excommunication of all those responsible for the Bishop's trial and sentencing. The case had become a *cause célèbre.* While some Catholic circles attempted to make a martyr of the Bishop, comparing him to the persecuted clergy of China, the popular sentiment sided with the couple. The Bishop had demonstrated a fantaticism and extremism out of all proportion, which rebounded against him not only in court but in the public squares. The assertion of the jurisdiction of the state appeared to be a rebuff to the idea that Italy was becoming a *repubblica papalina,* a little papal republic, in which clergymen were beyond the law. The decision became a campaign issue.[3]

More important was the promulgation on May 3, 1958, of a letter in the name of the Italian Bishops' Conference calling on all Catholics to "vote united" for the Christian Democrats. The letter was posted on church doors and read at masses all over Italy. There was no evidence that the Italian bishops had met in conference to approve such a letter. It appeared that a small num-

---

[3] A year later, a court of appeals reversed the sentence and stated that the courts did not have jurisdiction. By that time, little attention was focused on the incident and the reversal had no political repercussions.

ber of cardinals and archbishops had drafted and issued it in the name of the entire conference. This was the first time such open and public election instructions had been given. In July, 1949, Pius XII had issued a general excommunication of believing Marxists. Now all the other parties, including the non-Marxist ones, were more or less pushed beyond the pale. The purpose of the open letter appears to have been, not to attack the left— whose constituency was more or less immune to such orders—but rather to prevent certain bishops and other clergymen in the south from openly endorsing either the neo-Fascists or the Monarchists, who had by then split into two parties, the National Monarchist Party and the Popular Monarchist Party.

The other parties, especially the Radicals and the Republicans, who had allied for the election campaign, immediately protested this clerical intervention in the campaign, an intervention that was a violation of the Concordat of 1929. These protests proved useless, since the predominant Christian Democrats would never openly rebuff the Church, and were happy to get support in any case. The practice became standard, and the Bishops' Conference issued similar appeals in subsequent parliamentary and administrative elections. But little attention would be given to them, and their electoral consequences became negligible.

The parliamentary election of May 25, 1958, came at the end of a period of economic advance. In the early months of the year, however, the growth of the economy had slowed down, reflecting the current American recession in a limited way. The Christian Democrats could point to the progress made on the economic front, even if political affairs had been stalled for some time. Its election slogan was "Progress without adventures," to reassure its more conservative voters that the problem of relations with the Socialists was not to worry them.

The election produced small increases for both the Christian Democrats and the Socialists over their 1953 representation. The results in the Chamber are shown for both elections in Table 5. These national figures do not give a real indication of the electoral consequences. A breakdown by electoral districts would demonstrate that the parties' positions had remained relatively stable in the north and that the gains and losses occurred prin-

TABLE 5

VOTE FOR THE CHAMBER OF DEPUTIES, 1953 AND 1958

	1953		1958	
Parties	Seats	Votes (Per Cent)	Seats	Votes (Per Cent)
Fascist	29	5.8	25	4.7
Monarchist	40	6.9	23*	4.8*
Liberal	14	3.1	16	3.5
Christian Democratic	261	40.1	273	42.2
Republican	5	1.6	7	1.4
Social Democratic	19	4.5	23	4.6
Socialist	75	12.7	84	14.2
Communist	143	22.7	140	22.7
South Tyrol People's	3	0.3	3	0.5
Other	1	2.3	2	1.4
Total	590	100.0	596	100.0

* These figures represent the totals of the two Monarchist parties. They reunited in 1960.

Source: Italia, Istituto Centrale di Statistica.

cipally in the south.[4] The big losers were the two Monarchist parties, whose strength had been mainly in the south and who now demonstrated that they were entering a decline. The economic transformations occurring in Italy had made their political impact. The southern subproletariat was becoming less susceptible to traditionalist Monarchist appeals and gifts of *pasta* or clothing to buy their votes. They now wanted more than pa-

---

[4] Two weeks before the Italian election, the French Fourth Republic fell as a result of the Algerian crisis, and General de Gaulle took over the government with emergency powers. The Italian Christian Democrats immediately seized upon the French crisis to argue that France's troubles were due to the failure of any party to get a majority, and called on the Italian electorate to rally around the largest party to ensure stability "without adventures." The Communists blamed France's troubles on the failure of the working class to remain united, an obvious attack on the autonomists among the Socialists. Some observers considered that this event influenced the Italian electorate, especially to the benefit of the Christian Democrats. I doubt it. The Italians most interested in, and affected by, French events were the inhabitants of the large northern cities. The Christian Democratic and Communist gains were largely in the south, among voters who knew little and cared less about what was happening in Paris.

ternalistic charity. The Christian Democrats were the principal beneficiaries of the Monarchist decline, but Communists, Socialists, Liberals, and Fascists also profited. Communist votes increased in the south to compensate for slight percentage losses in the north. (Since there was a large increase in the number of voters, the parties would have to gain votes just to remain in the same relative position.) The election proved once more that the political earthquakes of 1956 outside of Italy—de-Stalinization and Hungary—had little effect on the mass of Communist supporters.

On the whole, the election indicated a shift to the moderate left. The Communists had held their own; both Socialists and Social Democrats had gained. Even more interesting, however, were the shifts inside the parties, the result of the preference votes cast by the party electorate. The left-wing Christian Democrats made considerable gains, as did the autonomist Socialists. A new alternative to the stalemate of the previous year now appeared. But the apprehensions on the part of both these parties were still so strong that the deadlock would persist for more than three years, leading in the interval to new crises.

9

Fanfani's Failure

Fanfani, having directed the electoral campaign toward widening the gap between his party and the three parties to his right—the Liberal and the two Monarchist parties—now faced the problem of forming a new cabinet oriented toward the left. This involved overcoming strong resistance from within his own party and among the Liberals, the political groups committed to a relaunching of the old centrism. The immediate vehicle which these groups hoped to use was the Hungarian government's execution of three imprisoned leaders of the ill-fated 1956 revolt. Giuseppe Pella, the right-wing Christian Democratic Foreign Minister in the previous cabinet (which stayed on in a caretaker capacity until a new one was formed), denounced the executions in the most violent language, and as a sign of protest, summoned to Rome the Italian ambassador in Budapest. The large northern newspapers supporting the Liberal Party behaved in an identical manner. Pella's play for reappointment as Foreign Minister failed, however, since Fanfani's ambitions proved strong enough to resist these pressures.

Fanfani proceeded to construct a coalition of Christian Democrats and Social Democrats, taking for himself the portfolios of both the Prime Minister and Foreign Minister. The two-party coalition did not have a majority, but succeeded in obtaining the abstention of the seven Republicans as the condition for its accession to office. Fanfani made no serious effort to obtain Socialist support. He knew that important persons in his own party were opposed to it, as were influential Catholic groups outside the party, such as the Catholic Action Society and powerful ecclesiastical figures within the Church hierarchy. He himself was not yet ready to accept Socialist participation. With his integralist conception of Catholic politics, he envisioned social justice brought to the masses as part of the Catholic conquest of the whole society, not as justice achieved within a pluralistic society. Pietro Nenni stated, however, that the Socialists would not raise a general prejudicial opposition to the coalition, but would support or oppose each policy or bill on its merits.

Events outside of Italy did nothing to make the Socialists eager to participate in the government. In July, 1958, the Americans and the British invaded Lebanon to prevent the overthrow of the Lebanese Government from ending in a Communist takeover. The Italian Government supported its allies and defended their motives. The Anglo-American forces used the airport at Capodichino, outside Naples, as a transit station to move troops to the Middle East. The Communists naturally denounced the whole operation, while the Socialists criticized it on two grounds: It was, they charged, a classical example of the economic imperialism of English and American oil companies; second, it was intervention in the internal affairs of a foreign country. The Socialists, in the words of spokesmen such as Riccardo Lombardi, had opposed Soviet intervention in Hungary, and now opposed American intervention in Lebanon. All efforts by the far left to mobilize large demonstrations against American intervention met with little success. The government discouraged mass open-air meetings and parades. It permitted some speeches in theaters and meeting halls, but the turnouts were not impressive. The Communists tried to blame their weak showing on government "oppression," but it was perfectly obvious that the days were over when they could rally thousands of activists into the squares over issues that seemed remote from their supporters' immediate interests. Some commentators blamed the weak response on the heat wave that Italy was then suffering. Whatever the cause, the general indifference to the event was a conspicuous consequence.

Fanfani was convinced that Italy could and should play a more active role in international affairs, with a greater display of independence. Like President Gronchi, he did not believe that membership in the Atlantic alliance was identical with subservience to Italy's allies. They both saw that the decline of British and French power in Africa and the Middle East opened up the possibility for Italian political and economic penetration into those parts of the world. They approved of, and gave further backing to, Enrico Mattei in his search for exploration concessions and marketing deals for his state-owned oil-and-gas combine in the territories of the developing countries. And while they justified their politically motivated explorations as helping to maintain Western influence in Africa, their primary concern was with enlarging the Italian "presence" in the world.

A minor move made in the foreign-policy field was related to the ENI's expanding international operations. In the autumn of 1958, Mattei was working out an agreement with the Egyptian Government to create a jointly owned petroleum corporation. The 75% : 25% ratio of returns was again to be the basis of the agreement, as against the 50% : 50% ratio used by the large international Anglo-American oil consortium operating in the Near East. The agreement came roughly two years after the Anglo-French-Israeli political defeat over the Suez, and therefore rankled Italy's European allies politically as well as economically. Cyrus L. Sulzberger, the *New York Times* foreign-affairs columnist, charged that Fanfani was weakening NATO ties with his efforts to cultivate the Socialists at home and the Arab countries abroad. The Italian Government protested, and on November 26, 1958, United States Secretary of State John Foster Dulles publicly denied that Italy was weakening NATO.

One month after this little flurry, the Egyptian Government publicly announced the granting of an oil concession in the Sinai peninsula to the jointly owned subsidiary. A few days later, Fanfani made a formal visit to Cairo, and on January 8, 1959, a joint communiqué announced the signing of an economic and technical accord. On returning home, Fanfani found himself criticized for his apparent support of Arab neutralism.

Charging Fanfani with accepting or supporting Arab neutralism was not the same as charging that he embraced Italian neutralism, which was what his domestic enemies really wanted to claim. There is no evidence to substantiate the second charge, which was derived from the first, and much evidence to the contrary. On October 25, 1958, Italy had come out in opposition to de Gaulle's plan to create a "Big Three" directorate in NATO, but this can hardly serve as a basis for declaring that Fanfani was undermining the Western alliance. In fact, for the previous half-year he had been collaborating with his Western allies by quietly consenting to the construction on Italian soil of bases for American intermediate-range ballistic missiles with atomic warheads. Italy was to control the bases and missiles, the United States the warheads.

News of these negotiations had been leaking out ever since early 1958. At that time, Fanfani was not Prime Minister and Foreign Minister, but he was the dominant policy-maker behind Zoli's *monocolore* cabinet. The Italian Government had moved very cautiously on the issue, not only in view of the forthcoming elections but also in the knowledge that there was considerable opposition, by political figures as well as among the general public, to the installation of missile bases. A sample survey of opinion, taken in March, 1958, is given in Table 6. This indication of opinion

TABLE 6

ITALIAN ATTITUDES TOWARD MISSILE BASES, 1958

(In Per Cents)

Question: Do you favor the establishment of long-range-missile bases [in Italy] by the United States?

Response	Favor	Oppose	Don't Know	Depends
Total sample	30	39	29	2
By education level:				
Primary or less	25	39	34	2
Secondary	39	39	19	3
Superior, university	48	33	15	4

Source: Istituto Italiano dell' Opinione Pubblica, poll of March, 1958.

may provide some insight into the Italian Government's caution. By the summer of 1958, and after the elections were over, the Fanfani ministry could move a little more openly. In the Chamber of Deputies on September 30, an administration spokesman implied —though did not admit in so many words—that Italy would probably agree to the construction of the missile bases. On November 2, the Soviet Union protested this probability, a protest which the Italian Government rejected. This is the background for Dulles' rebuttal of Sulzberger's charge.

The final agreement on the bases was not completed until the following spring, after Fanfani's government had fallen. A communiqué from Washington on March 30, 1959, notified the world that Italy was the first of the Continental allies of the United States to accept construction of the bases. On April 21 and April 28, the Soviet Government again made public protests to Italy. Khrushchev warned that Italy would be among the first targets for atomic destruction in case of war. The next month, at the suggestion of the Italian Communist Party, he offered to create a Balkan Peace Zone in compensation for the de-atomization of Italy. The offer was repeated again in June, to be rejected once more.

The missile-base accords between Italy and the United States were never submitted to Parliament for approval and were never formally debated or voted upon. Consequently, the parties were never required to take a formal position on the issue, a requirement that would have strained the internal unity of several of them.[1]

It was not foreign policy, however, that made the life of the Fanfani government brief and difficult. At the time of its creation, predictions were made that finally things in Italy were really going to change and that the government would have a life of at least two years (compared to an average life for cabinets in postwar Italy of about nine months). It is true that in his capacity as Foreign Minister, Fanfani carried out a major reshuffling of the top levels of the Foreign Office hierarchy, putting his supporters among the career diplomats into the key positions.[2] His domestic

---

[1] In an interview with Guglielmo Negri on November 5, 1963, former President Gronchi declared that he was never officially informed by the government that an agreement with the United States had been concluded to construct the IRBM bases, nor was he ever officially informed of the 1962 decision to dismantle them: Guglielmo Negri, *La direzione della politica estera nelle grandi democrazie* (Milan: Giuffrè, 1964), p. 49, n. 100.

[2] Over the years, the career officers of the diplomatic corps, as in other ministries, had become factionalized into groups supporting various currents in the Christian Democratic Party.

problems, however, frustrated his hopes of carrying out a more dynamic foreign policy, and it was a combination of religious, economic, and party conflicts that finally brought him down. Although they were all occurring at the same time, it will be convenient to take them up separately.

In the Veneto and Emilia-Romagna regions, a financial scandal of vast proportions that had been brewing for some time finally burst into the open. A certain Commendatore Giuffrè had been involved in a number of get-rich-quick schemes and financial speculations, promising individuals and groups exaggerated returns (90 to 100 per cent) in a year for money they deposited with him. To cover his tracks and protect his position, he had become a generous supporter of Catholic charities and had cultivated close friendships with several members of the hierarchy of those regions. As it turned out, various clergymen, including high-ranking bishops, greedy or ingenuous or both, had put their own money and that of their parishes, dioceses, or orders into Giuffrè's hands, dazzled by the prospect of large earnings. The cabinet ordered an investigation, the results of which not only embarrassed the Christian Democratic Party and the Catholic Church but also strained relations with the allied Social Democrats.

Another religious issue involved government harassment of minor Protestant evangelical sects, usually stimulated by local priests in the areas where the sects were proselytizing. The police often broke up their meetings on the grounds that the sects were not provided with the necessary authorization for their meeting halls or churches, or that they were not led by authorized ministers. These issues had finally arrived in the Constitutional Court. On November 24, 1958, the Court ruled that Protestant sects could operate churches without police authorization. It also held, however, that Protestant ministers must have official recognition as ministers by the state. A number of the groups were led by lay preachers who were not so recognized. While the government had no control over the Court's decisions, it was nevertheless blamed by many conservative Catholics for failing to defend the interests of the Catholic Church adequately. There has never been much understanding or appreciation in Italy of the doctrines of separation of powers or checks and balances. The government is blamed

and held responsible for everything, even rain. Fanfani was considered deficient in the handling of the Giuffrè scandal, as well as
of other issues that brought embarrassment to Catholics.

His economic problems resulted from his sense of social justice,
the economic requirements of the time, and the suspicion of him
that was widespread among the leaders of private business. The
price of wheat in Italy was being supported at a rate well above
the international market price (although below the German market price). The importance of wheat in the Italian diet meant not
only that the poor suffered but that labor costs throughout the
economy were pushed up. Foodstuffs had more than 50 per cent
of the weight in the cost-of-living index, and most union contracts
had sliding-scale clauses that provided for automatic wage increases if the cost of living went up. Fanfani wanted to reduce
the support price of wheat but found himself in trouble with the
powerful Coltivatori Diretti, who claimed control of some sixty
Christian Democratic deputies in the Third Legislature. In principle, Paolo Bonomi, their leader, accepted the idea that support
prices were too high and would have to come down, but in practice he opposed their reduction. His function was to protect his
clients' income.

An additional economic dispute involved the construction of
atomic electric-power plants. The expanding demand for electric
power in the country could not be met by additional hydroelectric
plants since almost all the possible water sources were already exploited. Imported coal and fuel oil were expensive, and as a result
it was felt that atomic power would be economically feasible in
Italy—especially in the center and south—earlier than in many
other countries. For years, a debate had raged inside the country
between the supporters of privately owned atomic plants and the
champions of public ownership. The issue had divided the Christian Democrats and prevented the establishment of an atomic
policy for the country. The privately owned utilities wanted government support and subsidy of the initial atomic construction,
which would be very costly. For them, it was a life-and-death issue,
for they regarded atomic power as the dominant source of energy
in Italy's future, and unless they could participate in shaping an
atomic policy, their days were numbered. The supporters of pri-

vately owned utilities mobilized all their propaganda resources and political influence, as did the opposition. Television debates, newspaper articles, and party resolutions were all directed to the issue. Fanfani, spurred on by the left wing of his own party, by the Social Democratic allies, and by Enrico Mattei, made the choice for public atomic power. Two atomic plants were announced for construction, one by Agip-Nucleare, a subsidiary of the ENI, the other by SENN, a subsidiary of the IRI. On November 20, 1958, Agip-Nucleare began construction of its plant at Latina, south of Rome.

But the most serious of Fanfani's troubles was organizational. The issue of independent party power probably was the most damaging to the life of his government. In the fall of 1958, Fanfani was Prime Minister and Foreign Minister, as well as Secretary-General of his party. There was no doubt that he was trying to establish a degree of authoritative leadership such as no Christian Democratic politician had been able to exercise since the heyday of Alcide De Gasperi. He was even going beyond De Gasperi, in that he had for four years been engaged in constructing an effective party organization, something that De Gasperi had neglected. Fanfani did not want to be dependent on the Civic Committees of Catholic Action and on parish priests to round up and bring in the voters. It was not surprising that all those groups whose political power depended on their influence over a voting clientele viewed the creation of a strong party organization with fear.

If organization is one source of party strength, finances are another. In the late 1940's and early 1950's, during the period of De Gasperi's leadership, relations between the Christian Democrats and Confindustria had been amicable, and the party's financing had come mainly from big business. Church funds were directed toward those groups and individuals, such as Catholic Action and the clergy, that provided "free services" (in the financial, not political, sense) to the party. In the later 1950's Fanfani had found the contributions of big business reduced as Confindustria threw more support to the Liberals. By the time of the 1958 election campaign, the Liberals were receiving massive financial aid from the business community. The decline in large private contributions to the Christian Democratic Party organization (they were diverted to those right-wing factions and individuals within the party whose viewpoints were most congenial to business interests), coupled with Fanfani's goal of making his party less dependent on outside interests, had led him to seek other sources of funds. He found them in the publicly owned holding corporations, which derived their legal source of authority from the national state itself. But as *de facto imperia in imperium,* the IRI and the ENI were becoming major contributors to political parties to protect their own interests. Most of their money was going into Christian Democracy, although other parties were also beneficiaries. Undoubtedly, these contributions were a consideration in Fanfani's decision in favor of publicly owned atomic-power plants.

Thus, the Civic Committees, important Church leaders, and large-scale business all had reason to fear the direction of political events, which presaged a decline of their influence in Italian political life. And although Fanfani's actual policies and behavior were far less radical than his statements, these groups were perturbed over the possibility of an eventual coalition between Christian Democrats and Socialists, and the price that might have to be paid for bringing the Socialists into the government.

Added to these fears was the disgruntlement of other Christian Democratic notables over Fanfani's monopoly of the top governmental and party posts. All that was needed was the right occasion to move to the counterattack, and the tribulations of the Sicilian regional government provided the occasion. Sicilian resentments over neglect by Rome, historical feelings for local autonomy, the instability of the coalition in control of the regional government, all led certain Sicilian Christian Democrats to resist instructions emanating from central party headquarters in Rome. In October, 1958, Silvio Milazzo, a former protégé of Don Luigi Sturzo and now the Sicilian Christian Democratic leader, engaged in wrangling with Fanfani's Sicilian supporters. In order to form a regional government, he negotiated a new coalition, accepting support from the Communists and Socialists of the far left, and from Monarchists and *Missini* on the far right. Orders came from the national Christian Democratic headquarters for him to resign, but he refused. His followers were ordered to stop supporting him, which they refused to do. Milazzo was expelled from the party. On November 6, 1958, he founded a splinter Catholic party, the Sicilian Christian Social Union, which acquired local support.

At the Vatican and in Palermo, the Catholic Church had backed Fanfani's attacks on Milazzo's insubordination. The formation of the splinter party led to even more violent clerical criticism, especially on the part of Ernesto Cardinal Ruffini, Archbishop of Palermo. The growing local support of Milazzo's schismatic political behavior indicates, however, that behind the scenes Milazzo must have had some backing from sectors of the local Sicilian clergy, who were happy to spite the Cardinal, a northerner.[3]

Fanfani's defeat in Sicily weakened his whole position in Rome. With increasing boldness, his conservative enemies within the party broke party discipline in Parliament by voting against their own cabinet. On November 24 and December 4, the cabinet was defeated in secret votes on a bill to continue a special surtax imposed during the Suez Crisis of 1956 on the sale of gasoline. It was easy to deduce that Christian Democratic snipers had used this minor issue to put their own government in the minority. On December 6, Fanfani called for a roll-call vote and the snipers fell back into line. The government won by a vote of 294 to 286.[4] The Christmas-holiday recess postponed the disintegration of the government, but in January the attack was renewed.

The internal strains of the Christian Democratic Party during the fall and winter months of 1958 had been matched by similar strains among the Socialists. The struggle between autonomists and *carristi* continued. At an October, 1958, meeting of the Socialist Central Committee, Nenni found himself and his support-

---

[3] There have been charges, unproven but not out of the question, that Milazzo's original insubordination was encouraged by Mario Scelba, also a Sicilian, as a means of undermining Fanfani's position at the national level. It is hardly likely, however, that Scelba would have endorsed either the later alliance with the Communists and Socialists or the open schism within the Christian Democratic Party in Sicily.

[4] Under the Italian Constitution (Article 94), a defeat on a bill in Parliament is not the equivalent of a vote of no confidence, and the cabinet is not required to resign. A formal request for a confidence vote must be made by the government or by an opposition party, and this formal vote cannot take place sooner than three days after the motion is filed.

ers temporarily in the minority in their opposition to a resolution calling for continued close alliance with the Italian Communist Party. On October 30, Nenni resigned the secretary-generalship of his party in protest, but the Central Committee refused to accept his resignation. A party congress to face the question was called for January, 1959. As a result of careful prior electioneering, Nenni arrived at the congress with a majority of the delegates behind him. Three resolutions were offered to the delegates: the first, by Nenni, called for complete independence of the Socialists and the final rupture of the unity-of-action pact with the Communists; the second, offered by Tullio Vecchietti, leader of the *carristi,* called for renewal of the unity-of-action pact; the third, submitted by Lelio Basso, was a compromise between the two. Nenni's resolution won, the other two were rejected, and on January 19, Nenni was re-elected Secretary-General. He pledged himself to carry out a policy of Socialist independence and to remain, for the time being, in opposition to the government.

The Socialist decision strained relations within the Social Democratic Party, which shared the government with the Christian Democrats. Left-wing Social Democrats asserted that the decisions of the Socialist Party congress laid the basis for the immediate reunification of the two Socialist parties. Giuseppe Saragat considered reunification premature. The supporters of reunification, however, jeopardized the life of the government, for it was at this critical juncture that the snipers inside Christian Democracy renewed their attacks on Fanfani. In a secret vote on January 22, called to judge the government's handling of the Giuffrè scandal, enough of the snipers voted against the cabinet to leave Fanfani with only a one-vote margin in the Chamber of Deputies, 279 to 278. At this point, Ezio Vigorelli, a Social Democratic cabinet minister, resigned from the government to join the group advocating Socialist reunification.

Fanfani's majority had disappeared and he saw the possibility of nominally blaming another party for the cabinet crisis. On January 26, 1959, Fanfani submitted his government's resignation to President Gronchi. Five days later, in a personal crisis of nerves, he also resigned as Secretary-General of the Christian Democratic Party, bitterly criticizing the right wing of his party for deserting him.[5] Thus, January, 1959, marked the end of the first, hesitant approach to an opening to the left. President Gronchi delayed accepting Fanfani's resignation while he spent a week exploring alternative coalitions. Having found none, on February 3 he rejected Fanfani's resignation and asked the Prime Minister to resubmit his cabinet for a formal vote of confidence. Fanfani had no taste for this, however, and Gronchi was again required to construct a holding operation, to seek a routine administrative government until a new coalition could be found. And Antonio Segni was just the man for this kind of operation.

Segni's new government was a typical Christian Democratic *monocolore,* whose center of emphasis was shifted to the right. It was voted into office on February 15 with the support of his own party, as well as the Liberals, the two Monarchist parties, and the *Missini.* Since it had a majority without the support of the last group, the cabinet was not felt to be conditioned by the neo-Fascists. The restoration of a voting majority dependent on the Monarchists was a temporary encouragement to those two parties, and on April 3 they agreed to reunite, forming the Italian Democratic Party of Monarchist Unity. Earlier, on the opposite flank of the Christian Democratic Party, a minor schism had occurred when five Social Democratic deputies abandoned their party to form an autonomist Socialist initiative group, dedicated to reunification.

The re-establishment of a government, even a caretaker one, had the political significance of bringing the leftward evolution of Christian Democracy to a temporary halt. In organizational terms, the halt was more permanent. On March 16, Aldo Moro, a law professor from Bari, was elected Secretary-General of the Christian Democratic Party, filling the vacancy created by Fanfani's resignation. Moro made no attempt to reconstruct a tight party machine. Instead, he let the various factions, or "currents," as the Italians call them, have their own heads, trying to play the

---

[5] Fanfani's opponents within the Catholic world were not all party men. Ignazio Silone has written that Catholic bishops inside and outside of the Vatican supported the attacks on the energetic Tuscan. Silone specifically named Cardinals Tardini and Ottaviani: Ignazio Silone, "Apparati, religione, e politica," *Tempo presente,* March, 1959, p. 228.

role of mediator among them. In the following years, the currents would become parties within the party, each with its own organization, its own offices, its own press service and publications, its own finances. An exception to this broad generalization, however, was a center grouping of Christian Democratic notables and their followers. In the process of realignment of factions after Fanfani's fall and the disintegration of his Iniziativa Democratica, a meeting of leading Christian Democratic politicians was held in March, 1959, at the Convent of St. Dorothy. A loose coalition of these notables emerged, led by the party secretary, Aldo Moro, and the deputy secretary, Mariano Rumor (who comes from the Veneto region, a Christian Democratic stronghold that delivers a substantial number of deputies to Parliament). The grouping became known as the *Dorotei,* after the location of their meeting. Later, as Moro built up his personal following, it became known as the *Moro-Dorotei,* with Moro taking a slightly more progressive position than the moderate *Dorotei.* Further governments would hinge on the shiftings of these moderates right- or leftward, and they would always manage to have some of their key men become the crucial economic ministers, such as Emilio Colombo, later Minister of the Treasury.

The reactions of the general public to the political infighting were either those of contempt or of indifference. During the interregnum in February and March, Randolfo Pacciardi, a colorful leader of the small Republican Party, launched a movement to change the form of government from a parliamentary republic to a "presidential" regime, à la de Gaulle's Fifth Republic. Pacciardi was reacting to his political failures within his own party—it was gradually accepting the policy of an opening to the left while he was shifting to the right. His movement would remain small in subsequent years, but its open launching provided a pretext for the Communist Party on March 10, 1959, to call again for a popular front with Socialists and Catholics to defend the parliamentary system. The times were against a popular front, and the Communist appeal fell on deaf ears. Italian parliamentary government, however, was to face more serious dangers than Pacciardi in the near future.

10

The Economic Boom

The year 1958 had been one of relative economic stability, if not quite stagnation. Although the American recession of that year did not effect an inversion of the Italian upward economic trend, there was, nevertheless, a considerable slowdown in economic growth. In the summer of 1959, the growth rate spurted again, and until the end of 1963 Italy experienced an economic boom on a scale never before known in its history, surpassing in speed and in intensity the growth during the years prior to World War I, in which were felt the first major impact of industrialism.

A few relevant statistics may indicate the scope of this economic drama. By the end of 1963, the gross national product, which had been increasing steadily throughout the period, stood at 23,669 billion lire, or 138 per cent of the 17,114 billion lire figure for 1958.[1] New investment, from which results the construction of new facilities or the modernization of existing ones, was averaging close to 25 per cent of gross national product, slightly less in 1959/60, slightly more in 1961/62. And Table 7 shows the strikingly large increase in total investment from year to year. That total investments in the Italian economy in 1959 were 10 per cent greater than those of 1958 would seem to be sufficiently dramatic,

---

[1] Computation based on figures adjusted to 1958 market prices, in *Economic Surveys by the OECD: Italy, 1963* (Paris: Organization for Economic Cooperation and Development), p. 37; and *Economic Surveys by the OECD: Italy, 1965*, p. 39.

TABLE 7
ANNUAL INCREASE IN GROSS INVESTMENTS, 1958–62
(*In Per Cents*)

Year	Increase Over Previous Year
1958	1.6
1959	10.0
1960	20.3
1961	13.7
1962	13.4

Source: Giuseppe Scimone, "The Italian Miracle," in Hennessy, Lutz, and Scimone, *Economic "Miracles"* (London: The Institute of Economic Affairs, 1964), p. 176.

but that until the end of 1962, at the least, each percentage increase is itself not only larger but is moreover calculated each year on an ever larger base surely validates the term "economic miracle."

Naturally, the resultant increases in production varied in different sectors of the economy. Generally, the growth rate in agriculture was lower than in industry and services, so that agriculture's share of the total productivity declined steadily. By 1962, it had dropped to 16 per cent of gross national product, whereas in 1953/54 it had been over 25 per cent. Industrial growth was the highest of all three major sectors of the economy, and there the biggest increases occurred in the manufacture of automotive vehicles, household appliances, chemicals, petroleum products, and artificial fibers. The increases were due not only to the expansion of the domestic market but, even more, to a rapid growth of exports. This was a result of both the general prosperity of the international economy and the advantages Italy possessed in comparative prices and in design. Traditional Italian exports, such as citrus fruits, marbles, and textiles, were surpassed by the rapid growth of exports in manufactured items and machine tools.

The Italian boom continues to deserve the name "miracle" when compared with the economic activity for other countries in the Common Market, the EEC. In Table 8, it can be seen that for all the countries of the EEC, the over-all industrial growth rate for

TABLE 8

INDICES OF INDUSTRIAL PRODUCTION FOR EEC COUNTRIES, 1961–63

(1958 = 100)

Country	1961	1962	1963
Belgium	122	130	138
Luxembourg	117	112	114
France	116	123	129
West Germany	126	132	136
Netherlands	126	133	139
Italy	142	156	170

Source: *New York Herald Tribune* (Paris edition), December 9, 1964.

Italy was the highest. This growth was matched by expansion of foreign trade, higher for Italy than for all the European members of the Organization for Economic Cooperation and Development. Table 9 indicates the comparative foreign-trade expansion of

TABLE 9

OECD VOLUME INDICES OF FOREIGN TRADE, 1961

(1957 = 100)

Country	Imports	Exports
Italy	181	189
European member countries combined	140	136
France	126	154
West Germany	166	143
Netherlands	135	144

Source: *Economic Surveys by the OECD: Italy, 1963* (Paris: Organization for Economic Cooperation and Development), p. 22.

these countries for 1961.

A major source of revenue for Italy was the tourist boom, a result of the combination of general prosperity abroad and of the rapid increase in accommodations in Italy at relatively attractive prices. By the end of the period, however, Italian prices had so risen that the country was becoming exceedingly expensive for foreigners. As a consequence, the growth rate of foreign tourism slowed down, for other southern European countries—such as Yugoslavia, Greece, Spain, and Portugal—became more attractive

to the budget-conscious vacationer from the north. A further de-
pressant was the crowding of the principal Italian tourist centers,
with the ensuing traffic jams and noise.

The growth of Italy's foreign trade was the result of an expansion of exports and imports to all parts of the world: the Soviet
bloc, North and South America, Asia, and Africa. But it was especially the result of the large increase in Italian trade with the
other countries of Europe, the other members of the EEC. The
EEC had come into operation on January 1, 1958, and its first
consequence was a reduction of tariffs in several stages among the
six members—Italy, France, West Germany, the Netherlands, Belgium, and Luxembourg. This gave them preferential access to
each other's markets. As a result, Italy's trade with its fellow EEC
members rose more rapidly than its trade with the rest of the
world. Exports to other EEC countries rose from 28 per cent of
total exports in 1959 to 34.8 per cent of total exports in 1962. For
imports, the change was from 26.8 per cent to 31.2 per cent for the
same years.[2] Among the six member states, Italy had the largest
increase in intra-EEC trade, as is indicated by Table 10.

Not only had Italy been the major beneficiary from the expan-

TABLE 10
INTRA-EEC TRADE, 1958 AND 1963
(*In Millions of U.S. Dollars*)

	Imports			Exports		
Country	1958	1963	Increase (Per Cent)	1958	1963	Increase (Per Cent)
Belgium-Luxembourg	$1,462	$ 2,661	82	$1,377	$ 2,950	114
France	1,227	3,103	153	1,136	3,065	170
West Germany	1,896	4,275	125	2,406	5,279	119
Netherlands	1,518	3,059	109	1,337	2,662	99
Italy	687	2,491	263	608	1,788	194
Total	$6,790	$15,589	130	$6,864	$15,744	129

Source: Scimone, "The Italian Miracle," p. 198.

---

[2] Giuseppe Scimone, "The Italian Miracle," in Hennessy, Lutz and Scimone,
Economic "Miracles" (London: The Institute of Economic Affairs, 1964),
p. 197.

sion of trade within the Common Market, it had also been the prime beneficiary of other EEC institutions. The European Investment Bank, created to grant loans for economic development within the European Community, put more money into Italy than into any other member country. This is understandable, for among the six nations Italy contains the largest underdeveloped area. In 1961, Italian development projects received 54 per cent of the Bank's investments, while French projects received 24 per cent and West German projects 17 per cent. In 1962, Italy received 64 per cent of the Bank's total annual investments, while France received 12 per cent and West Germany 11 per cent.[3] The European Social Fund, created to promote employment opportunities and to retrain and resettle workers, was more helpful to Italy than to the other countries. Again, Italy was the major source of excess and unskilled labor within the EEC; the other countries had labor shortages. During two years of the Social Fund's life, Italy received grants worth $1.3 million, or about twice the amount that went to France or the Netherlands.[4]

One major goal that Italy failed to achieve was the free movement of labor within the Common Market. Although Italian workers were emigrating to other EEC countries—on either a time-contract or permanent basis—such emigration was accomplished under the legal authority of bilateral agreements worked out by the respective foreign offices. Italian emigration to Switzerland, not a member of the EEC, was as high (until Switzerland imposed restrictions in 1965) as to France or West Germany.

It can be seen why Italy would have been a more enthusiastic supporter of the Common Market than some of the other member countries, and more willing than some of the others, especially France, to convert the economic community into a political community. Yet, Italy did not refrain from behaving nationalistically when it was to its interest to do so, and to act independently of its Common Market partners, even in economic affairs. When, in early 1964, Italy encountered serious balance-of-payment difficulties, it negotiated a credit of more than $1 billion from the United States, which was granted on March 14, 1964. Italy had dealt

---

[3] *Ibid.*, p. 195.
[4] *Loc. cit.*

directly with the Americans. When the American credit was announced, the EEC Executive Commission publicly objected on the grounds that Italy had gone to the United States without informing the European Community, instead of working out its foreign-exchange problems with its partners through Common Market institutions.

The repercussions of the Common Market's success on Italy were political, as well as economic. If the Italian Government was more anxious than some others to convert the EEC into a political community, an important reason was due to the recognition that the other member countries had more stable and conservative populations than did Italy. Nowhere else in the EEC was there such a strong Communist Party, or even a Socialist Party as extremist as the left wing of the Italian Socialist Party. Within the larger community, consequently, the extreme left would be a much weaker minority than inside Italy. The moderate and conservative elements inside Italy would thus have their positions reinforced. This had been an original attraction of the EEC to them, and naturally a reason for the original hostility of the extreme left.

But the progress of the Common Market served to erode even that hostility, and eventually the last significant internal left-wing opposition to the European Community disappeared. The CGIL had been interested in the Common Market in 1957 (when it was first proposed), and Giuseppe Di Vittorio's then favorable reaction had had to be suppressed by a call to discipline within the Communist Party. By 1962, four years of EEC successes had also overcome Socialist hesitations (it will be recalled that they had abstained in the parliamentary vote of ratification), and had converted not only the CGIL but the Italian Communist Party itself. In the summer of 1962, the Communists took a public position in favor of the Common Market, and had to admit that the European Economic Community was forcing the party to re-examine its concepts about the "inevitable decadence of capitalism." Palmiro Togliatti speculated that the international class struggle might no longer make sense in Western Europe. In preparation for an autumn congress of the World Federation of Trade Unions, the CGIL announced that it was ready to go to the congress and openly defend the Community. The congress had been called by the Soviet-bloc trade-union federations to attack the Common Market, and the CGIL announcement created a furor. The congress was canceled, while at the same time the CGIL asked for representation at Common Market headquarters, a request opposed by the CISL.

Italian foreign trade continued to expand, apart from its growth within the Common Market. Trade with the Soviet bloc was developed, especially with the Soviet Union. Italian importation of Soviet crude petroleum expanded considerably on the basis of barter arrangements: Italian pipe line, manufacturing equipment, and petrochemical machinery were exchanged for the crude oil. Enrico Mattei first made this major agreement with the Soviet Government in 1959, paying a price for the oil calculated at roughly one dollar less per barrel than the price of Middle Eastern oil posted by the large international oil consortium. The deal caused an economic and political stir inside and outside Italy. The Italians were warned of the dangers inherent in becoming too dependent on Soviet sources of supply. Actually, Soviet crude oil amounted to about 30 per cent of all Italian petroleum imports.

The contract was renewed in November, 1963, for an additional six years at about the same average prices and quantities as in the previous agreement. This was concluded by Mattei's successors after his death in an airplane crash in 1962. However, in early 1963, his successors had negotiated an agreement with Esso International for the importation of additional crude oil from the Middle East. This appeared to indicate that the new ENI management was less committed to continuing the feud with the international oil consortium than Mattei had been. Italian oil consumption was increasing steadily, and while the 1963 agreement with the Soviet Government continued the average quantities purchased under the earlier contract, Soviet crude oil would occupy a declining percentage of total Italian consumption in subsequent years.

The increase in petroleum imports, and in the consumption of other raw materials, indicated the rapid expansion in the use of motor traffic and of power by both consumers and industry. More people were on the move than ever before, both in terms of getting on the highways and streets and in terms of shifting jobs and residences. In the former category, the dramatic increase is illustrated by Table 11, which lists the annual number of driver's

TABLE 11
DRIVER'S LICENSES ISSUED IN ITALY, 1952–62

Year	Licenses Issued
1952	225,090
1953	270,099
1954	292,957
1955	316,931
1956	319,431
1957	335,348
1958	358,760
1959	380,891
1960	500,581
1961	719,200
1962	1,250,400

Source: *La Stampa*, February 24, 1965.

licenses issued in the eleven-year period from 1952 to 1962. It can be seen that in the year 1962 alone, 531,200 new licenses were issued, more than the total number of licensed drivers in the country as late as 1960. The roads and streets of Italy were absolutely inadequate for the increased traffic, and the problem was aggravated by the growing number of tourists who arrived by car and by past urban construction patterns that choked traffic into narrow ways. In the countryside, a road-building program (of modest dimensions on the whole) was complemented by the construction of a few superhighways, the most spectacular of which was the toll road Autostrada del Sole. It linked northern and southern Italy, from Milan to Salerno. By the time of its completion in October, 1964, work had already begun on its extension from Salerno to Reggio di Calabria at the toe of Italy, and other new superhighways were on the drawing boards, at the contract stage, or in construction. The new system of highways could be expected to break down much of the isolation of one part of the country from the other, reducing provincialism and localism.

People were on the move not only in automobiles but in trains and buses, and many of them were looking for new jobs. During the five-year period of the boom, roughly 1.38 million persons abandoned agriculture to find jobs in industry or in services, about double the number that had fled from the land during the previous decade. The largest number came from the south, but there was also an exodus from central and northern rural areas. They moved to local towns of their own region, to the principal regional cities, to other regions of Italy, and to foreign countries. They came generally from the poorest agricultural areas, and for the first time in modern Italian history, they were not replaced by a quickly growing population. The consequence was that marginal mountain and hill farms were left abandoned, as well as others that lacked good soil or adequate water. This could permit conversion of such land to other agricultural uses, such as grazing, or to reforestation.

By the end of 1963, the proportion of the labor force engaged in agriculture had declined to 25.5 per cent. The exodus revealed the weaknesses of the land-reform program established a decade earlier. Almost 40 per cent of those peasants who were originally awarded land had left agriculture. Some of them sold out to fellow farmers, others among the new proprietors became so poverty-stricken that they simply abandoned previously expropriated lands. The success of the reforms was dependent to some extent on cooperation among the beneficiaries, but the highly individualistic and suspicious Italians—exaggeratedly so in the south—found it difficult, if not impossible, to develop the behavior patterns necessary for successful cooperative ventures.

The Sicilian land-reform program, promulgated by the regional, instead of the national, government, was the most dramatic failure. It had taken the form of "model" agricultural villages, and these proved to have little holding power over the assignees. When nonagricultural jobs became available elsewhere, they abandoned their allotments, with the consequence that by 1964 fifty of the fifty-four model villages were either almost or completely deserted.

The rural exodus led to a reversal of farm policy by the government. Whereas the original land-reform program of 1950 had been based on the policy of breaking up farms (on the assumption of permanent rural overpopulation), the new agricultural policy, adopted near the end of 1959 under the name Green Plan (Piano Verde), had as one of its goals the consolidation of farms. The Green Plan was not a plan, in the sense of real planning, but a system of authorized subsidies and easy credit for the agricultural sector, to be added to the already existing system of high agricultural price supports. The institution and elaboration of the plan, however, did little to encourage the peasants to remain on the land, and as jobs became available in urban areas, the desertion of agriculture continued. It was the young men who were naturally the most mobile and most willing to abandon traditional occupations, but their economic motivations were reinforced by sociological ones, for more and more peasant girls made it clear that they had no intention of marrying men who expected to remain peasants for the rest of their lives.

The industrial aspects of southern development left much to be desired. The 1957 law requiring state firms to direct 60 per cent of their new investments to the south was adhered to by some, not by others. The government did not have enough control over its subordinate agencies to impose its will effectively. The Cassa per il Mezzogiorno made commitments upon the basis of its own plans, which, in some cases, did not accord with changing cabinet policies. It had developed various local clienteles, and these used political influence to prevent effective implementation of new government policies.

The major change in cabinet policy was the decision to create "developmental poles" in the south. It was decided that instead of trying to implement a generalized program of development over the whole area, better economic sense was made by concentrating investments in a few "poles," key zones where a variety of factors—location, local resources, existing industry—increased the likelihood that further concentration of investments would be fruitful. This meant a policy of selection, or discrimination. It meant deciding that certain places had a future while others did not. The political pressure exerted to influence these decisions can easily be imagined. Typical bureaucratic delays, the result of incompetence, if not deliberate sabotage, worked to hamper implementation of the policy. These "poles" would require large investments in infrastructure, but many of the ministries concerned failed to include in their budget requests the funds to implement the decisions made by their political superiors. To be effective, the program would also require local agencies capable of recognizing development opportunities and collaborating with outside business. So "local development consortia" were to be created. But these consortia in the south were filled with lame-duck Christian Democratic politicians, local notables, men without qualifications to direct or innovate modern industry.

In spite of difficulties and discouragements, the south continued to pull ahead. However, growth in southern productivity was slower than in the center and north except in 1961, when good weather produced unusually bountiful crops. But a striking inversion of income growth occurred. Prior to 1959, the rate of annual per capita income had grown on the average more slowly in the south than in the center and north—3.2 per cent to 5.2 per cent. From 1959, average per capita income rose more quickly in the south than in the center and north—6.5 per cent as against 5.6 per cent. Since income was rising faster than productivity, increases in the southern standard of living were, in effect, the result of transfers of income from outside the area: from other parts of the country, or from abroad, through investments, subsidies, or remittances.

The shifts of population from rural to urban areas, from mountains and hills to the valleys, plains and coasts, from south to north, created tremendous strains on the recipient communities. The increasing population flooded into slums in the old centers and outskirts of the cities, creating social, educational, and transportation problems of the first magnitude. The towns and cities, ill equipped and ill financed for such problems, turned more and more to the national state to help finance new school construction, new streets, new water lines, new sewerage lines, and new health and sanitation services. The increased returns derived from local taxes were insufficient. Between 1959 and 1963, local-government expenses increased 83 per cent, while local-government income increased only 55 per cent. The total deficit of local governments increased in five years from 329 billion lire (1959) to 834 billion lire (1963), a deficit covered by loans from agencies of the national state or by the direct assumption of certain bills by the national state.

Local governments obtained their principal incomes from consumption taxes and real estate taxes. In the major cities, which felt the pressure most severely, real estate became a major source of speculation and quick gain, often fed by money derived from the evasion of income taxes. Contractors and land speculators made fortunes, and some of them would proceed to lose them. The pressure to build was so great, and the profits were so large, that zoning laws were violated, parks invaded, city administrations corrupted on an even larger scale than before, and construction codes ignored, with predictable increases in the number of jerry-built structures. Prices skyrocketed: between 1953 and 1963, prices of new buildings tripled, while the average price of construction land multiplied ten times, the biggest increases taking place in the last half of that decade. This meant, naturally, that land costs became an ever larger proportion of total construction costs. The growth of total construction costs was less dramatic because most construction jobs in Italy are considered unskilled, and the industry became a major absorber of low-paid peasant workers emigrating from the countryside. The real estate boom naturally had its effects on already occupied land and buildings, whose prices rose proportionately. Most of the new residential building was constructed in the form of expensive apartments. Only a relatively small amount of public housing for low-income families was built. There was, consequently, a shift of people within the city from lower- to higher-cost housing as incomes improved, and rent-control laws were gradually eliminated.

The construction boom was not limited to the large cities. The countryside, especially the scenic areas of the coast and resort areas of mountains, was overrun. The national parks were invaded, with the connivance of overcompliant public officials. The natural and historic beauty of one of the most striking countries of the world was seriously damaged. Protests by enraged intellectuals, organized in such associations as Italia Nostra (Our Italy), or institutes of urbanism, had little effect for a number of years. By the end of the period, however, the boom was beginning to falter. Thousands of expensive apartments were vacant, lacking sufficient buyers or renters in the upper-income groups, while millions of poor people desperately needed decent housing. The protests of the outraged intellectuals were having some impact on the political parties, and as the national government and many local governments shifted to the left, more attention was paid to enforcement of zoning rules. More importantly, a general overhaul of the laws on urban development was put under study. Expropriation of building land by public agencies was advocated to prevent speculative profits, and some urbanists were proposing that the expropriation prices be set back to those prevailing in 1958. The resultant shiver throughout the real estate world was sufficient to pull down the left-wing Christian Democratic Minister of Public Works, Fiorentino Sullo. His enemies charged, wrongly, that he was going to nationalize all the real estate in Italy, but there was no question that a collapse in the price of land for new construction would have brought a general decline in the price of all land. When the real estate boom was brought to a temporary halt, it was due, not to Sullo, but to the tight squeeze on mortgages and other forms of credit that was established in late 1963 to contain the ever more insistent inflationary symptoms.

Prices had been rising slowly throughout the 1950's, more slowly than the general increase in productivity. In the early years of the miracle, the increase in prices continued, but it was during the period 1962 through 1964 that the cost of living rose drastically. In 1962, the cost of living rose 5.8 per cent over 1961, in 1963, 8.7 per cent over 1962, and in 1964, 6.5 per cent over 1963.[5] Part of the reason for the price increases was the growth of domestic and foreign demand. Another part was the wage-price spiral, which in the years 1962 and 1963 was pushed up through the aggressiveness of the unions. The unions were stronger because of the general prosperity, a more sympathetic center-left government, and most importantly, rising levels of employment. By the end of 1963, Italy, for the first time in modern history, was on the threshold of a full-employment economy. Unemployment was estimated at only 3.6 per cent of the labor force. There was still underemploy-

---

[5] *Economic Surveys by the OECD: Italy, 1965*, p. 17.

ment in southern agriculture and featherbedding throughout public agencies and private enterprise, but nevertheless the category
of unemployed was approaching the category of unemployable
(defined in terms of long-run incapacity to get a job).

With this favorable situation, it is not surprising that the unions
made something of a comeback. This was especially true of the
CGIL, which had been losing out to its major competitors—the
CISL and the UIL—during the middle 1950's. In the boom years,
the CGIL reversed the tide because the workers felt more secure
against management pressure and because the CGIL changed its
tactics. It used its connections with the Communist Party to take
care of newly arrived workers from the rural areas—i.e., finding
them jobs and a place to live and providing them with some social life and institutional contacts.[6] In its general approach, the
CGIL abandoned its emphasis on mass collective struggles and
directed its attention to the individual factories and firms, to the
detailed demands and needs of particular categories of workers.
In collaboration with the other confederations, it made aggressive demands for higher wages and better working conditions.
Strike activity increased, in proportion to the workers' sense of
confidence, and the results were generally satisfactory to them.

From 1958 through 1964, wages in Italy rose 80 per cent. This
was the highest increase among all the countries of the Common
Market, and far above the rate of wage increases in Britain and
the United States. The comparative figures are given in Table 12.
The increases in Italy were sharpest in the last three years of the
period, and resulted from a combination of new wage agreements,
automatic cost-of-living adjustments, and employer-offered extras.

---

[6] Naturally, the other major union confederations, the Church, the Christian Democrats, and the Christian Associations of Italian Workers competed
with the Communists and the CGIL in these social-service and employment-
agency functions, but without the same success. The Christian Associations of
Italian Workers organized employment agencies for peasant women arriving
in the cities, finding them positions as domestic help. One worthwhile objective accomplished by the union confederations during this period was the
breaking of the power of labor contractors who had exploited the unedu-
cated and unskilled southern rural migrants in an earlier period. These operators, usually early migrants themselves, would recruit newly arrived emigrants
from their home areas, sell their labor to industries or construction companies, and collect a percentage of the workers' earnings.

TABLE 12

INCREASES IN WAGES AND PRODUCTION FOR SELECTED COUNTRIES, 1958–64
(*In Per Cents*)

Country	Increase in Wages per Worker	Increase in Production per Worker	Increase in Wage Cost per Unit Produced
Italy	80	32	36
West Germany	67	35	23
France	60	27	27
Netherlands	75	30	35
Belgium	35	32	3
United States	27	22	4
England	36	25	10

Source: "[European Economic Community] Quarterly Report on Business Cycles," April, 1965, as reported in *La Stampa*, April 10, 1965.

For, although Confindustria blamed the unions and the center-left government for the wage-price spiral that resulted, the fact was that employers were paying more than the contract rates in their efforts to raid other firms for workers and to keep their own workers from being raided by others. In a few specialized categories, the bidding was so extreme that wages surpassed the German rates and stimulated a limited return by expatriated Italians.

The largest increases were received by workers in the advanced sectors of the economy. The many workers in artisan shops, in agriculture, in retail stores, were less fortunate. The general rise in prices affected everyone, and it also hurt certain export industries. Several of these industries had depended in the past upon the low level of Italian wages for their competitive position in foreign and domestic markets. After 1962, however, wages were no longer low. Many industries—the textile industry furnishes a good example—had neglected recent modernization because there had been no incentive, and as the boom reached its peak, they found themselves with high wage costs and outdated production facilities. To sell abroad, they had to meet competition and cut their profits, making modernization even more difficult. The problem of technical modernization faced by Italian industry was a result of the constant necessity to match the continued modernization of plant and equipment taking place in other advanced industrial countries. Italy in the early 1960's was caught in the middle of a squeeze from both the advanced and the underdeveloped societies. With certain important exceptions, it was not yet a really advanced economy, but its salary levels were too high to stand the competition of the low-wage underdeveloped countries.

The difficulties of technical modernization in many industries were superseded by the difficulties of sociological modernization. Italian business had been organized in the past on a family basis, with the head of the family exercising autocratic, if not despotic, control. This pattern had begun to break down during the depression of the 1930's, when a number of families were forced to sell out to the IRI in order to survive. After World War II, as original founders died, the decline of family control continued, and the heirs were often incapable of managing the enterprises. For example, the Agnelli family, which had controlled Fiat, found it necessary to bring in Professor Vittorio Valletta to manage the firm after Senator Giovanni Agnelli died. By the 1960's, most large-scale businesses were no longer family-controlled, but rather were directed by executives who might have held little or no stock in the firm. The death of Adriano Olivetti in 1961 brought on a crisis in the following years in the Olivetti Corporation, the largest business-machine firm in Europe. The family was forced to sell its controlling stock holdings to a consortium of banks and other firms. The consortium brought in an outside manager to operate the business.

It is difficult to judge if Italian big business is still family-owned, even though not family-operated. The difficulty comes from the fact that, in spite of legislation to the contrary, concealment of stock holdings is still general. The apparent decline of family ownership, however, did not mean the decline of autocratic habits of authority. To a great extent, the "boss," whether the owner or a salaried executive, still ran the business as his private domain, tolerating little interference and delegating little authority. Huge firms with thousands of employees remained highly centralized, with all significant decisions, and many insignificant ones, kept in the hands of the few at the top. The inability, or refusal, to decentralize authority was a further handicap in the evolution of Italian industrial life to more modern forms of organization.

This failure was not unique to private industry. The publicly owned firms and the public administration, in the form of the traditional ministries, were cursed with the same oligarchic patterns of behavior. Enrico Mattei, for example, had run the huge ENI as a private empire, independent of both political superiors and his own subordinates, who were kept in the dark as to his plans. Many of his overseas investments—in the Middle East, North Africa, and Argentina, for example—turned out to be financial losses, the price paid for his drive for personal and national prestige. Before his untimely death, he was beginning to retrench, for the financial cost of his policies was becoming more apparent and his political opponents were becoming more vociferous in their attacks upon him. He turned to collaboration with the international oil industry, a shift continued and extended by his successors.

The distribution of wealth and power still remained lopsided, and the tax system did not redistribute income very satisfactorily. In 1964, 74 per cent of Italy's tax revenue was still being derived from indirect taxes and only 26 per cent from direct taxes. This was an improvement over 1958, when the corresponding figures had been 78 per cent and 22 per cent, but it was still the most regressive tax system in the EEC. Cheating and evasion of direct taxes was a general practice encouraged by the outmoded and rusty tax system.

By the end of the period, the country's spending spree was beginning to show its negative effects. In 1963, balance-of-payment difficulties were increasing rapidly as Italian imports climbed. The lira was becoming shaky. There was a capital flight, partly political in motivation. The spending spree on consumers' goods and luxuries was not matched by the necessary spending within the public-service sector. Appropriations for schools had increased in the years between 1958 and 1963, but the funds remained drastically inadequate. Ports, railroad networks, hospitals, public health services, urban renewal, had all been neglected. The repercussions on the economy were demonstrated by the shortage of qualified scientists, professional men, executives, and administrators, by the inadequate skills of a semitrained and semiliterate labor force, by the loss to North Sea ports of transit trade in goods for Central Europe, by the inadequate domestic transportation of goods.

The boom had carried into the modern world of well-being a larger number of Italians than ever before, but still a minority. About 25 per cent of the population had attained a decent level of comfort by Western European standards.[7] But a larger number remained far below that level, and an important segment still lived under conditions of marginal survival.

---

[7] The figure of 25 per cent is an estimate, used by former Minister of the Budget Ugo La Malfa in an address to the national congress of the Republican Party on March 29, 1965.

11

The Crisis of Parliamentary Democracy

The Segni government, created in the spring of 1959 to provide a period of domestic *détente,* lasted for little more than a year. As a minority government, backed by a coalition of center-right parties, it provided a political breathing spell in which the extreme tensions that had been generated by the crisis of Fanfani's fall could be moderated and harnessed. The new Secretary-General of the Christian Democratic Party, Aldo Moro, proved to be an extremely skillful mediator among conflicting factions, prudent and accommodating, although he lacked the mastery and authority of a De Gasperi. The business community also felt more secure under a moderate government; this feeling was reflected in an upsurge of investment and a revival of real estate speculation. Only the left-wing parties and organized-labor confederations could feel no pleasure at the political stalemate. Their antagonism was manifested in a series of strikes that erupted in one industry after another during the early summer of 1959. While these strikes were primarily economic—rather than political—in motivation, they reflected the hostility to the political solution reached in earlier months.

With the minority status of the cabinet, there was no leeway for positive moves in the domestic political arena, and the cabinet followed a policy of routine administration. In foreign policy, it followed its traditional policy of close friendship with the United States and promotion of European collaboration. General de

Gaulle visited Rome from June 23 to June 27, 1959, but failed in his attempt to gain Italian support for a Mediterranean pact under French leadership. President Gronchi announced in the name of the government that Italy always wanted close ties with France, but not at the expense of other NATO members. The following year, Italy again rebuffed the French President: the Italian Government rejected de Gaulle's proposal of a three-power NATO directorate, with France to speak for the Continental members. It objected to France's emphasis on "national independence within the alliance" and opposed the development of a national French nuclear deterrent. In the autumn of 1959, this loyalty to the United States and to NATO was rewarded by Italy's inclusion in the ten-member disarmament committee meeting at Geneva. The Italians had no original ideas for reaching a safe, controlled, and proportionate general disarmament agreement (neither had any other member country), but Italy's inclusion would give it a sense of participation in the larger events taking place in the world.

On Italy's own northeastern boundary, trouble that had been brewing for years erupted into open agitation and violence in the South Tyrol, the Italian province of Bolzano. The South Tyrol People's Party, representing the German-speaking majority in the province, felt that the majority's long-run existence was being threatened by the gradual emigration taking place in Italy from south to north. Early in 1959, the party began agitation against the De Gasperi–Gruber Accord of 1946. While its ostensible demand was the establishment of a separate autonomous region for the province of Bolzano, its real goal was the eventual secession of the province and its return to Austria. Only in this way could its ethnic character and way of life be preserved in the long run. The agitation in the South Tyrol provoked counteragitations in Rome and in other Italian cities. Segni stated firmly that Italy would not countenance any revision of the accord. The Austrian Government intervened in March, 1959, to charge Italy with violations of the De Gasperi–Gruber Accord and threatened to take the issue to the United Nations. Pro-Austrian terrorists initiated a policy of bombing, both inside and outside the South Tyrol, which produced more counterdemonstrations in other parts of Italy.

In September, 1959, in anticipation of the annual meeting of the United Nations General Assembly, anti-Italian demonstrations took place in Innsbruck, Austria, capital of the North Tyrol and the center of Tyrolese agitation and subversion. On September 21, Bruno Kreisky, the Austrian Foreign Minister, formally charged on the floor of the General Assembly that Italy was pursuing a policy of social and economic discrimination against the German-speaking population of Bolzano. He asked the United Nations for a resolution that would call on Italy to grant regional autonomy to the province.

Foreign Minister Pella, representing Italy, responded to the charges skillfully. The Italian Government knew it was leading from strength. Pella denied the charges of discrimination and countered with the claim that Italy was extremely liberal in its treatment of the German-speaking inhabitants, more so than the De Gasperi–Gruber agreement required. Pella argued that in any case the treatment of Italian citizens was a domestic question and outside the jurisdiction of the United Nations.

This last claim made no impact on the General Assembly, but in all other respects the Italian position was in effect upheld inside the United Nations. The General Assembly refused to condemn Italy or to make any specific recommendations to the two countries. Austria raised the issue again in a note sent to Italy on May 29, 1960. Asking for "true autonomy" for Bolzano, the Austrian Foreign Office stated that unless its demands were met, it would put the question on the United Nations agenda once more. Italy responded by offering to send the dispute to the International Court of Justice for a decision, or else to engage in direct negotiations. Austria rejected international adjudication, for it knew perfectly well that the creation of a separate regional government for the province of Bolzano was not required by the De Gasperi–Gruber Accord. On July 17, 1960, Austria inserted the problem once again on the agenda of the General Assembly. The General Assembly debated the issue in its autumn session and on October 27 passed a resolution recommending bilateral negotiations between the two countries as the best means of re-

solving the dispute. The solution could not have been more satisfactory to the Italians.

Bilateral negotiations between Italy and Austria were carried
on sporadically in the following years, but as of 1965 no conclu-
sive agreements had been reached; fundamentally, the status quo
in the province was maintained.[1]

Italy's international success was due to reasons other than the
persuasiveness of Italian arguments. None of Italy's allies in the
West wished to weaken further an already feeble Italian Government by inflicting a diplomatic defeat upon it. And, as the Italians
were ready to point out behind the scenes, encouraging Pan-Ger-
man nationalism in the South Tyrol was not conducive to the
wider peace of Europe. If German revisionism were successful in
changing the Italian boundary, it would stimulate even further
all the German refugee movements and nationalist groups in Germany proper and thereby threaten the status of the German
eastern boundary. This was an argument that had appeal to the
Eastern European countries as well.

The Italian success on the South Tyrol issue at the international level was not matched at home in the province itself. In
subsequent years, the terrorist campaign expanded, rather than
subsided, and it continued to spread outside the provinces of Bolzano and Trento into other areas of northern Italy. The resentments and antagonisms in the zone directly affected became
further inflamed, making local attempts at accommodation more
difficult. Within the South Tyrol People's Party, moderate forces
were weakened and extremist elements bolstered. There was no
national party in Italy ready to do battle for the principle of self-
determination for the people of the South Tyrol.

The mixture of foreign and domestic concerns inherent in the
problem of the South Tyrol was reproduced in even greater degree in the ambivalence of Italian attitudes toward the larger
problems of East-West relations. The movement toward a *détente*

---

[1] There is some question as to Kreisky's personal commitment to the Austrian case. Certainly, the delicate balance between Catholics and Social Democrats in Austria would be upset if eventually the conservative, nationalist, and
Catholic peasants of the South Tyrol became Austrian voters. The Social
Democrats had nothing to gain.

in Soviet-American relations was accelerated by Premier Khrushchev's celebrated meetings with President Eisenhower at Camp David in September, 1959. International reconciliation had always been feared by right-wing groups within Italian politics, both lay and clerical, for they considered their domestic fortunes to be brightest within an international atmosphere of extreme tension. In its election propaganda, the Catholic Action Society always attempted to re-create the ambiance of the Czechoslovak *coup d'état* of early 1948 or the Budapest uprisings of 1956. Former Foreign Minister Gaetano Martino, in a Liberal Party campaign speech of early 1958, had warned that a relaxation of international tension would benefit left-wing elements in Europe and "make it possible in six months for Communist elements within the various countries to occupy positions of predominant power."[2]

Within the conservative group of cardinals in the Vatican, the visit of the Soviet Premier to the United States caused grave concern, and a series of unsigned editorials in *L'Osservatore romano* expressed serious criticism of the whole concept of East-West negotiations. The visit of the two leading world statesmen stimulated imitations, however, and in the fall it became known that President Gronchi had received an invitation to pay a state visit to Moscow, which he was eager to accept. Vatican pressure to prevent Gronchi's trip was enormous. It was pointed out that a reciprocating invitation would have to be extended to Khrushchev, which would bring the leader of the Communist world to the center of the Catholic world. The demonstration that the Italian Communist Party would organize to greet Khrushchev could easily be imagined. Gronchi was persistent, however, and he presumably threatened to go to Moscow whether or not the cabinet approved. Finally, the first week in November, the government authorized the trip for early 1960, after assurances had been received that Khrushchev would not make a return visit to Rome.

When President Eisenhower visited Rome in early December, 1959, he was greeted warmly by the government and enthusiastically by the Communists, Socialists, and other parties of the

---

2 Gaetano Martino, *L'idea liberale nella politica estera italiana* (Rome: Partito Liberale Italiano, 1958), pp. 13–14.

left and center who supported the reduction of international tension and the doctrine of peaceful coexistence. The next month, in burning indignation, Alfredo Cardinal Ottaviani publicly denounced "men of high responsibility in the West . . . who say that they are Christians [but] shake the hand that slapped Christ in the face."[3] Although Christian Democratic Gronchi was the direct target of Ottaviani's remarks, Eisenhower was the indirect one. Gronchi left for Russia in early February and soon learned that life in Moscow could be as difficult as in Rome. Apparently, his efforts to play the role of mediator between East and West were rather sharply discouraged. If Russians wanted to come to terms with Americans, they did not need Italian go-betweens.

At the domestic level, the minority government's incapacity to make basic policy decisions favored the status quo and was unquestionably one of the factors encouraging big business to proceed with its plan for expansion. But Italian political life was not quiescent. From both the right and the left, the respective attacks upon each other and upon the center continued. In May, 1959, the right-wing parties and press had opened up a barrage of criticism against Mattei, the ENI, and its principal newspaper organ, *Il Giorno* of Milan, accusing all of them of neutralism and, in some cases, of pro-Soviet bias. On June 1, Urbano Cioccetti, Mayor of Rome and a right-wing Christian Democrat, refused to approve a celebration of the fifteenth anniversary of the Allied liberation of Rome on June 4, 1944. His communal government was dependent on the votes of the *Missini* for its majority.

At the same time, the left was continuing to move forward electorally. Administrative elections for the regional governments of the Val d'Aosta and of Sicily, and for the provincial government of Ravenna, were scheduled for the late spring and summer of 1959. On April 13, the Vatican newspaper, *L'Osservatore romano,* issued a warning against voting for the Communist Party or for parties supported by the Communists. In Sicily, an excommunication decree was issued by the Archbishop of Palermo, Ernesto Ruffini, against anyone who would do so. Clerical intervention was ineffective in all cases. In the Val d'Aosta, a popular-front

---

3 *New York Times,* January 8, 1960.

coalition of Communists, Socialists, and the local Union Valdo-
taine won the regional election. On May 30, the Communist-
Socialist coalition governing the province of Ravenna won
re-election with an increase in votes over the previous majority.
And in July, in Sicily, Silvio Milazzo's schismatic Christian Social
Union improved its position, as did his left-wing allies. When
the Sicilian regional parliament met to elect a regional government, *L'Osservatore romano* issued a warning against re-electing
Milazzo as president of the region, but on July 28 the regional
parliament proceeded to do just that. Milazzo obtained the support of his own party, the Communists, the Socialists, and rebel
Christian Democrats.

The general trend of events, as indicated by the results of these
local elections, was not lost upon the national leadership of the
Christian Democratic Party. The shift to the left in the underlying strata of the population was apparent, and Aldo Moro, Secretary-General, felt that his party had to respond to this historic
trend if it were to have a long-run future. He finally convinced
the moderate and conservative leaders of his faction, the *Dorotei,*
that their party would have to approach the left. He and they felt
that if handled prudently and cautiously, the opening would not
be disastrous for them or for the party. At a national congress of
the Christian Democrats held in Florence at the end of October,
1959, Moro gradually unveiled his plans. In a major policy address, he defined the Christian Democratic Party as a "popular
and anti-Fascist" party, at a time when at the national level and
in many local governments his party was dependent on the votes
of Liberals, Monarchists, or *Missini,* who were spokesmen more
for the classes than the popular masses. Right-wing Christian
Democratic leaders, such as Pella, Andreotti, and Scelba, grudgingly went along with the new emphasis. The congress concluded
with an agreement between the *Dorotei* and the left wing of the
party, whose leadership was resumed by Fanfani, returned once
more to political activity. Moro would reject extremist support
from right-wing parties for any future government. Since the old
centrism was also impossible because the Social Democrats and
Republicans would no longer accept it, an opening to the left
appeared to be the only other choice.

If these conclusions appear clear in retrospect, they were not so clear at that time. It took several more months before the Liberals became convinced that under the cover of a government supported by the right, the *Dorotei* of the Christian Democrats were cautiously moving in the opposite direction. As the Liberals became aware of the development, their criticisms of the government increased, and in the major northern and central cities the large newspapers that supported them, such as *Il Corriere della Sera* of Milan and *La Nazione* of Florence, became more aggressive and violent. Large-scale industry threw its money and economic pressure behind the effort to block this evolution. ENI and IRI money was being similarly used, but for the opposite purpose. Fanfani's followers inside the Christian Democratic Party were increasing their attacks on the cabinet for relying on right-wing support. The Liberals finally withdrew their support of the government, and on February 24, 1960, Segni presented his cabinet's resignation to President Gronchi.

This resignation initiated a major crisis that lasted for months and threatened the very existence of democracy in Italy. Segni's resignation had come as the result of decisions reached by the *direzione* of the Christian Democratic Party, without having been preceded by any parliamentary debate or by any vote of no confidence. On February 29, Cesare Merzagora, Christian Democrat, resigned in protest from the presidency of the Senate, delivering a bitter speech in which he charged that Parliament had been reduced to an "organ without a voice at the crucial moments of Italian life."[4] He went on to condemn the "atmosphere of corruption [that] weighs on Italian political life, polluted by speculation and unlawful financial activities."[5] To many political commentators Merzagora's action appeared to be aiming toward the destruction of the party-parliamentary system and its replacement by a presidential one, as in France.

The parties were still struggling to reorganize a government, and with the endorsement of a majority within his own party's *direzione,* Moro began to negotiate for a revival of Segni's pro-

---

[4] The complete text of the statement can be found in Armando Saitta, *Storia e miti del '900* (Bari: Laterza, 1960), pp. 938–41.

[5] *Loc. cit.*

visional Christian Democratic *monocolore,* to be supported this time by the parties to the immediate left—the Social Democrats and the Republicans. Since the votes of all three parties would be insufficient to provide a parliamentary majority, Moro was prepared to negotiate for the Socialist Party's abstention, and Segni, who had accepted Liberal and Monarchist backing throughout the previous year, was willing to accept this indirect Socialist support. The Socialist price was the nationalization of the electric-power industry.

As the news of Moro's maneuvers leaked out, the conservative elements in Italian society, lay and clerical, moved to the attack. They were not yet ready to accept Moro's conviction that "historical inevitability" required Christian Democracy to open to the left. Under the stimulation of the private electric-power industry, Confindustria exerted its pressure. The Coltivatori Diretti did likewise. But the most effective restraints came from Church circles. The Catholic Action Society denounced the idea of the acceptability of Socialist support. Cardinals Ottaviani (Curia), Siri (Genoa), and Ruffini (Palermo) used their influence behind the scenes.[6] Faced with these pressures, Segni abandoned his efforts to form a government. Fanfani was willing to try in Segni's place, but clerical condemnation induced him to withdraw also.

Moro was confronted with the prospect of another cabinet dependent on the right, which he felt was both pragmatically and historically wrong. He refused to accept Liberal and Monarchist conditions and, instead, recommended a stopgap Christian Democratic administrative government that would not be identified with any political trend. It would be ready to accept votes from any source except Communist, on the grounds that the cabinet would be temporary and would have no political coloration. President Gronchi suggested that the man to lead the experiment was the Christian Democrat Fernando Tambroni, who had the reputation of being mildly leftist and who had had cabinet experience as the Minister of the Interior in several previous gov-

---

[6] Cardinal Siri was chairman of the Bishops' Commission for the Supervision of the Catholic Action Society. Ruffini was a leader of the conservative wing, as was Ottaviani, Prosecretary of the Holy Office.

ernments. Tambroni, ambitious and cynical, was more than ready to consent.

On March 25, one month and one day after Segni's original resignation, Tambroni's administrative cabinet was sworn in before President Gronchi, who gave it his endorsement. Tambroni asked Parliament for backing on the grounds that his cabinet was only temporary, that its functions would be limited to routine administration and to compliance with the constitutional requirement that the annual budget be passed by the end of June. On April 8, his cabinet received a vote of confidence from the Chamber of Deputies by a figure of 300 in favor to 293 opposed. Included in Tambroni's small majority were 271 Christian Democratic votes, 5 Monarchist votes, and 24 *Missini* votes. It was clear that the neo-Fascist votes had been determining; without them the government would have been rejected.

All Moro's efforts to present his maneuvers as nonpolitical could not gainsay the hard fact that for the first time since 1943 the Fascists were back in a crucial position of leverage at the national level. Left-wing Christian Democrats were not ready to accept the identification of their party with Fascism. Had not De Gasperi in 1948 defined Christian Democracy as a center party moving to the left? Had not Moro just six months ago called his party a "popular and anti-Fascist" party? Within two days, three left-wing Christian Democratic ministers—Giulio Pastore, Fiorentino Sullo, and Giorgio Bo—resigned rather than accept the Fascist votes. Others threatened to do likewise. On April 11, Tambroni submitted his government's resignation to the President of Italy. Gronchi held it in reserve while he explored the possibility of other choices.

Even before the vote in the Chamber, Fanfani had indicated his readiness to try for another agreement with the Socialists in case Tambroni failed to get a majority. Gronchi now let him go ahead informally, but Vatican cardinals again interposed what amounted to a veto. By April 22, Fanfani had given up once more, and the following day Gronchi rejected Tambroni's resignation. He told the Prime Minister to fill the vacancies in his Cabinet in order to govern.

The interference of the Catholic hierarchy had been behind

the scenes, but visible to active political and journalistic circles. To justify clerical intervention, *L'Osservatore romano* published an unsigned editorial (usually attributed to Cardinal Ottaviani or Cardinal Siri) entitled, "Basic Principles." It asserted the right of the Church to issue political instructions, arguing: "The Catholic can never overlook the teaching and instruction of the Church; in every field of his life he must base his private and public behavior on the guidance and instructions of the hierarchy."[7] The editorial went on to claim that collaboration with the Socialists was contrary to Catholic doctrine in principle. It added, inconsistently however, that "collaboration with those who do not admit religious principles may arise. In that case, it is up to the ecclesiastical authority, and not to the choice of the individual Catholic, to decide on the moral lawfulness of such collaboration."[8] This was, indeed, an open assertion of the right to dictate the choice of political alliances to Catholic politicians. The implication that collaboration with Fascists was morally acceptable, but collaboration with Socialists was not, was equally obvious. Of course, the Fascists claimed to be good Catholics, the heirs of the party of reconciliation between the Church and the Italian state.

More than two months had passed between the fall of the Segni cabinet and the final installation of Tambroni's administrative government. The Prime Minister now set about converting his stopgap, nonpolitical cabinet into an active political one. He already had the support of most business and industrial groups, which did not hesitate to praise him in their press. The stock market flourished. Now he announced a whole new spate of legislative bills, decrees, and executive orders hardly consonant with the role of a temporary place-saver that was pledged to step down in a few months. He proclaimed that bills would be introduced to reform the Senate, local finances, and the bureaucracy, to lower prices, and to increase government spending on highways, railways, and housing. He ordered reductions in the prices of sugar and bananas (controlled by government agencies), automobile

---

[7] An English translation of the editorial was published in *U.S. News & World Report,* May 30, 1960, pp. 73–74.

[8] *Loc. cit.*

gasoline (through ENI price leading), all designed to make himself popular with the public, especially with the middle classes, for whom the automobile was becoming a necessary status symbol. Later, price reductions were announced for bread, pharmaceuticals, fertilizers, cement, and automobile licenses. Postal and railroad workers received needed raises. He promised something for almost every group in Italian society: more government spending, more subsidies to industry and agriculture, to the south, to the islands, and to northern shipbuilding interests. And at the same time he promised to cut taxes. His Minister of Finance, Giuseppe Trabucchi, suggested that a law requiring the registration of stock transactions be repealed. He was not successful, but he had hoped to legalize the practice—then and still widespread—of concealing dividend income and capital gains. Tambroni's efforts to win popularity included the lavish distribution of honors: new *commendatori, cavalieri,* and *grand' ufficiali* were created on a scale and with a speed never known before or since.

Tambroni's demagoguery stimulated fears of his future ambitions, fears aggravated by the newly acquired respectability of Fascism. To press its advantage, the MSI announced its intention of holding its national congress in Genoa at the end of June. Genoa was a center of the resistance movement, where wartime partisan activity had been effective and widespread. It was easy to foresee possible trouble. The Italian governments of the past had often refused to permit meetings and conventions of left-wing parties on the grounds that they would lead to disturbances of the peace. The *Missini* knew, however, that Tambroni could not afford to stop a congress of a party upon which his government depended. On the contrary, they expected the police to provide them with the necessary protection. They were unquestionably engaged in a display of strength, anxious to demonstrate, if not to abuse, their newly acquired position.

On June 30, riots broke out in Genoa when groups of young anti-Fascists who were milling around the MSI meeting hall formed a protest demonstration that swelled rapidly, and by the following day, the area around the meeting hall was besieged. The demonstrators, who appeared to have joined together spontaneously, included individuals from a variety of parties and political groups. Later efforts to attribute the Genoa riots to the Communist Party do not appear to be justified. In fact, the Communists were caught unprepared at the outset. Some of them considered that an extreme right-wing pro-*Missini* government in Italy was the best one to further the Communist cause in the long run.

The Communist Party soon realized, however, that it would have to get on the anti-Fascist bandwagon. The Communists also saw in the situation the possibility of escaping from their progressive isolation by re-creating the wartime atmosphere and unity of the anti-Fascist popular front. It then quickly used its extensive network and party machine to organize demonstrations in other parts of Italy. A general strike was called in Reggio Emilia, in the "red belt." A number of deaths occurred in the ensuing violence. Protest rallies were held in numerous other cities, under Communist stimulation but often with the support of other political groups. By mid-July, ten demonstrators in various parts of the country had been killed and many others wounded.

Under Tambroni's orders, the police had been heavy-handed in their control of the unrest. As a former Minister of the Interior, he was prone to see police clubs as the solution to his problems. Visualizing himself as the object of conspiracies in which he felt many of his fellow Christian Democrats were participating, he appeared ready to use on his colleagues in his own party the dossiers that he had been able to accumulate during his years at the Ministry of the Interior. He also had been tapping the telephones and checking the mail of some of his own cabinet members.[9] When, however, he was challenged to produce the evidence of conspiracy, for some reason he backed down.

How far Tambroni went or was prepared to go is still debated. How seriously democracy in Italy was endangered remains a speculative subject. Phone tapping and mail checking had gone on before and have probably gone on since. What else was done in the way of threats or suppression of the press is uncertain. What became certain, however, was that the days of Tambroni's

---

[9] On the whole problem of the Tambroni episode, see K. Robert Nilsson, "Italy's 'Opening to the Right': The Tambroni Experiment of 1960" (Ph.D. dissertation, Columbia University, 1964).

government were numbered. The depth of anti-Fascist feeling in the country had turned out to be far more profound than was expected. On July 1, he had been forced to suspend the MSI congress. The following day, the *Missini* announced that they would no longer support his cabinet. And Aldo Moro could now use the crisis to demonstrate to an alarmed Church hierarchy and a concerned business community not only that Christian Democracy could not afford to be identified with Fascism but that Italy had no alternative but to move to the left.

12

The Opening to the Left

Before that alternative could be openly accomplished, however, two more years would elapse, in which the necessary adjustments in policy and attitude on the part of both Christian Democrats and Socialists would gradually, and in many cases, grudgingly, take place. In the meantime, the country needed a government, even if only an interim one, but a government free of any identification with Fascism.

Even before Tambroni's resignation, Moro had begun negotiations with the Social Democrats and Republicans for the formation of a "democratic coalition" to give parliamentary support to a new "administrative" cabinet. These parties, together with the Christian Democrats, did not have a sufficient majority, however, and because of the difficult and very special circumstances, the Liberals were approached for their support. The Liberal Party agreed, provided that the government not be used as a cover for an opening to the left. To insure further the security of the cabinet, negotiations were also opened with the Socialists for their abstention. The Socialist agreement to abstain, which was properly interpreted as a positive endorsement of the new government, provided the necessary condition for later developments.

The *direzione* of the Christian Democratic Party authorized Fanfani to head another *monocolore* interim cabinet, which in due course received the confidence of Parliament on the basis of the party agreements reached beforehand. Fanfani defined his government as one of "democratic restoration." This very description was an indication of the nature of its predecessor. While the four parties that voted in favor of the cabinet were precisely those that had composed the old centrist coalitions, it was not the intention of Moro and Fanfani to revive the old centrism. Fanfani defined the basis of his one-party cabinet as a system of "parallel convergences," without any policy agreement other than to "restore democracy."

The price of Socialist abstention was one that any proponent of the opening to the left would pay gladly. Administrative elections were scheduled for the fall of 1960. The electoral laws provided for proportional representation in all communes over 10,000 in population. In the election of the provincial councils, however, a prize of two-thirds of the seats was given to the list that elected a simple majority of the council, using single-member districts. This voting system exerted a strong pressure on the minor parties to merge (for the provincial election) with the major ones, and had been one factor in the Socialist-Communist presentations of joint tickets. The Socialists now asked that the provincial councils be elected by a system of proportional representation. Those Christian Democrats who were interested in the opening, knowing that the ability of the Socialists to run separate tickets would aid their gradual separation from the Communists at the local as well as the national level, got their party's consent. The Christian Democrats, also, would have to endure a separation, for other small parties that previously had participated in Christian Democratic provincial lists would now be able to run their own tickets. In the future, provincial governments would have to be constructed on the basis of coalitions formed after, rather than before, the election. In September, the law changing the provincial election to one of proportional representation was pushed through Parliament.[1]

An additional innovation of indeterminate, but potential, significance was the introduction of television campaigning. Televi-

---

[1] In 1964, the electoral laws were further modified to extend the proportional representation system to communal elections for all communes over 5,000 in population.

sion was initiated in Italy in 1954 by the government, which controlled radio and television broadcasting through an IRI corporation. Unlike the British BBC, the Radio-Televisione Italiana delivered news and comments in such a form as to favor the party in power, always the Christian Democrats. Neither its minor allies nor the opposition parties had ever had a chance. They had protested over the years without effect, but finally in 1960 the television program "Tribuna politica" was introduced in the months preceding the administrative elections. Here the secretaries-general of all the parties had an opportunity to face the camera in a question-and-answer session conducted by both friendly and hostile journalists. Now they could present their respective points of view directly to a national audience. The program was continued in differing formats in subsequent years, so that television became another imponderable in the operations of Italian political life.

On November 6 and 7, 1960, the administrative elections were held. In Table 13, the over-all results for the provincial councils

TABLE 13
PROVINCIAL ELECTION RETURNS OF 1960 COMPARED WITH
1958 ELECTIONS TO THE CHAMBER OF DEPUTIES
(In Per Cents)

Party	1958	1960	Difference
Fascist	4.8	5.9	+1.1
Monarchist	4.8	2.9	−1.9
Liberal	3.5	4.0	+0.5
Christian Democratic	42.4	40.3	−2.1
Republican	1.4	1.3	−0.1
Social Democratic	4.5	5.8	+1.3
Socialist	14.2	14.4	+0.2
Communist	22.7	24.5	+1.8
Other	1.7		

Source: Italia, Istituto Centrale di Statistica.

are compared to the political elections of 1958. The principal gainer, in percentages, was the Communist Party, the main losers, the Christian Democrats and the Monarchists.

In an address to the Chamber on November 25, Nenni announced that with the elections of November 6 the "truce" established during the previous summer could be considered ended, and for all purposes the Socialists once more could be considered in the opposition. Nenni's intention was not to attempt an overthrow of the government, but rather to use the ending of the truce as a basis for negotiating openings to the left at the local level. Since Liberal Party support for the truce had been conditioned precisely on a pledge by the Christian Democrats not to negotiate an opening to the left at the national level under the cover of "parallel convergences," the Socialist attempt to end the truce could pave the way for a shift of alliances. The supporters of the opening were convinced that it could proceed better if attempted first at the local levels, and negotiations to this effect were begun once the election results were in.

Within each of the four parties directly concerned, there were minorities opposed to the attempted opening. On the left wing of the Socialist Party, the *carristi* and the followers of Lelio Basso, a left-wing dissident, considered any collaboration with bourgeois forces or Social Democrats a betrayal of the working class. On the right wing of both the Social Democratic and the Republican parties, there were minorities favoring the old centrism or even collaboration with the parties of the right. (Pacciardi had appeared on platforms with neo-Fascists; and he was a man who had once been a leader of the International Brigades in Spain.) And within and without the Christian Democratic Party, strong opposition to any deals with Socialists still existed. On November 23, however, two days before Nenni's speech, the *direzione* of the Christian Democrats had agreed that local alliances with the Socialists could be made where feasible. The only stipulation was that Christian Democrats could not form local governments which included or depended on the support of Communists or neo-Fascists.

It took months of negotiations and long, hard bargaining before many local center-left governments were brought into existence. On January 21, 1961, the first local center-left government was created for the city of Milan, to be followed in February and March by similar governments for Genoa and Florence. By the end of spring some forty such local governments had been formed in north and central Italy, in those areas where the left-wing groups within Christian Democracy and the autonomist forces within the Socialist Party were strongest. But many older-style alliances were in existence at the same time: centrist governments, Communist-Socialist governments, and center-right governments. These last flourished especially in the south, where Christian Democrats often continued collaboration with Monarchists and in some cases neo-Fascists, in spite of the prohibition laid down by the party's central executive board.

The northern local center-left governments had not been created without continued opposition from within Church circles. The Catholic Action Society fought the trend bitterly, as did high churchmen such as Cardinals Ottaviani and Siri. In the spring of 1961, Cardinal Siri of Genoa, chairman of the Italian Bishops' Commission for Supervision of the Catholic Action Society, wrote to Aldo Moro, warning against the formation of local coalitions that included Socialists.[2] But the power of Catholic Action and its leaders had declined considerably. Its president, Luigi Gedda, had bitterly fought the leftward evolution of the Christian Democratic Party throughout this whole period. His influence had been present in Fanfani's downfall in January, 1959. His publications had attacked Moro's declarations to the Christian Democratic congress of October, 1959. He had supported Tambroni's opening to the right in the spring of 1960. He had attempted to build up the Catholic Action Society as a counter-altar to the Christian Democratic Party, potentially its successor should the Church hierarchy ever decide to abandon the party. His war against the left-wing Christian Democrats was unconcealed from the autumn of 1959 on. He even attacked the moderate *Dorotei* for their apparent opportunism and lack of ideological rigidity. The collapse of Tambroni's government was a severe blow to Gedda. The refusal of even conservative Christian Democrats to follow him in his attacks upon the party was another one. These conservatives preferred to resist the center-left evolution from inside the party rather than to split from it. The failure of the intransigent wing

---

2 See the *New York Times*, March 3, 1961.

of Catholic Action to induce large numbers of Catholics to vote "blank ballots" in the administrative elections of November, 1960, was another defeat.

From the beginning of 1961, the political power of Catholic Action was substantially on the decline, a regression due not only to its inability to halt the leftward direction of the Christian Democratic Party but also to changes in the atmosphere within the Church hierarchy. Pope John XXIII had succeeded Pope Pius XII in the autumn of 1958, but for the first two years of his pontificate he had been feeling his way slowly and moving cautiously. In 1960, he began to affirm his progressive views in a manner that was careful but that nevertheless enabled the leaders of Christian Democracy to stand up to the assault of conservative Catholic groups. It was John who, as Patriarch of Venice, had wished the Socialists a successful congress in 1957. In 1961, Pope John acted more vigorously. On April 11, the occasion of an official visit by Prime Minister Amintore Fanfani to the Vatican in connection with the celebrations of the centenary of Italy's unification, the Pope took the opportunity to express publicly his warm sympathies for the Prime Minister, the man most identified among Christian Democrats as the proponent of the opening to the left. In September, 1961, the Sicilian Christian Democrats accepted Socialist support in the regional legislature to obtain a majority capable of maintaining a Sicilian regional government. The move had been publicly condemned by Catholic Action and by Cardinal Ruffini of Palermo, as well as by the other Sicilian bishops. Threats of excommunication had been made broadly before the event, but when the alliance was formed no public reprisals ensued.

The publication in 1961 by Pope John XXIII of his first major encyclical, *Mater et magistra* (*Mother and Teacher*), was a further step in weakening the conservative wing of Catholic society. The encyclical's broad endorsement of a mixed economy, its rejection of the uncontrolled free market, its call to bring the disinherited into the social and political order, its emphasis on social justice and economic development, could all be legitimately deduced in its application to Italy as backing for the direction being pursued by Moro and Fanfani and as a rejection of the policies advocated by Catholic Action.

John XXIII was preparing for the Second Vatican Council, which would begin the following year, and he wanted to shift the focus of Church attention from Italian politics to the larger questions that the ecumenical council would face. In December, the Pope addressed Catholic Action leaders and advised them to concentrate on spiritual, rather than political, functions, advice repeated in an editorial in *L'Osservatore romano*.[3] Gedda was transferred from the presidency of Catholic Action to the presidency of the Civic Committees, replacing Ugo Sciascia in the latter post. While Gedda was succeeded by his close collaborator Agostino Maltarello, who shared his predecessor's outlook, the symbolic significance of Gedda's removal was not lost upon attentive political observers.

The weakening of the position of the right wing within the Catholic spectrum during 1961 also weakened the position of the right wing outside the Catholic world. The Liberal Party was faced with a dilemma as to the strategy it should pursue. It could accept Nenni's assertion that the administrative elections of November, 1960, brought to an end the special conditions of truce that had justified the Fanfani *monocolore* based on "parallel convergences." It could argue that the formation of the center-left local governments in early 1961 violated the conditions under which it had agreed to support the cabinet. If the Liberals wanted to precipitate a government crisis they had reasons to justify such an action. There were groups within the Liberal Party calling for this very step, but Giovanni Malagodi opposed such a policy and was able to get majority endorsement for continued Liberal backing of the cabinet. It was relatively easy for him to demonstrate that the minority cabinet was following a *de facto* centrist policy (which is what the Liberals advocated), even if it were more desirable to participate directly in the cabinet. The Socialists, in their party congress of February, 1961, still showed themselves to be bitterly divided over collaborating with the Christian Democrats and Social Democrats. The Christian Democrats, like the

---

[3] *L'Osservatore romano*, December 13, 1961.

Socialists, were not committed to the proposition that the center-left experiments at the local level must inevitably achieve a logical completion at the national level. The situation was still fluid, and the Liberals finally concluded that it was best to leave it that way.

Another factor inducing caution was the fear that pulling down the cabinet might bring about an early parliamentary election. The regular five-year term for the Chamber of Deputies would expire in 1963, but President Gronchi's seven-year term of office would end in 1962. Gronchi was understood to be eager for another term, but his reputation had been badly damaged by his original support of Tambroni in 1960. It was felt that he might seize upon a new crisis as an excuse for dissolving Parliament, in the hope that a new parliament might prove more favorably inclined toward him.[4] Article 88 of the Constitution prevents the President from exercising his power of dissolution within the last six months of his term. This meant that the potential danger would exist until November of 1961, and none of the parties desired an anticipation of elections.

So the cabinet of "parallel convergences" continued, but under its apparent immobility, action was being taken, at both the governmental and party levels, to work for a future center-left coalition. In February, 1961, an old Fascist law that prohibited both the migration of peasants to the city without a guarantee of a job and the offering of a job to anyone not a registered resident of the locality was finally abolished. The Constitutional Court had challenged this law years before, but it had taken time until the government finally eliminated it. The old law had been ignored in fact, and peasants had been on the move throughout the postwar period. By 1961, however, the flight from the land was reaching a peak, and hundreds of thousands of people were living in places where they had no legal residence. But they could not register to vote or register in unemployment offices in their new towns of residence. The left parties had fought for the abolition of the old law on both political and constitutional grounds. The Christian

---

[4] It must be recalled that the President of the Republic is elected by both houses of Parliament in joint session.

Democrats, fearful of how transplanted peasants would vote in the newly inhabited urban and suburban slums, had delayed for years, but finally gave in. The pressures of the left, and the mobility of a people in the midst of an economic boom, could not be resisted indefinitely.

Other steps were taken during the year to lay the groundwork for an eventual Christian Democratic–Socialist convergence. On March 24, a special parliamentary commission was formed to study the problem of the lack of economic competition. The Christian Democratic Party established a study group to examine the problems connected with national planning, or "programming," as the Italians preferred to call it (to make it sound less Marxist). In May, 1961, the government announced that equalization of electricity prices throughout the country would be imposed upon the electric-power industry, the first of two stages to begin the following September. A Christian Democratic study commission was established to analyze the problem of urban planning and zoning, one of the most chaotic and corrupt aspects of Italian life, and one that was becoming even more chaotic and corrupt because of the boom.

On July 11, 1961, Nenni presented to Parliament a Socialist motion of no confidence to prepare the way for restructuring the cabinet. He argued that the period of emergency was over, that in the year since July, 1960, democratic legality had been established, and that it was now time for the parties interested in the center-left to clarify their positions. Nenni's timing proved to be bad, and the vote was lost. The center parties were not yet ready to commit themselves, nor was his own party. The move boomeranged on him; he was condemned by his potential allies, and was subjected to renewed attacks from the Communists and the *carristi*.

In September, the Christian Democrats held a conference at San Pellegrino to discuss their ideology. The left wing dominated the conference and it was clear that an intellectual basis was being laid for an historic "meeting" with the Socialists. Professor Pasquale Saraceno, the most influential economist connected with the party, made a strong argument for national programming as the only means of eliminating the historic disequilibria of Italian society. He maintained that the natural forces of the market could not break through age-old underdevelopment, as the experience of the Italian south during the previous decade and the experience of other underdeveloped areas demonstrated. The following month, the National Council of the Christian Democratic Party issued a call for a party congress to settle fundamental policy. The date of the congress, set for the end of January, 1962, provided further time to organize for the internal battle that would take place and also provided another excuse for prolonging the life of the government now that the original one (fear of Gronchi's ambitions) had expired.

While the country waited for a decision in internal affairs, Fanfani busied himself in trying to play the role of mediator abroad. In the summer of 1961, he visited first the United States and then the Soviet Union. He arrived in Moscow during the Berlin crisis of August, 1961, but learned to his chagrin that the Russians were not any more disposed to take his suggestions than they had been earlier to take Gronchi's.

The national congress of the Christian Democratic Party began at Naples on January 27, 1962. A decision on opening to the left was the purpose of the congress, and Moro and Fanfani had prepared the ground carefully. To reduce the foreign-policy obstacles, Pietro Nenni had published an article in the January, 1962, issue of the American review *Foreign Affairs,* in which he announced to both the American and Italian interested publics that the Socialists, although opposing NATO in the past, had no intention of insisting on Italy's withdrawal from the alliance in the present. He wrote: ". . . we have never raised the question of withdrawal [from NATO] for two reasons. First, because to do so would convict us of demagoguery; and second, because to withdraw under present conditions would jeopardize the European equilibrium, which though it is dangerously unstable does contribute to the maintenance of a truce between the two opposing blocs."[5]

On January 11, 1962, the Central Committee of the Socialist Party voted a resolution stating that the party did not expect Italy

---

[5] Pietro Nenni, "Where the Italian Socialists Stand," *Foreign Affairs,* January, 1962, p. 221.

to desert its alliances, but merely insisted that NATO's obligations must be limited to Europe and given a "purely defensive interpretation." The Central Committee approved, by a majority vote, both the resolution and a report by Riccardo Lombardi in which a "defensive interpretation" was meant to include an absolute denial of atomic weapons to West Germany.

Reinforced by these Socialist pronouncements, Moro was able to concentrate the argument on domestic issues. While the right wing of the Christian Democrats, led by Mario Scelba, opposed the opening, the great majority of delegates was ready to try the policy on an experimental basis, without committing the party to it irrevocably. Tactical expediency required this approach, for the Social Democrats and Republicans had already announced that their support of Fanfani's cabinet of "parallel convergences" was to be considered terminated as soon as the results of the Christian Democratic congress were known. The announcement was intended to force the Christian Democrats to make a clear-cut choice, and to bolster Moro's position within his own party by cutting off the only other feasible alternative, a return to centrism. Moro was thus successful in carrying the large majority of the congress with him and emerged victorious with a final resolution authorizing the party executive directorate to construct a center-left government with the support though not the direct participation of the Socialist Party. The resolution promised continuation of a pro-Western foreign policy, and did not require that the Socialists split immediately with the Communists at local governmental levels, in the CGIL, or in various cooperatives. Moro had argued that a successful center-left policy would produce these splits as an eventual consequence.

The Christian Democratic congress ended on February 1. The next day, Fanfani presented his cabinet's resignation to President Gronchi. After three weeks of negotiations with the Social Democrats, Republicans, and Socialists, Fanfani presented a new government composed of his own and the two small parties. There had never been any intention to have Socialist participation, nor did the Socialists want it at this time. They were involved, however, in the elaboration of the program that Fanfani intended to present to Parliament and to the people of Italy. Both Mario

Scelba and Giuseppe Pella, the most prominent of the conservative Christian Democrats, refused posts in the cabinet.

Fanfani's program contained seven major policy declarations: (1) establishment of governments for all nineteen regions of Italy —fourteen regions were still without them (this was a somewhat nebulous promise, however); (2) reform of the public administration; (3) a three-year program for school development, including the establishment of a unified junior high school;[6] (4) the gradual abolition of *mezzadria* ("sharecropping"); (5) the establishment of economic programming for "just and harmonious social development," including new legislation for urban planning and zoning; (6) elimination of the private electric-power industry; and (7) fidelity to the North Atlantic Treaty Organization.

The program was unquestionably center-left, yet there were elements in it that raised Socialist doubts. The commitment on regional governments contained all kinds of hedging. The school statement was a compromise that avoided the delicate issue of illegal state subsidies to private, mainly confessional, schools. There were differences as to the method of eliminating the private electric-power industry; the Socialists argued for nationalization, while some Christian Democrats preferred "IRIzation" (the buying up of a controlling stock interest by IRI corporations). For these and other reasons—the most important of which was the firm *carristi* disapproval of the whole idea of collaboration—the Socialist Party decided to abstain, rather than vote for the government. Nenni announced in Parliament, however, that Socialist abstention must be interpreted as favorable to the government. The right-wing parties—Liberal, Monarchist, and *Missini*—voted against the cabinet. The Communists did too, but Palmiro Togliatti justified their negative vote on the bases of the two issues of fidelity to NATO and the vagueness of the commitment to regional governments. He insisted that the Communist opposition was limited to these two issues, and was not a general opposition to the center-left. In this respect, the Communists were more mod-

---

[6] The establishment of the unified junior high school meant that the child's future life was to be determined by a decision made at the age of fourteen, rather than eleven, as had been the case previously. The choice of secondary school determined the choice of future vocations open to the child.

erate than the Socialist *carristi,* who revealed anarcho-syndicalist orientations by charging their comrades with transformism[7] and desertion to the class enemy.

The establishment of the first center-left government created an uproar in the press and in business circles, especially within Confindustria. The intensity of the attacks, the barrage of accusations of betrayal, the predictions of economic disaster, knew no limitations. The stock market declined more drastically than before. Yet the government was moving slowly, with the *Dorotei* restraining precipitate action. Gronchi's term was expiring in May, and the *Dorotei* anticipated that in the battle over the succession they might need the votes of right-wing parties. This is precisely what they did need. While the Socialists, Republicans, Social Democrats, and some left-wing Christian Democrats insisted that the new President of the Republic should be identified with, and committed to, the center-left, the *Dorotei* imposed the choice of a conservative Christian Democrat upon their party. Antonio Segni was their man, and it was becoming apparent that this was a price Moro had had to pay the past January to get their support for his policy. The three lay parties put forward the candidacy of Giuseppe Saragat, the leader of the Social Democrats. A victory for him would remove one of the obstacles to the reunification of the two Socialist parties, since it would leave Nenni in an unchallengeable position of party leadership.

It took nine ballots before the *Dorotei* were able to get Segni elected. Insurgent left-wing Christian Democrats refused to support Segni in the early ballots, proposing instead their own candidates: Gronchi, Piccioni, Fanfani. They would never go over to Saragat, however. After the sixth ballot, Fanfani released his followers, and the insurgents came back into line. Then the *Dorotei* negotiated with the right-wing parties and Segni was finally elected on the ninth ballot with the support of the Liberals and the Monarchists. So in a very early stage of its existence, the new center-left coalition was racked with dissension.

The three-party coalition continued with its program. The pre-

---

[7] Transformism can be defined as a betrayal of ideological principles in return for power, prestige, or material rewards. Historically, it has been applied to the Italian left.

censorship of stage plays was abolished, but not of movies. A special parliamentary commission was established to investigate the Mafia. A withholding tax on stock dividends was passed in the hope that it not only would produce income-tax revenue that was escaping payment but would also smoke out the real ownership in Italian industry. Both hopes turned out to be unwarranted, however, and in 1964 it was "temporarily" suspended.

In May, 1962, Budget Minister Ugo La Malfa of the Republican Party presented the government's reasons for, and methods of, national programming. In an address on the state of the economy, he announced that the biggest economic boom ever known in Italy's history had failed to establish a balanced economic system but, on the contrary, had aggravated the gaps, between north and south, industry and agriculture, modern and backward industries, that were dividing Italian society. He insisted that continuation of current patterns would not overcome these disequilibria, that democratic government programming was the only solution. An interministerial committee on programming would be set up with the Minister of the Budget as its chairman. An assisting technical committee composed of experts—including representatives from the major categories of Italian economic life, industry, agriculture, commerce, and labor—started its work in September under the chairmanship of Professor Pasquale Saraceno.

On June 16, 1962, the cabinet presented to Parliament its bill on the electric-power industry. The bill provided for nationalization of the industry, including those firms already owned by the IRI and ENI. A new and separate agency, ENEL (Electrical Undertakings Trust), would be created to administer the plants. A generous cash price was to be paid to the firms in ten annual installments.[8] The short-run inflationary impact would be reduced by permitting the firms, most of which were diversified with large operations outside of electric utilities, to invest in other areas of business.

The decision to nationalize the electric-power industry had both economic and political motivations. Economic complainers against

---

[8] Municipalized electric-utility companies were given the option to sell out to ENEL or to continue independently. In subsequent years, most of them chose to continue operating independently.

the industry charged it with a reluctance to cooperate in the development of the south, and with noncompliance and evasion of the prices set for electric power by the Interministerial Committee on Prices (which fixed prices for the sale of energy and of other basic necessities, including medicines). Politically, the industry was felt to be responsible for the conservative and uncompromising line followed by Confindustria since 1955, and for the shift in financial and journalistic support away from the Christian Democrats to the Liberals. The decision of the majority of the Christian Democrats to support nationalization may very well have been the result of the party's reaction to this treatment in the previous years, rather than of ideological principle or economic conviction.

During the following months, the battle over nationalization held the center of political attention. The fight inside and outside Parliament was bitter. Led by the Liberals and by Confindustria, the battle was fought with a variety of techniques: parliamentary obstruction, stock-market decline, threats and intimidations, newspaper proclamations of disaster. The Christian Democrats promised that there would be no future nationalization of other industries; the Socialists announced that they would not insist on further nationalization on principle, but would examine and judge the future development of the various sectors of industry. The attempt on the part of Confindustria and the Liberals to forge a united front in defense of the ideological principle of private enterprise failed. Many large firms and industries not directly affected refused to rally to the cause. Such giants as Fiat and Montecatini (chemicals) stayed clear of the struggle.

In reality, there was little doubt about the outcome. Most Social Democrats, Republicans, Socialists, and left-wing Christian Democrats were committed to nationalization of the industry. The Communists, after criticizing the bill in detail and suggesting various amendments that were not accepted, announced their support of the government's measure. Thus, many more than enough votes existed to offset any potential sniping that conservative Christian Democrats might attempt. There was no possibility of repeating the events of January, 1959, which had brought Fanfani down. In the fall, nationalization was approved in the Chamber of Deputies by a vote of 404 to 74. The Senate vote was of similar proportions. A number of Christian Democrats abstained or absented themselves.

The nationalization bill did not consolidate the relationships between the two principal parties of the center-left. The fight over the presidency of the republic still rankled, for Fanfani's refusal to support Saragat was not yet forgotten. On the other hand, the dominant moderates within Christian Democracy, the *Dorotei,* were worried about the effects of the nationalization battle on their conservative supporters and were already hedging on the next major issue, the creation of regional governments for the regular regions. The reason they gave was the unwillingness of the Socialists to guarantee that they would never form coalitions with the Communists in those regions—Emilia-Romagna, Tuscany and Umbria—where there was a long experience of Communist-Socialist collaboration at lôcal and provincial levels. Nenni responded by offering direct Socialist collaboration in a center-left national government after the 1963 parliamentary elections. The *carristi* objected violently. Later, Nenni offered to examine the question of regional center-left alliances (where the strength of the parties made such alliances possible) if the four parties would agree to, and pledge themselves to act together for the application of, a five-year program to be enacted after the election. The *carristi* threatened a split.

On November 10, the Christian Democrats turned Nenni's offer down. It was becoming obvious that they wanted to conduct the coming electoral campaign by emphasizing moderation and prudence, to stave off the Liberal Party attraction to the conservative wing of their electorate. The Socialists, on the other hand, were worried about losing support to the extreme left. Not only were the *carristi* of the Socialist Party threatening a split, but in October, 1962, the Communist Party had abandoned its cautious waiting and had launched an outright attack on the center-left, concentrating on the Socialist Party.

Communist hesitations had been the product of both domestic and international complications. The Party could not ignore the effects of the boom and of the Common Market on Italian society. An editorial by Togliatti in his weekly, *Rinascita,* on August 25, 1962, had openly accepted reformism as a suitable method to achieve socialism. He had argued that while his Party accepted the elaboration of gradual reforms, on a democratic basis, it did so with the goal of achieving a truly socialist society. His differences with the Social Democratic parties of Western Europe, he claimed, were not over the method of reform, but over their abandonment of socialism as the final goal. He speculated that the classical class struggle no longer made sense in Western Europe, and in September the Party openly reversed its former negative judgment of the European Economic Community.

These trends within Italian Communism were naturally not shared by all Party members. A more orthodox group, getting moral and perhaps financial support from Communist China, opposed the acceptance of this program. The growing public dispute between Russia and China over peaceful coexistence, and the Chinese charges of revisionism, became reflected in battles inside the Party. The reopening of the attack on the center-left and on the Socialists helped to limit internal Communist dissidence. At the Party congress held in Rome in December, 1962, Frol Kozlov, representing the Russian Party, openly attacked the Chinese Party. The Chinese delegate responded, attacking not only the Russians but also the Italians. Togliatti reacted by endorsing the Russian position and further recommending to the two major disputants that they handle their disagreements in private and resolve them by negotiation.

By the end of 1962, the positions being taken by all the parties were in anticipation of the coming parliamentary elections. In January, 1963, the tensions between the Christian Democrats and Socialists over the postponement of the commitment to regional governments almost precipitated a cabinet crisis. Aggravating the tension was a dispute over the assignments to the top posts of the new electric-power agency, ENEL; the Christian Democrats had skimmed the cream of the patronage, leaving their allies embittered. The Socialists, with an electorate that was traditionally "against the government," had no desire to be identified with it, especially when the benefits of such identification were negligible. The Christian Democrats preferred not to enter the campaign identified as an ally of the Socialists. An open crisis was avoided, however, when cooler heads within both parties argued that a crisis would just advance the election date and, more important, be an open admission that the policies of the two parties had failed. The crisis was postponed, and on February 18, 1963, Parliament was dissolved for elections scheduled for April 28.

13

The Testing of the Center-Left

The end of the third legislature inaugurated one of the strangest campaigns in Italian electoral history. The cabinet routinely remained in office until the elections were over, while the country, prosperous as never before, was subjected to an assault of unwarranted proportions from both extremes. One would have thought, from observing the propaganda of the parties of the right (with the Liberals in the forefront), that country, religion, morality, and Western civilization had been betrayed by unscrupulous Christian Democrats, subverted by alien ideologies. At the other extreme, the Communists were denouncing a perfidious Socialist Party that had betrayed the workers, better off than ever before, to the class enemy. These bombardments put the two principal parties of the center-left on the defensive. To meet the attacks, the Socialists announced that they were returning to a position of noncommitment for the future. The Christian Democrats likewise declared that their obligation was ended; they would feel free to decide which way to go after the election returns were in. The two minor parties warned, however, that they would support only a new center-left government.

Meanwhile, international events contributed to maintaining a future for the center-left. De Gaulle had vetoed Britain's entry into the Common Market the previous January. The Italian reaction the following month was a refusal to sign an agreement, already initialed, accepting the association of former French African colonies and protégés into the EEC. Anti-Gaullism was one thing all four center-left parties had in common. By June, 1963, however, Italian-French relations had been smoothed. The removal of the intermediate-range-missile bases from Italian soil, in the spring of 1963, undoubtedly helped to improve the Socialist attitude toward the government.[1] The decision of the Americans and Italians that Italian ports would not be needed for bases for the American Polaris submarines that were replacing the land-based missiles also pleased the Socialists.

During the election campaign, two other events of international importance occurred that would have ramifications in internal affairs. On March 6, 1963, Pope John XXIII received Premier Khrushchev's daughter and son-in-law in private audience. The impact on the world and on Italian politics was stunning. Domestically, the gesture symbolized a reversal of the 1949 general excommunication of Marxists by Pope Pius XII. Although six days later the Italian Bishops' Conference published its by now routine pre-election instructions to Catholics to vote united for the Christian Democratic Party, this letter could not offset the impact of the visit. The wording attacked atheistic Communism specifically, rather than Marxism or socialism. Its intentions were interpreted to be as much an attempt to hold conservative Christian Democrats from the attractions of the Liberals as it was a warning against Communism.

On April 10, 1963, Pope John published his second major encyclical, *Pacem in terris (Peace on Earth)*. The significance of the document was universal; its consequences for Italian life were apparent in three of its fundamental characteristics. First, it was addressed to "all men of good will," not just to Catholics. Second, it gave major emphasis to the principle of freedom of conscience. Third, it endorsed the possibility and rightness of collaboration for peace and social justice between men who differed on ideological grounds. Consequently, it was, in effect, reversing the *Osservatore romano* editorial of May 17, 1960, "Basic Principles," which

---

[1] While the decision to remove the missile bases was justified on the grounds of their obsolescence, it may have been related also to the American-Russian agreements that brought the Cuban crisis to an end in October of 1962.

had declared collaboration between Catholics and Marxists to be immoral. Inside Italy, it could easily be interpreted as an endorsement of the center-left. On a larger scale, along with the visit of Khrushchev's relatives, it could be considered an acceptance of the Communists as within the bounds of respectability.[2]

A little over two weeks later, on April 28, the elections for the fourth republican legislature took place. The results, compared with the 1958 vote, as shown in Table 14, clearly indicate the ad-

TABLE 14

VOTE FOR THE CHAMBER OF DEPUTIES, 1958 AND 1963

Parties	1958		1963	
	Seats	Popular Vote (Per Cent)	Seats	Popular Vote (Per Cent)
Fascist	24	4.8	27	5.1
Monarchist*	25	4.8	8	1.7
Liberal	17	3.5	39	7.0
Christian Democratic	273	42.4	260	38.3
Republican	6	1.4	6	1.4
Social Democratic	22	4.5	33	6.1
Socialist	84	14.2	87	13.8
Communist	140	22.7	166	25.3
South Tyrol People's	3	0.5	3	0.4
Other	2	1.2	1	0.9
Total	596	100.0	630	100.0

* The Monarchist figure for 1958 represents the totals of the two Monarchist parties. They were reunited in 1960.

Source: Italia, Istituto Centrale di Statistica.

vances made by the Communists, who received more than one-fourth of the total vote after five years of the greatest and most widespread prosperity ever known in Italian history. The Liberals doubled their small vote. The Social Democrats made moderate gains; the Socialists ended with a small gain in absolute numbers,

2 In spite of the anti-Communist barrage of the previous decade, the Catholic and Communist groups inside Italy had always been in contact with each other, both inside and outside of the political sphere. The Communist Party was too large and too rooted in Italian society to have been kept at arm's length, on the margins of Italian life.

but a percentage loss because of the larger total vote. The Monarchists were the big losers, while the Christian Democrats also suffered a significant drop.

The recriminations began immediately, especially over the large increase in Communist votes, an increase registered throughout all parts of the country. It was evident, also, that the Christian Democrats had lost both to the right and to the left. Fanfani's center-left policy was blamed for the loss of votes to the right. Pope John was blamed by the conservatives for the Communist gains. They claimed his actions and statements had released the inhibitions of many voters, especially women, who voted Communist for the first time because they felt that they could now do so without fear of reprisals from the Church. These recriminations were politically motivated, of course, designed to influence the formation of a subsequent government. Aldo Moro, however, gave a more profound explanation of the results. He pointed out the significant transformations of a society in the midst of an industrial revolution. He mentioned the vast migration from the country to the city, from south to north; the urbanization and proletarianization of the peasants; the emancipation of women from the home and from age-old traditions and restrictions. He alluded to the specific causes of discontent, such as rising prices, the lack of housing, the inadequacy of public services in the mushrooming outskirts of the cities. He admitted that the Communists had been better able to exploit these discontents than had the other parties. They had gained support from urbanized peasants who, in their former villages, had previously voted Christian Democratic or, in the south, Monarchist. They had made inroads in the left wing of the Socialist electorate, especially in the "red-belt" areas of Emilia, Tuscany, and Umbria. They had gathered the mass of the protest vote.

The four parties that had supported the former center-left coalition still controlled over 60 per cent of the seats in Parliament, if they could agree on a program. In May, negotiations were begun for a new coalition, and Fanfani, pushed aside as the scapegoat for the Christian Democratic losses, was succeeded by Moro directly, who tried to form a new government. Fanfani was bitter at such treatment and refused to enter a new cabinet. Moro proceeded very deliberately with his negotiations. He hoped to strengthen his hand with a Christian Democratic success in the Sicilian regional election, which was scheduled for early June. His hopes were realized. Milazzo's schismatic party suffered a severe defeat, and the Christian Democrats felt more secure nationally. Then the death of Pope John delayed progress toward a cabinet until his successor, Pope Paul VI, the former Giovanni Battista Cardinal Montini, was installed. At this point, negotiations accelerated and the leaders of the four center-left parties arrived at an agreement which committed them to a relaunching of their program.

On the evening of June 16, Pietro Nenni brought the program to a meeting of the Central Committee of the Socialist Party. There he saw his autonomist majority split. The dissidents, led by Riccardo Lombardi, argued that the new program was deficient. The commitment to establish regional governments was too vague; the law on urban planning and zoning was not tough enough; the criteria for economic programming were too imprecise; the deadlines for the enactment of these bills were too loose. These were the official reasons. Unofficially, the *Lombardiani* were involved in a maneuver to scuttle Moro and restore Fanfani, in whom they had more confidence.

With his majority temporarily gone, Nenni and his secretariat presented their resignations to the Central Committee, which refused to accept them. Moro's attempt to form a cabinet had thereby collapsed, and the only course of action was to hold new elections, or else establish another caretaker government. The right-wing Christian Democrats, encouraged by the results of the Sicilian regional vote, wanted new national elections. This threat of new elections played into the hands of those who preferred a caretaker government, because the Socialists felt themselves in no condition to face such elections so soon. On June 19, Giovanni Leone, the Christian Democratic Speaker of the Chamber of Deputies, formed still another minority *monocolore*. Leone assured the Socialists that he had only two purposes: to get the budget passed by June 30 as required by law, and to provide the time for the Christian Democrats and Socialists to pull their respective parties together. The Socialists would hold a party congress in

October to decide on fundamental policy. All Leone asked of the Socialists was that they abstain on the vote of confidence.

The Socialists realized that to vote against Leone would practically guarantee new elections. Both Nenni and Lombardi apparently felt that Leone's pledges and his party's commitment to relaunch the center-left were honest. The autonomist majority inside the Socialist Central Committee was reconstituted and the party agreed to abstain. The Social Democrats and Republicans did likewise. Leone's *monocolore* was safe and his government was voted into office over the opposition of the Communists, Liberals, and *Missini*. The Monarchists, too, abstained.

During the summer, Moro pulled his party majority together by able maneuvering. In early August, the Christian Democratic National Council issued a strong call for the constitution of a four-party government of the center-left after the Socialist Party Congress. It was a specific invitation for direct Socialist cabinet participation; the purpose was to aid the autonomists within the Socialist Party in their campaigning prior to the congress. In foreign affairs, the international *détente* between the United States and the Soviet Union also helped to reduce points of friction between the prospective partners. The agreement between the two superpowers in June, 1963, to establish a "hot line" between Washington and Moscow was approved by the Italian Government. The moratorium on nuclear testing in the atmosphere, which Russia and America negotiated the next month, was endorsed by all Italian circles except extreme-right supporters of the Cold War. On only one foreign issue was there potential disagreement. The American proposal for a NATO multilateral atomic force was advocated by many as a way of providing a substitute for the proliferation of national atomic arsenals, and the Christian Democrats looked upon it in this light. The Socialists, however, considered this an indirect way for the Germans to get to the atomic trigger, and so were generally opposed. The Italian Government's agreement in 1963 to "study" the proposal postponed any final commitment and headed off a possible source of friction for the prospective coalition. Since France rejected the proposal and other NATO members were hesitant, a final Italian decision was not urgent.

During the summer and fall of 1963, the peak period of the boom, the price level was still rising and the Italian balance of payments was becoming shaky. A capital flight of substantial proportions occurred, principally to Switzerland. The conservative parties claimed the flight was due to stupid government economic policies; the left-wing parties claimed it was politically motivated to undermine a prospective relaunching of the center-left. In September, the Bank of Italy tightened credit policies. In October, the Leone government initiated cautious measures to control prices and rents and to stop the flight of capital. Together with the squeezing of profit margins, these measures served to discourage new investments.

On October 24, the party congress of the Socialist Party convened and within a brief time it became clear that the reconstituted autonomist group had a small but workable majority. Over the violent protests of the *carristi,* the congress voted to take the revolutionary step of participating directly in a bourgeois government. On November 6, the Leone cabinet resigned and Aldo Moro began negotiations for a four-party coalition. This time he succeeded and on December 4 his new cabinet was announced with himself as Prime Minister and Nenni as Deputy Prime Minister. After sixteen years, the Socialists were finally out of what Nenni called "the ghetto of isolation." The new Deputy Prime Minister pledged the enactment of a five-year program that would go into effect in June, 1964, the establishment of regional governments, and new reforms in education, city planning, and agriculture. On foreign policy, the Socialists reiterated that they considered Italy's obligations to NATO to be strictly defensive and limited to Europe.

Opponents of the agreement within both the major parties of the coalition were restive and unhappy. The right wing of the Christian Democrats, led by Scelba and Pella, threatened not to vote for the new government in the forthcoming vote of confidence. They controlled approximately thirty deputies. In justifying their insubordination, they claimed that too many reforms had been conceded to the Socialists without any guarantees that the Socialists would split with Communists in local, provincial, and future regional governments. On December 16, however, a sharp editorial in *L'Osservatore romano* condemned any breach of Catholic party discipline and unity. The potential dissidents retreated immediately.

In the Socialist Party, there was no higher outside authority to impose obedience on agitated and bitter minorities. Charging a betrayal of the working class, the *carristi* broke party discipline; about 20 per cent of the Socialist parliamentarians voted against granting confidence to the new government. Although the cabinet still had plenty of votes to spare, the Socialist Party had no choice but to punish the dissidents. In reaction, the *carristi* broke away, and in January, 1964, formed a third Socialist party, taking the name Italian Socialist Party of Proletarian Unity (PSIUP), which had been used by the Socialists during the war. Not all of the Socialist antagonists of the center-left policy split off, however, for a number of them preferred to fight their battle within their party. The parliamentary loss of about 20 per cent appeared to represent fairly accurately the Socialist loss among the rank-and-file supporters, for in elections in 1964—such as the one in May to establish a new government for the special region of Friuli–Venezia Giulia, and the administrative elections of November—the Socialists lost an over-all average of about 20 per cent of their voting support to the new party. In the trade unions, however, the Socialist loss was more serious. A substantial number of the top Socialist leaders of the CGIL, including Vittorio Foa, the president of the Metallurgical Workers' Federation and the theorist of syndicalism, were leading schismatics. Their dissidence gravely weakened the Socialist presence at the upper levels of the largest Italian labor confederation.

The new government and its program were under pressure and criticism from the very beginning of 1964. In January, Aldo Moro, the Prime Minister, resigned his post as Secretary-General of the Christian Democratic Party. The party did not want the same man to occupy the two key roles in Italian political life. Moro was replaced by his Deputy Secretary-General, Mariano Rumor, a leading *Dorotei*. In February, the agricultural reform bill was postponed in time and watered down in content when presented to Parliament, in an effort to placate disgruntled Christian Democratic conservatives. The inflation was spiraling, the heavy deficits in the country's balance of payments were still rising, the stock market was still declining, and the business community was demanding the jettison of reforms that would be not only expensive but negative in their effects on business confidence.

The initial and hesitant deflationary measures enacted by the interim Leone government the previous October had been inadequate. At the end of February, the cabinet issued new and severe regulations, raising interest rates, increasing consumption and excise taxes, instituting a new supertax on automobile sales, restricting installment buying, and suspending the new withholding tax on dividends from stocks. On March 14, the American Government granted a credit of over $1 billion to Italy to handle the loss of foreign-exchange reserves. It was a demonstration of faith in the future of the Italian economy and also an indication of American support for the center-left government.

Domestic assaults continued. In March and April, Amintore Fanfani, the original executor of the opening to the left, launched a series of attacks on his own offspring, claiming that the center-left was "not irreversible." In May, 1964, Guido Carli, the Governor of the Bank of Italy, called for a moratorium on new wage agreements, and a spreading-out of the cost-of-living increases built into existing union contracts. At the same time, the *Dorotei* Minister of the Treasury, Emilio Colombo, leaked sections of a private report that blamed the inflation on the wage-price spiral generated by the wage increases of the previous years. His report was also an indirect attack upon the five-year program being drawn up by his cabinet colleague Antonio Giolitti, the Socialist Budget Minister. Essentially, Colombo was arguing that a plan based on coercing the business community into behaving on a basis of social consciousness or civic duty could never work in Italy. Italian businessmen had to be accepted for what they were, and the kind of ambiance should be created that would restore their confidence and their profits. The implications were spelled out by Robert Marjolin, the French vice-president of the executive board of the EEC. He publicly criticized the Italians for not taking sufficiently drastic financial measures to counteract inflationary pressures, and he urged a balanced governmental budget and the dismissal of high-cost reforms.

All of the trade-union confederations refused to accept Carli's call for a wage freeze, especially when there was no freeze on profits and little effectual collection of income taxes. Colombo's leak had practically plunged the government into another crisis, and by June the coalition was disintegrating. In that month, Moro announced to the Chamber of Deputies that the sole object of his policy was stability—political, monetary, and fiscal. Reforms would have to be postponed twelve to eighteen months. It was at this point that it was learned, almost by accident, that the *Dorotei* Minister of Public Instruction, Luigi Gui, had inserted into his budget, behind the back of Socialist Budget Minister Giolitti, a small fund to begin the financing of Catholic parochial secondary schools.[3] The three lay parties immediately objected. Their ministers resigned and the government fell.

All efforts to form a different kind of coalition failed, and by the middle of July the four parties were negotiating once more. At the end of the month, an agreement was reached. Christian Democrats accepted the postponement of the school-aid problem. They repledged their commitment to the enactment of the agreed reforms, but later, and in a diluted form. It was a center-left program with some of its teeth filed down, if not pulled. The same ministers were back at their posts with few exceptions, the most conspicuous being the replacement of Antonio Giolitti, who had been a Communist until 1957, by the less controversial Socialist Giovanni Pieraccini. A few more outraged Socialist parliamentarians went over to PSIUP. A large number, led by Riccardo Lombardi, remained in the party but announced, in effect, that they no longer felt the center-left had any real life. They would oppose Socialist participation in the government from their minority position within the party, but accept the decisions of the majority. The potentiality of another schism was thus ever present.

The new cabinet was formed in time for the August vacations, and political activity was limited. Two personal misfortunes in that month laid the bases for future conflict. Antonio Segni was struck by a cerebral thrombosis early in August, and although he was out of danger after several weeks, it became apparent that he

---

[3] Catholic elementary schools, but not secondary schools, had been receiving public funds for years.

would be left semiparalyzed. A short time later, Palmiro Togliatti died of a stroke while visiting Russia. His deputy, Luigi Longo, moved smoothly into the succession, but Longo had neither the ability nor the authority of his predecessor, and rivalries among leading Communists for new positions would gradually emerge.

The major concern of both the general public and the government remained the business cycle. The anti-inflation policy had produced a recession. Prices kept rising, although less steeply. But in 1964 consumption started to fall, especially in hard goods, consumer durables, and investment goods, but also in textiles. The real estate market collapsed as high mortgage and interest rates, combined with uncertainty about future urban-planning legislation, served to induce both buyers and builders to delay. Unemployment rose as production declined. Layoffs were coupled with a failure to fill job vacancies when they occurred. Employment in industry declined by 325,000 workers for the year.[4] Underemployment figures rose even faster than those for unemployment as firms reduced their operations to three-quarter time, half time, or one-quarter time. The flow of peasants from the country to the city gradually slowed down to a trickle, and a flow in reverse even began to take place. The recession in 1964 was not as drastic as that in 1947. It began from a situation of almost full employment and from a much higher level of economic activity and standard of living. But people's expectations had risen and they were not much impressed with the argument, obvious but irrelevant, that they were still a lot better off than they had ever been before.

Two favorable factors in 1964 served to moderate the impact of the recession: crops were excellent as a result of favorable weather conditions and previous investments in increasing productivity, and exports expanded substantially while imports declined with domestic demand. The continued growth of exports was the result of general prosperity among Italy's principal foreign customers. It was also a consequence of the desire of Italian firms to maintain their hard-won positions in foreign markets.

---

4 (Italian) Istituto Centrale di Statistica, as quoted in *La Stampa*, March 30, 1965.

They were willing to see their profits squeezed in order to hold on. The combination of higher exports and lower imports brought about a sharp improvement in Italy's trade and payments balances. Whereas in 1963 Italy had a deficit of $1,250 million in its balance of payments, in 1964 it had a surplus of $764 million.[5]

While the improvements in Italy's international financial position had become apparent to its economic ministers and banking authorities by the summer of 1964, the declining domestic economy was becoming a matter of greater concern. The tight money policy began to be eased in September. The banks were encouraged to make loans. Public works, which had been slowed down in the past year to reduce budget deficits, were accelerated. A speedup was ordered in projects such as public-housing development and school construction. In November, the special supertax levied on the sale of automobiles was removed. The state took over some of the contributions previously paid by employers to social insurance funds in order to help cut labor costs. By the end of 1964, the government had definitely shifted from a restraining to a propulsive economic policy, while trying at the same time to keep the price level stable. Since the early months of 1965 showed only a slight increase in domestic business activity while prices remained fairly stable and exports continued high, the government issued a decree on March 15, 1965, incorporating a wide range of antirecession measures.[6] Local governments were authorized to borrow large sums from the central state for local improvements, schools, hospitals, streets, and water and sewer lines. National entities were given funds for highway, port, and railroad building and repairs. Procedures for implementing public-works projects were simplified and accelerated. State-owned corporations were urged to speed up their plans for expansion. More liberal credit facilities were authorized for private business. Social insurance payments, unemployment benefits, and family allowances were increased to put more money into circulation.

While all these efforts to improve the public sector were needed, and in fact long overdue, it took a sharp recession in the construc-

---

[5] *Economic Surveys of the OECD: Italy, 1965*, pp. 19–20.
[6] In May, Parliament converted the decree into law.

tion industry to get action. But the delays and inefficiencies of the public bureaucracy, the complicated procedures and system of review, the legal requirements of codes that were a half-century to a century out of date, all served to slow down the actual application of policy decisions made at the top. At the private level, easier credit did not mean a quick decision to engage in new investment. With plenty of existing plant and labor not being used full time, the availability of money was in itself not enough to induce new private investment. So although business was gradually reviving in 1965, there was little evidence that any significant dent was being made in the reserves of the unemployed.

The action taken in the last quarter of 1964 and the first quarter of 1965 had been almost completely the work of the executive branch. Parliament was practically at a standstill. At the beginning of November, it adjourned so that the parliamentarians could campaign in the administrative elections, scheduled for November 22. During the fall, however, Parliament had brought forth the second major reform which the center-left was able to accomplish. It passed a law that would gradually abolish sharecropping: existing sharecropping contracts would be allowed to expire, but no new contracts could be made or old ones renewed, and at the time of expiration, the landowner would have to sell, with the sharecropper having first option to buy. If the two could not agree on a price, the provincial agricultural agent was empowered to establish an arbitrated price. The law provided for forty-year loans at 1 per cent interest, to enable the sharecroppers to buy the land, and thirty-year loans at 2 per cent interest for equipment and supplies. Thus an ancient institution would be finally eliminated and an ancient ideal (the land to the peasants who work it) partially achieved. Whether the peasants would want the land if another industrial boom got under way would be determined only in the future.

Before the administrative election, the Bishops' Conference issued its standard call for all Catholics to vote united for the Christian Democratic Party. The returns in seventy-four provincial elections, compared to the previous year's parliamentary election returns in those provinces, are shown in Table 15. These over-all results hide some of the major trends, however. The

TABLE 15

ELECTION RETURNS IN 74 PROVINCES IN 1964 COMPARED WITH
1963 ELECTIONS TO THE CHAMBER OF DEPUTIES

(*In Per Cents*)

Parties	1963*	1964
Fascist	5.0	4.99
Monarchist	1.7	0.93
Liberal	7.0	7.96
Christian Democratic	38.2	37.36
Republican	1.3	1.17
Social Democratic	6.3	6.68
Socialist	14.2	11.30
PSIUP		2.91
Communist	25.6	26.02
Other	0.7	0.76
Total	*100.0*	*100.00*

* The 1963 results are for the 74 provinces in which elections were held in 1964; therefore, they do not coincide with the 1963 figures for the whole country.

Source: La Stampa, November 25, 1964.

Christian Democratic vote increased in the centers of the cities and in the north, while it declined in central and southern Italy, with the exception of Sicily.[7] The Communist vote increased in northern and central Italy and in the peripheries of the cities, while it also declined in the south. In the country as a whole, the Socialist decline was almost perfectly matched with the votes received by its left-wing splinter group, PSIUP. The Liberals continued their general increase throughout the country, but on a smaller scale. On the whole, the parties of the center-left coalition suffered a slight decline. Since the country was in the midst of a recession, it may be said that they survived fairly well, although the indications of widespread unrest could hardly be ignored.

On November 30, *L'Osservatore romano* sadly criticized those Catholics who had not voted Christian Democratic. Repeating its

[7] Unofficial explanations of the Sicilian increase are that the Mafia threw its support to the Christian Democrats in return for their burial of the parliamentary report on the Mafia.

condemnation of voters who mistakenly endorsed atheistic Communism, it used stronger language in attacking liberalism, insisting that the Catholic could not support the liberal theory of the separation of Church and State, in which religion becomes a private matter. It concluded that liberalism would never be able to weaken Communism.

This recognition of the lack of Catholic unity, of the temptations of Communism on the left and the Liberal Party on the right, was just one effort to hold together a bitterly divided party. During the preceding year, the factions within Christian Democracy had crystallized even further. On the extreme left, some Christian Democrats were engaged in a "dialogue" with the Communists, examining the possible areas of common belief, as well as the possible trends in their respective ideological orientations.[8] The most advanced Catholic group, in this respect, was centered, in Florence, around Christian Democratic Mayor Giorgio La Pira, who accepted the votes of the Communist members of the Communal Council in early 1964 in order to keep his center-left administration in office.

The Communist Party had been trying to escape from the political isolation, local and national, into which it had been placed by Socialist participation in the government. It was also engaged in a struggle to understand and to cope with the evolution of events in Italy and Western Europe. Divided by the reactions inside Italy to the Russian-Chinese dispute, by the efforts to cope with the postwar prosperity in the Western world—an economic phenomenon not easily explained by Marxist dialectic—by its declining ability to bring Italian youth into the Party in spite of its voting gains,[9] the party leadership had gradually moved to a verbal compliance with the more standard, if still qualified, procedures of political democracy. In 1963, it announced that if the Party came to power it would still accept the existence of opposi-

---

[8] The most elaborate result of this dialogue can be found in the volume edited by Mario Gozzini, *Il dialogo alla prova* (Florence: Vallechi, 1964).

[9] In 1965, Giorgio Amendola acknowledged that while over 50 per cent of the Italian workers were under thirty years of age, less than 10 per cent of Communist Party members were under thirty. The Party membership was aging. See Giorgio Amendola, "Il partito in fabbrica," *Rinascita*, May 29, 1965, p. 1.

tion parties (limited to those parties willing to participate in the construction of a Socialist society), and that it concurred in the principle of majority-and-minority votes and accepted the possibility of losing an election after once winning one. Its internal debates became more open to the external world, and various leaders were more willing to take contradictory positions in public. Giorgio Amendola went so far as to advocate majority-and-minority voting on specific issues inside the Party organs, although he rejected the open acknowledgment of organized factions, which existed in any case. While outsiders differed as to the sincerity and reality of these professions of democracy, it was evident, nevertheless, that the Party was alive and moving, that the internal dissatisfactions were real, that the political world could not wash its hands of the whole development by writing it off as fraudulent.

By 1964, the Communists had openly divided in a debate over the best means of escaping from isolation. One group, headed by Amendola, advocated launching a new drive for the creation of a united party of the working class. Amendola argued that neither Communism nor Social Democracy had succeeded, and could not succeed, in constructing a Socialist society in Western Europe, and he called for the creation of a new party "neither Leninist nor Social Democratic." The other group, led by Pietro Ingrao, argued for a direct Communist-Catholic dialogue, disregarding the Socialist parties for the time being, concentrating instead on attracting the Catholic masses, negotiating with the Catholic political, economic, and social organizations and with the Church itself.

These differing strategical conceptions were to be tested shortly. Although it had been apparent for months that Segni would never recover completely from his stroke, his resignation as President of the Republic had been delayed to save the Christian Democrats from an additional source of division before the elections. During this period, Cesare Merzagora, presiding officer of the Senate, had functioned as Acting President. With the administrative elections over, Segni resigned and Parliament was faced with choosing his successor. The three lay parties of the coalition again agreed on Giuseppe Saragat's candidacy for the office. The *Dorotei* imposed Giovanni Leone's name on the Christian Democratic Party without negotiating with other factional leaders. When the parliamentary balloting began, these two candidates quickly took the lead, while the other parties ran favorite sons. As one ballot succeeded another, it became apparent that Fanfani's supporters were not voting for Leone, while the left-wing Christian Democratic trade-unionists and intellectuals were throwing votes to Giulio Pastore, the former president of the CISL.[10] Then, slowly, it also became apparent that this time there would not be a repetition of the previous election. The *Dorotei* could not re-establish discipline, and together with the right-wing parties they did not have enough votes to win. The Socialists threw Nenni's hat into the ring. All the candidates were now negotiating with the Communists for their votes, which the latter refused to deliver while they themselves debated what to do. Amendola argued for support for the Socialist candidates. Ingrao argued that the Communists should vote for Fanfani. But Ingrao could not demonstrate that even with Communist support Fanfani could get enough votes from his own party. The Vatican successfully "advised" Fanfani to withdraw his candidacy. Nenni finally withdrew his name in favor of Saragat. The *Dorotei* eventually gave up and decided to accept Saragat. Amendola carried the debate in his own party and Saragat was elected President of the Republic. Dissident Christian Democrats refused to switch to the Social Democrat when the party leaders did, however, so that the Communist votes were necessary for Saragat's majority.

It had taken twenty-one ballots to elect a President of the Republic, during which time those who formed the interested and attentive public looked on, with fascination at first, and then with greater and greater disgust. The inadequacies of the parties, the ineffectiveness of Parliament, could not have been more

---

10 In 1964, the Christian Democrats were organized in four major factions. On the right was *Centrismo Popolare,* the group led by Scelba, Pella, and Gonella; in the center was the largest faction (almost one-half the members of the party's National Council), the *Moro-Dorotei,* a loose coalition led by Moro, Rumor, Colombo, and Flaminio Piccoli. On the left were two groups, the *Nuove Cronache* or *Fanfaniani,* and the *Nuove Forze,* composed of Catholic trade-unionists and the intellectuals who came from an association known as the *Sinistra di Base.* Pastore was its most prominent spokesman.

graphically demonstrated. The principal party, Christian Democracy, had almost reached the point of disintegration. The political system itself appeared to be undermined. Monarchists used the spectacle to moralize about the virtues of monarchical succession. Pacciardi once more denounced the parliamentary system and called for a presidential regime, with the President to be directly elected by the voters. Some of the more fearful citizenry prepared themselves for a shift in allegiances in case the political system crumbled.

The new year saw a slow pulling together of the government. The Socialists thought they could utilize the temporary defeat of the *Dorotei* and the state of disarray of the major party to push it further to the left. This turned out to be a false hope. At the end of January, 1965, the Christian Democratic National Council issued a unity declaration. The declaration was an attack on Communism, practically the only subject the factions could agree on in public. *L'Osservatore romano* and other Catholic publications criticized the party severely. Pope Paul VI ostentatiously revived the Catholic Action Society, a warning to the Christian Democrats that the Church had other choices. He also attacked those Catholics who believed in dialogue with Communists. One after another, the principal Catholic organizations—Coltivatori Diretti, the ACLI, the CISL—issued denunciations of the "dialogue."

Under the circumstances, it was not surprising that Ingrao's strategy had suffered a failure. This did not mean a victory for Amendola's point of view, however. In April, 1965, the Communist Central Committee launched an appeal for a new "superparty" of the working class. On close examination, it turned out that the Communists were calling for a confederation of parties in which each would keep its identity. This was different from Amendola's original call for a new party that would not be Communist. It was a relaunching of the concept of the popular front. A large superparty could take up once more the task of negotiating with the Catholics, and on a more equal basis. The Social Democratic and the Socialist parties turned down the Communist call immediately. PSIUP expressed interest. In the meantime, in a number of local governments formed after the administrative elections, Socialist councilors had shifted away from the traditional alliance with the Communists to form center-left local administrations. Inside the CGIL, the Socialist trade-unionists were more restive and unhappy than ever before over that labor confederation's attacks on the government. By May, 1965, in a number of local Chambers of Labor, the Socialist union officials had organized an open minority opposition to the Communist leadership. The Socialists were not yet ready to abandon the CGIL, however, since they were fearful of losing what was left of their contact with their working-class base.

On the other side of the political spectrum, a different abandonment appeared to be in process. In the spring of 1965, Giovanni Malagodi announced that the Liberal Party accepted the social commitments of modern society, that programming was not an evil if carried out on a democratic and noncoercive basis, and that his party was ready to participate in the common effort to organize a better future for Italians. Liberal renunciation of the conception that all would be well if only the market economy and private entrepreneurs were left alone was taken with a considerable amount of disbelief by center-left protagonists. Malagodi, however, had overcome some strong opposition among very conservative Liberals to go even this far. The move was interpreted to mean the abandonment of the frontal assault on the center-left by Confindustria. The skeptics considered it merely a shift in tactics, others a recognition by some elements of the business community that nineteenth-century ideas were inadequate in a twentieth-century world. Gianni Agnelli, the son of the founder of Fiat, in arguing the importance of collaboration between business leaders and the government, admitted the difficulty for Italian business executives "to move out of the old defenses and behavior patterns, which have little relationship to the requirements and atmosphere of a modern enterprise, in a country that would like to be modern."[11]

In the spring of 1965, the four-party coalition was shaky. All major government activities had been in a state of semisuspension from the beginning of November, 1964, until the following March, when the cabinet could once more pull itself into working

---

[11] Quoted by Gianni Baldi, "I due poteri," *Il Mondo*, June 1, 1965, p. 2.

order. Fanfani replaced Saragat as Foreign Minister, and another Christian Democrat, Giuseppe Medici, resigned to make way for the Social Democrat Edgardo Lami Starnuti, so that the Social Democrats could have the representation in the cabinet to which they felt entitled. This minor reshuffle left a number of Christian Democrats and Socialists unhappy. The parties of the coalition were divided over issues of foreign policy and the meaning and timing of their program. The Socialists openly criticized the growing American military intervention in the war in Vietnam and the American military intervention in the uprising in the Dominican Republic. The Christian Democrats dutifully defended their American ally, although Foreign Minister Fanfani concentrated on calling for negotiated solutions, rather than on making justifications. At the end of 1965, Fanfani, as President of the United Nations General Assembly for the 1966 session, would transmit private messages to the United States Government from his friend Giorgio La Pira. This communication concerned the latter's interview with the leaders of North Vietnam. American publication of the messages led to a sarcastic attack by La Pira against the United States. Fanfani resigned in embarrassment, further weakening the Moro cabinet. On January 21, 1966, the government fell, again over a school issue.

In domestic affairs the Church's pressure on the government to close a Rome performance of the play *The Deputy*, which was critical of Pius XII, produced resentment among the lay parties. Since the Christian Democratic Minister of the Interior, Paolo Emilio Taviani, used the Concordat of 1929 to justify his closing of the play, the Socialists announced that revision of the Concordat would be one of the issues on their future agenda. Reform of the school system was another source of friction. A temporary compromise was reached that continued the public financing of confessional elementary schools, but excluded Catholic secondary schools from public funds.

Disputes over patronage and over the major economic issues strained relations within and among the coalition parties most seriously, however. The new five-year program set forth by the Socialist Budget Minister, Giovanni Pieraccini, in March, 1965, was attacked by the left wing of his own party, led by Riccardo

Lombardi, as insufficient and inadequate. Although the majority of the Socialist Central Committee finally approved it, the minority was a large one. In a meeting of the Christian Democratic National Council, Fanfani attacked the program as a "book of dreams," while his supporters were clamoring for more positions in the cabinet. From business and industry came criticisms of the program for not making economic efficiency the prime goal, while the political leaders insisted that relatively full employment must be the first goal. All the labor confederations rejected the program's assertion of an incomes policy in which future wage increases would be kept proportionate, in general, to increases in productivity. Although the CISL and the UIL proclaimed that their wage demands would be responsible ones, they would not accept the incomes policy in principle. The CGIL violently attacked the policy, thereby aggravating the dissension between Socialist union leaders on the one hand and the Communist and PSIUP leaders on the other. In fact, however, the unions were all too weak and the business conditions were too precarious to enable them to pursue effectively a higher goal.

Although business conditions were improving in the first part of 1965, the situation was still so uncertain that the dangers of renewed inflation preoccupied the economic and financial ministers. In June, it was announced that the five-year program and the reform of the schools would be postponed until 1966,[12] although Pieraccini claimed that the government was already making decisions according to the program. The activation of the regular regional governments was barely mentioned, and the bill on urban regulation appeared to be in suspension. The Governor of the Bank of Italy was calling for the containment of wage increases and the restoration of profits to induce new investment by entrepreneurs. He argued that public expenditures had to be controlled to avoid inflation. The Socialist Party could look ruefully at the apparent necessity to accept more delay for costly reforms, and its more impatient left wing could reassert its conclusion that

---

[12] School reform would be costly and produce only long-run benefits. School construction put unemployed laborers to work immediately and therefore provided short-run benefits. However, educational reform was given first priority *after* economic revival.

the center-left had failed and that it was time for the Socialists to get out of the government.

The vast majority of the Socialists were not yet ready to accept this pessimistic conclusion. In addition, they had now received positions on almost every board, committee, agency, and bureau in government, at the national, provincial, and local levels. New vested interests had rapidly been created. As a result, at the Socialist Party congress of November, 1965, Lombardi and his supporters were in such a small minority that they dared not repeat their demand to abandon the government. Nor did they threaten to create still another schism. As a result, Nenni, who resumed the post of Secretary General, was able to lead a party more united than it had been in years, and to put through a resolution approving a policy of reunification with the Social Democrats.

The Communists could do little more than accuse the Socialists of betraying the working class. At their own party congress held at the end of January and beginning of February, 1966, the Communists concentrated on an appeal to the Catholics, praising the Ecumenical Council, denouncing state atheism, and applauding the efforts of Pope Paul, Foreign Minister Fanfani, and Giorgio La Pira to promote a peaceful settlement in Vietnam. Luigi Longo called for a direct dialogue with both the Christian Democratic Party and the Roman Catholic hierarchy. The Vatican rejected this effort to instrumentalize the Pope's efforts for peace. The Christian Democrats answered that the center-left government was the only possible one for Italy; even Scelba abandoned his opposition to it. The cabinet had fallen in January, 1966, after still another clash over schools, this time at the nursery level. But on February 23, 1966, a new center-left ministry was created, leaving both the Communists and Liberals again in opposition. Both were in increasing isolation, and both were increasingly unhappy. There were still more than two years until the next parliamentary election (1968), and perhaps a renewed prosperity could do what the last boom had not done—moderate the attractions of a powerful party of the extreme left and provide the necessary lubrication to keep Socialists and Christian Democrats together and to keep the internal feuds of the Christian Democrats within reasonable limits.

14

Conclusions

On April 25, 1965, the Italian nation celebrated the twentieth anniversary of the liberation of the Po Valley from the Nazi-Fascist occupation. Among the various addresses honoring the occasion, two expressed somewhat different evaluations of the intervening decades. In comparing the aspirations of the Resistance movement with the results achieved in the postwar period, Giorgio Bo, a left-wing Christian Democrat and Minister of State Participations, could happily assert:

> Twenty years later we can say that we have translated the aspiration to liberty into laws and institutions that shelter our country from authoritarian temptations and plots; we have given a first realization to the anxiousness for social justice, having faced, after the initial reconstruction period, the age-old problem of elevating the southern regions and all the depressed areas; we have given to the world of labor a prestige and authority hitherto unknown, proposing for the first time in history the necessity of redistributing the wealth, accomplishing reforms, beginning a process of profound modification of our national society.
>
> In respect to popular participation in the governing of public affairs, we have seen the overcoming of the ancient ideological barrier between the Catholic and Socialist masses, which has enlarged the area of democracy. Perhaps incomplete and partial, these are realizations on the plus side of the ledger in the effort to translate the fundamental ideals of the Resistance into contemporary reality.[1]

[1] *Stampa Sera,* April 26, 1965.

Ugo La Malfa, Secretary-General of the Republican Party, also noted that Italy was no longer the provincial, depressed, and autarchic nation of the Fascist period. He emphasized, nevertheless, that its development had not been balanced or homogeneous, so that in Italian society—

> . . . unquestionably now much richer in material goods and resources, we find aligned privileges, injustice, waste, and backwardness.
>
> Recognizing the progress and errors made, and above all, retaining in the present the grand ideals of the Resistance, we must seek to promote a democratic society, livelier in its parties, more effective in all its institutions, more just and equitable to its great mass of laborers.[2]

Both speakers were, to some degree, correct, even if one stressed how far Italy had come and the other how far it still had to go. For both were recognizing that Italy had been through a revolution in the twenty years since the end of the war, and that, as in all revolutions, the results were very incomplete and the ultimate ideals far from realization. The revolution was not a violent one; it involved neither a *coup d'état* nor a civil war, nor was it directly political, for the formal institutions of the parliamentary system remained as they had been created by the Constitutional Convention of 1946/47. It was Italy's second industrial revolution, a continuing one, which had transformed and was transforming Italy from a primarily agricultural and rural society to a predominantly urban and industrial society. In 1942, 48 per cent of Italy's labor force was occupied in agriculture; at the beginning of 1965, only 25 per cent was in agriculture, while 41 per cent was in industry and 34 per cent in tertiary activities.[3]

These flat figures indicate, but do not reveal, the force and consequences of a revolution that established a degree of mobility never known before, ruptured the old, static social structure, and tore millions from their original habitations and traditional ways of life. The rapid urbanization imposed hardships and inadequacies upon a people whose leaders were neither prepared to meet, nor shown to be capable of meeting, the problems. Italian

---

[2] *Loc. cit.*

[3] The figures were provided by the (Italian) Istituto Centrale di Statistica, as published in *La Stampa*, March 30, 1965.

literature of the 1950's and the 1960's reflected the bitterness of the shock, the personal price paid by the migrants especially, but by others as well. The second industrial revolution was being carried out with the help of social workers and sociologists, with the help of medical, unemployment, and old-age insurance, as well as of other benefits (financially small but nevertheless real), yet its human consequences were as uprooting and as alienating as the original impact of the factory system on the transplanted English farmhands in the early nineteenth century.

Vertical mobility, though still far less significant than geographic shifts, was another feature of the period. A landless farm laborer or a sharecropper who became a peasant proprietor was undoubtedly rising in the social scale, as were peasants and workers who, formerly unskilled, became partially or completely skilled workers. The modernization of industry created new categories of clerks and other white-collar employees. The greater variety of jobs and of required skills became the basis of a new system of stratification. The pressure to classify was so strong in Italian society, the tradition of hierarchy so pervasive in all social, political, religious, and economic institutions, that the bitterness attendant upon the discrimination of rank still served as a psychological offset to the gradually increasing material well-being. But the most important gap remained the one between the "cultivated" class and the popular masses. For in Italy real vertical mobility was achieved through only one channel, the formal educational system. If you were not a university graduate, a *dottore,* you were nothing. (Men like Enrico Mattei or Giuseppe Di Vittorio were exceptions to prove the rule.) And while investigators disagreed on details, all analysts of the university-student population were certain that only an insignificant number, 1 to 5 per cent, of university students were of worker or peasant origin.

This, perhaps even more than the traditional clerical-laical struggle, was why the schools and school reform were such a bone of political contention in the postwar period. The educational system, aristocratic and humanistic in tradition, was under attack not only for its inadequacies in preparing youth for the professional, scientific, and administrative requirements of the modern world, but for its structure and curriculum that segregated a leisured from a nonleisured class. Thus, Parliament had to use precious hours of debating time while the Latin and Greek requirements of the secondary schools were raked over by the orators of the left to become another weapon in the class struggle. And, in 1965, the center-left coalition had to do internal battle to agree finally that school reform had first priority for whatever money might be available in the public treasury after day-to-day expenditures and investments in income-producing and employment-creating projects were provided for.

The mobility of the population and the extension of elementary and secondary education to more sections of society were gradually nationalizing the Italian people culturally and socially. The spread of radio and television was having a similar effect. Since the population movement was primarily from south to north, some disaffected northerners judged the behavior changes to be something closer to a "southernization," what with the northern adoption of long afternoon siestas and late dining hours, the acceptance of Neapolitan pizza, and the political and bureaucratic extension of Bourbonic statalism and red tape. A crucial development in the opposite direction, however, was the gradual nationalization of the Italian language. Italian, a literary language derived from the Tuscan, was written and sometimes spoken by an educated upper class. Now it was spreading horizontally to all parts of the country, especially to the south, as the number of students attending the secondary schools increased. Vertically, it was ceasing to be the language of a class. Under the pressure of a confluence of diverse social levels, it was being transformed—by regionalisms, dialects, and slang—into a new and alive national language. At the time of Italian unification, a patriot of the Risorgimento, Massimo D'Azeglio, had reputedly exclaimed, "We have made Italy; we must now make Italians!" A century later, his hopes were, perhaps, coming into slow realization.

The slow cultural assimilation of the people was nevertheless proceeding faster than the evolution of a sense of social and civic consciousness, not to say solidarity. The average Italian still felt little obligation or responsibility to those outside his family or outside his circle of personal friendships. The larger social world was still alien and potentially or actually hostile, to be feared or to be manipulated by the fortunate minority who had influential connections. The attitude toward the state and its legal and political institutions was ambivalent. There was a growing recognition among ordinary people of the numerous and various ways in which their personal futures were affected by the decisions of public authorities. Nevertheless, while turning to the state for the welfare it provided to the poor, or the special benefits and protections it granted to the rich or powerful, the beneficiaries remained hostile and suspicious. Fear, expected as a natural component of totalitarian regimes, was still widespread in all sectors of a nominally democratic society. The fear felt by those in power was reflected in the ubiquitous presence of the national police forces—the Pubblica Sicurezza and the Carabinieri—as well as the continued importance of the Prefect, the *Questore* (Chief of Police), and the Ministry of the Interior.

A critical example may be found in the reaction of the Catholic hierarchy to the attempt to perform Rolf Hochhuth's *The Deputy* in Rome early in 1965. Never in the history of united Italy has the Catholic Church been as powerful and influential as in the two postwar decades. Yet its fear of the performance of a play critical of the late Pius XII caused it to exercise all its pressure upon the Christian Democratic Party to have the performance stopped. Minister of the Interior Taviani ordered the play closed and had the performers and director temporarily arrested, justifying his action with the Concordat of 1929, which forbade any offense to the sacred character of the city of Rome.[4] As is the usual consequence of action taken in fear, the move boomeranged. The play was given attention and publicity of a sort it never would have been accorded, and sales of the Italian translation of its text jumped sharply. The debate in Parliament over Taviani's action openly divided the government coalition. Both the Socialists and the Republicans put revision of the Concordat on the agenda for future action.

Twenty years of the republic and substantial economic progress had not yet created the social and political consensus necessary for the legitimization of the state and its institutions. Neither

---

[4] The Concordat was obviously useless in preventing performances in other cities, and a few such did take place.

Parliament nor the cabinet nor the presidency of the republic
had acquired prestige, although some distinguished and outstanding men had honored Italian public life by their presence and
participation. Parliament and the parties that ran it were in crisis.
Their incapacity to function effectively was exposed for the entire
nation to see at the time of the presidential election of December,
1964. It is true that in 1965 the direct threats to parliamentary
institutions were negligible. Only the neo-Fascists and the Monarchists, plus Pacciardi's movement for a plebiscitary presidential
republic, openly attacked the party parliamentary system. All the
other parties, Communist included, upheld it. But Communist
commitment to the system could be questioned legitimately. And
there were Catholic integralists both inside and outside the Christian Democratic Party, of the right and the left, who did not accept the postulates of a pluralistic society.

Most of these potential threats to the political system neutral-
ized each other by their mutual antagonisms, enabling democracy
and political freedom to survive. For they did survive, and with
the exception of occasional excess zeal on the part of censors or
prefects, Italy could honestly claim a respectable place among the
free societies of the world. There was present a liveliness of discussion, a ferment of ideas, a variety of opinions, and a vigor in
their expression remarkable in a country still so pervaded by fear.
Perhaps this liberty was protected, not so much by widespread
commitment to it in principle, as by the Babel of conflicting
voices that drowned each other out; perhaps because words were
discounted heavily in practice by substantial doses of popular and
elite skepticism.

Neither skepticism nor temporary equilibria provide sufficient
bases for the long-run maintenance of public institutions. These
require both adequate administration and supportive myths. If at
the top level of administration, the party-political level, Italy was
functioning badly, the lower, bureaucratic level provided no
adequate substitute. Both the personnel policies and the administrative codes were out of date. Personnel policies were directed
toward providing jobs and security rather than encouraging enterprise and ambition. The public service was overloaded with low-

and high-level supernumeraries, while at the professional levels there were shortages, since neither pay scales nor promotion policies could draw the limited number of ambitious young scientists and professionals from the attractions of an expanding economy. Civil service examinations in the fields of engineering, archival work, and science were taken by few applicants.[5] The legal basis of Italian administrative practice was aimed at preventing fraud and corruption, in which it was a clamorous failure, rather than at promoting efficiency and speed. As a result, to get something done required breaking the law. In two notorious scandals in 1964, Professor Felice Ippolito, former executive director of Italy's National Council for Nuclear Research, and Professor Domenico Marotta, former head of the Higher Institute of Health, were indicted for violations of administrative codes. These two men, who were rare Italian examples of top-level scientist-executives, found themselves legally pilloried because they had been trying desperately to overcome in a hurry Italy's backwardness in their respective fields. In 1965, the Socialist Minister of Public Works, Giacomo Mancini, renounced an effort to speed up the placement of public-works contracts (his aim was to stimulate a depressed construction industry) because the parliamentarians felt that the new procedures would encourage even greater corruption.[6]

---

[5] In June, 1965, Luigi Preti, the Social Democratic Minister Without Portfolio in charge of Reform of the Public Administration, announced that he aimed at a 20 per cent reduction of personnel at the directive level of the public administration. This was to be achieved, not by firing, but by not filling vacancies as they occurred through death, retirement, or resignation. Whether he would succeed in his ambition, under the pressure to find positions for the flood of graduates from the law schools who looked to the government to get them established, was debatable. The study of the public administration and agitation for its reform had been going on since 1945 without visible results. In the last analysis, only a full-employment economy could provide the social and economic basis for the rational application of technological and personnel reform of the administration. It could then cease to be used as a sponge to soak up the excess labor in Italian society.

[6] The new procedures would have permitted provincial public-works officers to negotiate contracts directly rather than use the time-consuming system of public bids, bids which then needed final approval in Rome. See *La Stampa*, April 10, 1965.

Two decades had eroded a number of myths that had flourished in the immediate postwar period. On the far left, the old Marxist formulas were felt to be inadequate, even if they were not formally rejected. Communists talked about the "renewal" of Marxist thought, but this renewal was merely the replacement of one label with another. Thus, the old myths of a "dying capitalism" and the "proletarianization" of the masses, both untenable in the light of the economic and social evolution of postwar Italy in particular and of the advanced countries of the Western world in general, were replaced by the new rationalization of "neo-capitalism," which explained as little as the earlier phrases. In the period of the exposure of Stalinism and the Hungarian uprising, the myth of the "Soviet fatherland" had crumbled, first for the Socialists and later for the mass of Communists. The myth of the revolutionary overthrow of an exploitive social order had faded away. The top leadership of the extreme left-wing parties had never really believed in it from the beginning of the postwar period, knowing full well that even if it were possible domestically, American intervention would put an end to it in short order. Only a small number of "Chinese" within the Communist Party, and the ideological visionaries of PSIUP, still preached revolutionary doctrines or felt that a concrete possibility of revolution existed in Western Europe.

Within the variegated camp of Christian Democracy, the myth of a "peasant civilization," elaborated by some of its more conservative members, had been destroyed by the second industrial revolution. Not only was the majority of the population now living in urban areas, but urban tastes, habits, and outlooks were gradually spreading to the countryside, at least in the northern and central regions. In reverse, rural habits were imported into the cities, which were jammed with first- and second-generation peasant immigrants. The consequences for the party were both practical and ideological, and involved more than just bewailing the urban "dechristianization" of transplanted rural masses.[7]

---

[7] It is, of course, a debatable proposition that rural life is more Christian than urban life. There seems little doubt, however, that Church attendance is higher in the countryside and villages, and that the rural faithful are more responsive to the directions and instructions of the clergy.

Votes were lost by a party whose strength lay in rural areas and small towns and villages.

The myth of Catholic unity was exposed in all its falsity, not only by the indifference of the majority of the population to the regular appeals of the bishops to "vote united," but within the Catholic party itself. The intraparty struggles, the violent competition for power engaged in by factions and their leaders, the wide divergences in programmatic beliefs, all indicated that unity was based on external discipline, not internal cohesion. The Church imposed a unity from above, accepted as an act of obedience. A secondary source of unity was the realization that schism would bring loss of power and of all the perquisites deriving therefrom. (This same realization was one factor holding the Communists together.) The Christian social program, which provided the rationalization for the party's existence, meant so many different things to so many different Christian Democrats that its unifying power was negligible. This is easily illustrated by the results of the conference of the National Council of the party, held at the end of January, 1965. All the factions were able to agree upon was a denunciation of Communism.

Western European Union had provided an ideal for a minority throughout the postwar period, although it had never caught the imagination of the masses, who were only beginning to escape from cultural provinciality to a wider realization of nationality.[8] The roughness of the road to European unity, the obstacles to its realization set up especially by President de Gaulle, had brought a sobering of the early enthusiasm. Within the Italian ruling class, a slight nationalistic reaction was occurring, although it would perhaps be too strong to call it a revival of old-style nationalism. Nevertheless, the public ceremonies of April 25, 1965, celebrating the twentieth anniversary of the Resistance uprising, and the ceremonies a month later, on May 24, 1965, honoring the fiftieth anniversary of Italy's entry into World War I, brought out a military display of patriotic symbols, as well as a rash of

---

8 It could be, and has been, argued that the relative lack of political nationalism among the Italian masses would make it easier to develop a European consciousness, and that Italy, of all the Western European countries, was least handicapped in this respect.

nationalistic oratory, not seen or heard on such a scale in the previous twenty years.[9]

A stated and important political goal was the "reconciliation of the popular masses with the state." Former President Gronchi had referred to it in his inaugural address of 1955, when he spoke of "those working masses and middle classes whom universal suffrage has conducted to the doorstep of the state's edifice without introducing them effectively to where political direction is exercised."[10] The ideology of the opening to the left and the presence of the Socialist Party in the cabinet were based upon bringing at least a part of the working masses into a representative participation in the government of the country.

Yet this is another example of the nominalism of labels and identifications in Italian politics and culture, behind which there is often a contradictory reality. For the gap between the popular masses and the leadership of the organizations that speak in their name is so great that the participation of the latter represents no involvement of the former. The largest organization of the working masses is the CGIL. It claims 3.5 million members. In preparation for its Sixth Congress, which took place at Bologna between March 31 and April 5, 1965, it asserted that about 100,000 members participated in meetings held at various levels. This is less than 3 per cent of the membership. If one reduces the claim of 3.5 million members to 2.5 million, the participation of the rank and file rises to 4 per cent.

Nevertheless, this 4 per cent might as well have stayed home, because the selection of the delegates to the congress was negotiated by the leaders of the Communist, Socialist, and PSIUP parties. They arbitrarily distributed the seats among their officers, the Communists taking about 56 per cent, the Socialists 28 per cent, and the PSIUP 16 per cent. There were no competitive elections held, for the Communists probably would have received

---

[9] There is a nice historical irony involved when one considers that the government celebrating Italy's entry into World War I was a coalition whose two leading parties were Catholic and Socialist, for in 1915 the Socialist Party and the Italian Catholic community had been the strongest opponents of Italian intervention in the war.

[10] The text of the speech can be found in Giovanni Gronchi, *Discorsi d'America* (Milan: Garzanti, 1956), p. 99.

more seats than they took. They were willing to grant seats to the Socialists above their effective strength within the CGIL to reduce the potentialities of a Socialist schism. There is no indication that the mass of members of the CGIL, or of the other confederations, feel that they have any effective influence on the policies of their unions or the designation of their leaders.[11] They nevertheless feel closer to their unions than to the parties that dominate them.[12] It is in this real sense that to speak of Socialist, or Christian Democratic, or even, hypothetically, Communist participation in the government as bringing the working masses into the state is to confuse appearance with substance. Senator Bo claimed that the creation of the center-left government witnessed the crumbling of the "ancient ideological barrier between the Catholic and Socialist masses," but the wider gulf between the masses and the ruling and political classes was not yet bridged. The prestige and authority of labor was the prestige and authority of the leadership; to work with one's hands in either the factory or on the farm granted no prestige or authority in Italian society, even if the Constitution did describe Italy as a "democratic republic founded on labor."

The destruction of numerous myths by two decades of experience leaves room for others to take their place. One of the newer ones is the ideology of "democratic programming," even if one considers it to be a variation of older Socialist myths.[13] Could this be an effective substitute for older ideologies? Effectiveness should be measured against two criteria: its appeal must become emotional and psychological, internalized so that it becomes a stimulus to and justification of action; it ought to have a reasona-

---

11 *La Stampa*, March 31, 1965; Giorgio Galli, "Le alchimie sindacali," *Il Mondo*, April 20, 1965; Domenico Sforza, "Questioni sindacali," *Il Mondo*, April 13, 1965.

12 Giorgio Amendola wrote bluntly that the Communist Party's impact on the workers was negligible; that even when they participated in strikes, or voted Communist, the workers acquired neither a general political conscience nor a revolutionary class conscience. See Giorgio Amendola, "Il partito in fabbrica," *Rinascita*, May 20, 1965, p. 1.

13 See Joseph LaPalombara, "Decline of Ideology: Myth, Reality, or Selective Perception," paper read at the 1964 Annual Meeting of the American Political Science Association (mimeographed).

ble correspondence to reality. It was too early to measure programming against the first test; in 1965, it was already doubtful that it could pass the second.

The five-year program introduced in Parliament in May, 1965, by Socialist Budget Minister Giovanni Pieraccini consisted of government indicators, or "guide lines," plus "indirect" means of influencing the decisions of private operators. Its nature was clearly and openly recognized by the Secretary-General of the Socialist Party, Francesco De Martino.[14] In a television interview on May 27, 1965, he indicated that programming did not involve "coercion" of private or public firms, but rather creation of the circumstances that would impel them to the kind of decisions the government desired them to take in the interest of its general development program.[15] But if the only means available to the government were guide lines and indirect stimuli (spending and tax policies, monetary and credit policies), would the government now be doing anything that it had not been doing earlier, before the opening to the left? How would it differ from the Vanoni Plan of 1955, which, in reality, was not a plan? Would the economic operators respond to the government's indirect stimuli? The trade-union confederations had already announced that they would not accept in principle the incomes policy built into the program. The Communist CGIL leaders were attacking it violently. The private-business community had demonstrated in the past that the government's southern development programs and the indirect stimuli built into them were insufficient compulsions. Had they changed enough? Would they follow the guide lines; would they respond to the government's incentives and disincentives?

It could be argued that they were inclined to do so. In 1965, the Liberal Party was accepting the welfare capitalist state, through Giovanni Malagodi, although some of his more conservative party and business supporters accused him of engaging in a transformistic betrayal. Whether the shift was purely nominal or reflected more profound movements of thought and feeling remained un-

---

[14] De Martino replaced Nenni as Secretary-General of the party when Nenni became Deputy Prime Minister.

[15] The text of De Martino's interview is reprinted in *Avanti*, May 28, 1965.

certain. But Malagodi was calling for a dialogue with the Socialists to examine their respective positions.

The Socialists, on the other hand, denied that democratic programming was their basic goal. They asserted that this objective
was the best available under the given political conditions, a
policy that could get the support of a parliamentary majority. But
De Martino continued to insist that the Socialists had "chosen the
path of gradual reforms because this corresponds to the world in
which we are living and to the tradition of our party. This does
not mean, however, that we renounce our basic objectives. We do
not accept reformism as a marginal correction of the capitalistic
system."[16] He argued that while his party had cordial relations
with many of the Social Democratic and Labor parties of Western
Europe, it differed from them because "in our opinion the Social
Democratic parties have abandoned the struggle for socialism,
substituting for it a society of well-being, while we want to continue our struggle for the radical transformation of society."[17]

In spite of these pronouncements, however, the majority of the
party would probably have settled gladly for a welfare capitalist
state that provided a substantial measure of well-being for the
Italian people. So there was developing a slow but perceptible
consensus encompassing the more advanced Liberals of the right
to the more moderate Socialists on the left. Twenty years of uneven economic progress and more uneven political progress were
constructing a new, heterogeneous majority around something
that could be called, in American terminology, a "New Deal"
ideology. It had yet to be formulated in contemporary Italian
terms.[18] Any given formulation would probably be rejected by
the many differing groups, each with its particular traditions and
terminology. The expired Action Party, that collection of intense
and argumentative intellectuals and fighters, had foreseen it in
the 1940's and had formulated it under the name "liberal socialism." They had fallen apart and failed, earning the disdain of

---

16 From an interview granted by De Martino to the weekly journal *L'Espresso*, published in the issue of May 23, 1965.

17 *Loc. cit.*

18 One recent effort to do so is found in Roberto Guiducci, *New Deal
Socialista* (Florence: Vallecchi, 1965).

more practical and cynical political operators. Yet they may very well have had a more accurate vision of the Italian future than their more successful competitors.

Two dynamic and exciting decades produced vast change, and change produces crisis. It is trite to note that Italy was going through a crisis of change; it is important to recognize also that a large part of Italy was suffering a crisis of stagnation. Beyond a few "islands" of large-scale investment—such as Bari, Brindisi, Taranto, Catania, Salerno, and Syracuse-Augusta, the south was still afflicted with its secular miseries. Away from the coasts, the interior appeared ageless and changeless. It might be argued that the exodus of people was itself a crisis of change, but people had been leaving the south in large numbers since the 1880's. The exodus was nothing new. An answer to the problem had yet to be found.

But modern Italy and modern Italians were not waiting passively for others to find the answer, nor were they merely borrowing formulas from others. If they found myths coming from the East unacceptable, neither were they uncritically assimilating those from the West. My use of the phrase "New Deal" was intended to make certain trends comprehensible to the American reader, not to assert that the Italians were lifting their ideas and patterns of life from America wholesale. They were applying their own critical intelligence, finding Italian solutions to their problems. They had many serious problems, but the years between 1945 and 1965 had clearly demonstrated their will and their determination to face up to them within a framework of political democracy.

Glossary

ACLI: Associazioni Cristiani di Lavoratori Italiani (Christian Associations of Italian Workers).

AGIP: Azienda Generale Italiana Petroli (Italian General Petroleum Agency).

CGIL: Confederazione Generale Italiana del Lavoro (Italian General Confederation of Labor).

CISL: Confederazione Italiana Sindacati Lavoratori (Italian Confederation of Workers' Unions).

CISNAL: Confederazione Sindacati Nazionale Lavoratori (National Confederation of Workers' Unions).

CLN: Comitato di Liberazione Nazionale (Committee of National Liberation).

ENEL: Ente delle Imprese Elettriche (Electrical Undertakings Trust).

ENI: Ente Nazionale Idrocarburi (National Hydrocarbons Trust).

FIL: Federazione Italiana del Lavoro (Italian Federation of Labor).

IRI: Istituto di Ricostruzione Industriale (Institute for Industrial Reconstruction).

LCGIL: Libera Confederazione Generale Italiana dei Lavoratori (Free Italian General Confederation of Workers).

MSI: Movimento Sociale Italiano (Italian Social Movement).

PSIUP: Partito Socialista Italiano di Unità Proletaria (Italian Socialist Party of Proletarian Unity).

SENN: Società Elettronucleare Nazionale (National Nuclear Electric Society).

UIL: Unione Italiana del Lavoro (Italian Union of Labor).

Bibliography

ADAMS, JOHN C., and BARILE, PAOLO. *The Government of Republican Italy*. Boston: Houghton Mifflin Company, 1961 (paper).

AGLIANÒ, SEBASTIANO. *Questa Sicilia*. Milan: Mondadori, 1950.

ALBERTONI, ETTORE (ed.). *La generazione degli anni difficili*. Bari: Laterza, 1962.

ALFASSIO GRIMALDI, UGOBERTO, and BERTONI, ITALO. *I giovani degli anni sessanta*. Bari: Laterza, 1964.

ALMIRANTE, GIORGIO, and PALAMENGHI CRISPI, F. *Il Movimento Sociale Italiano*. Milan: Nuova Accademia, 1962.

ALMOND, GABRIEL A. *The Appeals of Communism*. Princeton, N.J.: Princeton University Press, 1954.

ALMOND, GABRIEL A., and VERBA, SIDNEY. *The Civic Culture: Political Attitudes and Democracy in Five Nations*. Princeton, N.J.: Princeton University Press, 1963.

ANDREOTTI, GIULIO. *Concerto a sei voci*. Rome: Della Bussola, 1945.

――――. *De Gasperi e il suo tempo*. 2d ed. Milan: Mondadori, 1965.

AQUARONE, ALBERTO. *Grandi città e aree metropolitane in Italia*. Bologna: Zanichelli, 1961.

Atti e documenti della Democrazia Cristiana 1943–1959. Rome: Cinque Lune, 1959.

Atti del VII Congresso nazionale della Democrazia Cristiana. Rome: Cinque Lune, 1961.

BADOGLIO, PIETRO. *L'Italia nella seconda guerra mondiale*. Milan: Mondadori, 1946.

BALDUCCI, ERNESTO. *Papa Giovanni*. Florence: Vallecchi, 1964.

BANFIELD, EDWARD C. and L. F. *The Moral Basis of a Backward Society*. Glencoe, Ill.: The Free Press, 1958.

BARBADORO, IDOMENEO. *La federconsorzi nella politica agraria italiana*. Rome: Lavoro, 1961.

BARBAGALLO, CORRADO. *La questione meridionale*. Milan: Garzanti, 1948.

BARBANO, FILIPPO. *Partiti e pubblica opinione nella campagna elettorale*. Turin: Giappichelli, 1961.

BARBERI, BENEDETTO. *I consumi nel primo secolo dell' Unità d'Italia 1861–1960*. Milan: Giuffrè, 1961.

BARBERIS, CORRADO. *Le migrazioni rurali in Italia.* Milan: Feltrinelli, 1960.

BARBERO, GIUSEPPE. *Riforma agraria italiana.* Milan: Feltrinelli, 1960.

BARTOLI, DOMENICO. *L'Italia burocratica.* Milan: Garzanti, 1965.

———. *Vittorio Emanuele III.* Milan: Mondadori, 1946.

———. *Da Vittorio Emanuele a Gronchi.* Milan: Longanesi, 1961.

BARTOLI, GIANNI. *Italia ritorna.* Bologna: Cappelli, 1960.

BARZINI, LUIGI. *The Italians.* New York: Atheneum Publishers, 1964.

BASSO, LELIO. *Il Partito Socialista Italiano.* Milan: Nuova Accademia, 1962.

BATTAGLIA, ACHILLE. *I giudici e la politica.* Bari: Laterza, 1962.

——— (ed.). *Dieci anni dopo.* Bari: Laterza, 1955.

BATTAGLIA, ROBERTO. *Storia della Resistenza italiana.* 2d ed. Turin: Einaudi, 1953.

BEDESCHI, LORENZO. *I cattolici disubbidienti.* Naples: Vito Bianco, 1959.

BELLÒ, CARLO (ed.). *Lettere al presidente 1948–1953 (Carteggio De Gasperi–Malvestiti).* Milan: Bonetti, 1964.

BENEDETTI, DANTE. *De Gasperi politico e statista.* Rome: G.D.M., 1949.

BERENSON, BERNARD. *Sunset and Twilight: From the Diaries of 1947–1958.* Edited and with an Epilogue by NICKY MARIANO. New York: Harcourt, Brace & World, 1963.

BERTONI, JOVINE, DINA, and MALATESTA, F. *Breve storia della scuola italiana.* Rome: Riuniti, 1961.

BO, GIORGIO. *Verso lo stato moderno.* Florence: Vallecchi, 1961.

BOCCA, GIORGIO. *I giovani leoni del neocapitalismo.* Bari: Laterza, 1963.

———. *Miracolo all' italiana.* Rome: Avanti, 1962.

———. *La scoperta dell' Italia.* Bari: Laterza, 1963.

BONESCHI, MARIO (ed.). *Verso il regime.* Bari: Laterza, 1960.

BONOMI, IVANOE. *Diario di un anno.* Milan: Garzanti, 1947.

BUONAIUTI, ERNESTO. *La Chiesa e il comunismo.* Rome: Bompiani, 1945.

———. *Pio XII.* Rome: Riuniti, 1964.

BUR, JACQUES. *Stato e Chiesa: Di fronte alla scuola.* Milan: Vita e Pensiero, 1962.

CADORNA, RAFFAELE. *La riscossa.* Milan: Rizzoli, 1948.

CAFAGNA, LUCIANO. *Il Nord nella storia d'Italia.* Bari: Laterza, 1962.

CAIZZI, BRUNO. *Olivetti.* Turin: U.T.E.T. (Unione Tipografico-Editrice Torinese), 1963.

CALDERONI, UGO. *I cento anni della politica doganale italiana.* Padua: Cedam, 1961.

CANALI, PAOLO (ADSTANS). *Alcide De Gasperi nella politica estera italiana.* Milan: Mondadori, 1953.

CANNARSA, SPARTACO. *Dal fascismo alla repubblica. Il senato: Agonia, morte e rinascita.* Rome: La Politica Parlamentare, 1962.

CANTRIL, HADLEY. *Faith, Hope, and Heresy: The Psychology of the*

Protest Voter. Princeton, N.J.: The Institute for International Social Research, 1958.

CAPITINI, ALDO. *Danilo Dolci*. Florence: La Nuova Italia, 1964.

————. *Discuto la religione di Pio XII*. Florence: Parenti, 1957.

————. *L'obiezione di coscienza in Italia*. Florence: La Nuova Italia, 1964.

———— (ed.). *Atti della costituente sull' art. 7*. Florence: La Nuova Italia, 1964.

CARLYLE, MARGARET. *The Awakening of Southern Italy*. London and New York: Oxford University Press, 1962.

————. *Modern Italy*. Rev. ed. New York: Frederick A. Praeger, 1965.

CAROCCI, GIAMPIERO. *Storia del parlamento italiano*. Bari: Laterza, 1964.

CARPI, FABIO. *Cinema italiano del dopoguerra*. Milan: Schwarz, 1958.

CARRILLO, ELISA A. *De Gasperi: The Long Apprenticeship*. Notre Dame, Ind.: University of Notre Dame Press, 1966.

CASINI, TOMMASO. *Lo Stato italiano: Principi ed ordinamento*. Bologna: Mondo Moderno, 1961.

CATALANO, FRANCO. *L'Italia dalla dittatura alla democrazia 1919–1948*. Milan: Lerici, 1962.

CATTI DE GASPERI, MARIA R. *De Gasperi uomo solo*. Milan: Mondadori, 1964.

CAVALLARI, ALBERTO. *L'Europa su misura*. Florence: Vallecchi, 1964.

CENTRO DI AZIONE LATINA. *Italia economica 1961*. Milan: Giuffrè, 1961.

CENTRO DI RICERCHE INDUSTRIALI E SOCIALI. *Immigrazione e industria*. Milan: Comunità, 1962.

CENTRO ITALIANO RICERCHE DOCUMENTAZIONE. *Annuario politico italiano*. 3 vols. Milan: Comunità, 1963–65.

CESAREO, GIOVANNI. *La condizione femminile*. Milan: Sugar, 1963.

CEVA, BIANCA. *Cinque anni di storia italiana 1940–1945*. Milan: Comunità, 1964.

CLOUGH, SHEPARD B. *The Economic History of Modern Italy*. New York: Columbia University Press, 1964.

COLOMBO, ARTURO. *Rapporto sull' università italiana*. Milan: Comunità, 1962.

COMITATO NAZIONALE PER LA PRODUTTIVITÀ. *L'economia italiana ha bisogno di laureati*. Rome: S.P.E.I., 1961.

COMPAGNA, FRANCESCO. *Lauro e la Democrazia Cristiana*. Rome: Opere Nuove, 1960.

————. *La lotta politica italiana nel secondo dopoguerra e il Mezzogiorno*. Bari: Laterza, 1955.

————. *Mezzogiorno d'Europa*. Rome: Opere Nuove, 1958.

————. *La questione meridionale*. Milan: Garzanti, 1963.

CONTI, GIOVANNI. *La costituente*. Rome: La Voce, 1956.

CORBINO, EPICARMO. *L'economia italiana dal 1860 al 1960.* Bologna: Zanichelli, 1963.

CRAVERI, RAIMONDO. *Politica e affari.* Milan: Garzanti, 1964.

CROCE, BENEDETTO. *Quando l'Italia era tagliata in due.* Bari: Laterza, 1948. English translation by SYLVIA SPRIGGE. *Croce, the King and the Allies: Extract from a Diary, July 1943 to June 1944.* London: Allen & Unwin, 1950.

————. *Scritti e discorsi politici 1943–1947.* Bari: Laterza, 1963.

DAVIS, M. S. *All Rome Trembled.* New York: G. P. Putnam's Sons, 1957.

DEAKIN, FREDERICK WILLIAM. *The Brutal Friendship.* New York: Harper & Row, 1963.

DE CASTRO, DIEGO. *Il problema di Trieste.* Bologna: Capelli, 1953.

DECHERT, CHARLES R. *Ente Nazionale Idrocarburi.* Leiden: Brill, 1963.

DEGLI ESPINOSA, AGOSTINO. *Il regno del sud.* Rome: Migliaresi, 1946.

DEGLI OCCHI, C., and OPERTI, P. *Il Partito Nazionale Monarchico.* Milan: Nuova Accademia, 1962.

DEL BO, DINO. *La crisi dei dirigenti.* Florence: Vallecchi, 1964.

DELL' AMICO, L. *Il mestiere di comunista.* Rome: Opere Nuove, 1962.

DELZELL, CHARLES F. *Mussolini's Enemies: The Italian Anti-Fascist Resistance.* Princeton, N.J.: Princeton University Press, 1961.

DE MARIA, GIOVANNI. *Problemi economici e sociali del dopoguerra.* Milan: Malfasi, 1951.

DE MAURO, TULLIO. *Storia linguistica dell' Italia Unita.* Bari: Laterza, 1963.

DE MICHELE, MARIO. *Scultura italiana del dopoguerra.* Milan: Schwarz, 1958.

DE ROSA, GABRIELE. *Alcide De Gasperi: I cattolici trentini sotto l'Austria.* Rome, Storia e Letteratura, 1964.

DICKINSON, ROBERT E. *The Population Problem of Southern Italy.* Syracuse, N.Y.: Syracuse University Press, 1955.

DI FENIZIO, FERDINANDO. *La programmazione economica 1946–1962.* Turin: U.T.E.T., 1965.

DI STEFANO, CARLO. *La censura teatrale in Italia.* Bologna: Cappelli, 1964.

DOLCI, DANILO. *Report From Palermo.* New York: The Orion Press, 1959.

————. *Waste.* Translated by R. MUNROE. New York: Monthly Review Press, 1963.

EINAUDI, LUIGI. *Lo scrittoio del presidente.* Turin: Einaudi, 1956.

EINAUDI, MARIO et al. *Communism in Western Europe.* Ithaca, N.Y.: Cornell University Press, 1951.

————. *Nationalization in France and Italy.* Ithaca, N.Y.: Cornell University Press, 1955.

EINAUDI, MARIO, and GOGUEL, FRANÇOIS. *Christian Democracy in Italy and France.* Notre Dame, Ind.: University of Notre Dame Press, 1952.

FACCHI, PAOLO (ed.). *La propaganda politica in Italia 1953–1958.* Bologna: Il Mulino, 1960.

FALCONI, CARLO. *La Chiesa e le organizzazioni cattoliche in Italia.* Turin: Einaudi, 1956.

————. *Il pentagono vaticano.* Bari: Laterza, 1958.

————. *Pope John and the Ecumenical Council.* New York: The World Publishing Company, 1964.

FANFANI, AMINTORE. *Anni difficili ma non sterili.* Bologna: Cappelli, 1958.

————. *Autunno 1956: La Democrazia Cristiana e i problemi internazionali.* Rome: Cinque Lune, 1957.

————. *Centro-Sinistra '62.* Milan: Garzanti, 1963.

————. *Dopo Firenze.* Milan: Garzanti, 1961.

FERRARA, MARCELLA and MAURIZIO. *Conversando con Togliatti.* Rome: Cultura Sociale, 1953.

————. *Cronache di vita italiana 1944–1958.* Rome: Riuniti, 1960.

FOFI, GOFFREDO. *L'immigrazione meridionale a Torino.* Milan: Feltrinelli, 1964.

FREE, LLOYD A. *Six Allies and a Neutral.* Glencoe, Ill.: The Free Press, 1959.

FREE, LLOYD A., and SERENO, RENZO. *Italy: Dependent Ally or Independent Partner?* Princeton, N.J.: The Institute for International Social Research, 1956.

FRIED, ROBERT C. *The Italian Prefects: A Study in Administrative Politics.* New Haven, Conn.: Yale University Press, 1963.

FUÀ, GIORGIO, and SYLOS LABINI, PAOLO. *Idee per la programmazione economica.* Bari: Laterza, 1963.

GALASSO, GIUSEPPE. *La riforma agraria in Calabria.* Rome: Opere Nuove, 1962.

GALATI, VITO. *La Democrazia Cristiana.* Milan: Nuova Academia, 1962.

GALLI, GIORGIO. *La sinistra italiana nel dopoguerra.* Bologna: Il Mulino, 1959.

GALLI, GIORGIO, and BELLINI, F. *Storia del Partito comunista italiano.* Milan: Schwarz, 1958.

GALLI, GIORGIO, and FACCHI, PAOLO. *La sinistra democristiana.* Milan: Feltrinelli, 1962.

GHIROTTI, GIGI. *Italia mia benchè.* Milan: Comunità, 1963.

————. *Il magistrato.* 2d ed. Florence: Vallecchi, 1963.

GIOLITTI, ANTONIO. *Il comunismo in Europa.* Milan: Garzanti, 1960.

————. *Riforme e rivoluzione.* Turin: Einaudi, 1957.

GIORDANO, RENATO. *Il mercato comune e i suoi problemi.* Rome: Opere Nuove, 1958.

234 *Bibliography*

GIOVANNINI, ALBERTO. *Il Partito Liberale.* Milan: Nuova Accademia, 1962.

GODECHOT, THIERRY. *Le parti democrate-Chrètien italien.* Paris: Libraire Générale de Droit et de Jurisprudence, 1964.

GONNELLA, GUIDO. *L'attuazione della costituzione nel triennio 1955–1958.* Rome: Società Nuova, 1958.

GORRESIO, VITTORIO. *Italia a sinistra.* Milan: Rizzoli, 1963.

GOZZER, GIOVANNI. *I cattolici e la scuola.* Florence: Vallecchi, 1964.

GOZZINI, MARIO (ed.). *Il dialogo alla prova.* Florence: Vallecchi, 1964.

GRAHAM, ROBERT A. *Vatican Diplomacy: A Study of Church and State on the International Plane.* Princeton, N.J.: Princeton University Press, 1959.

GRASSI, L. *L'adulterio femminile in Italia.* Milan: Comunità, 1963.

GRIFFITH, WILLIAM E. (ed.). *Communism in Europe: Continuity, Change, and the Sino-Soviet Dispute.* Cambridge, Mass.: The M.I.T. Press, 1964.

GRIMAL, PIERRE. *Alla ricerca dell' Italia.* Milan: Martello, 1961.

GRINDROD, MURIEL. *The New Italy: Transition from War to Peace.* London: The Royal Institute of International Affairs, 1947.

———. *The Rebuilding of Italy.* London: The Royal Institute of International Affairs, 1955.

———. *Italy.* New York and London: Oxford University Press, 1964 (paper).

GRONCHI, GIOVANNI. *Discorsi d'America.* Milan: Garzanti, 1956.

GUARIGLIA, RAFFAELE. *Ricordi 1922–1946.* Naples: E.S.I. (Edizioni Scientifiche Italiane), 1950.

GUGLIELMI, ANGELO. *Vent' anni d'impazienza.* Milan: Feltrinelli, 1965.

GUIDUCCI, ROBERTO. *New Deal Socialista.* Florence: Vallecchi, 1965.

HOLBIK, KAREL. *Italy in International Cooperation.* Padua: Cedam, 1959.

HOROWITZ, DANIEL L. *The Italian Labor Movement.* Cambridge, Mass.: Harvard University Press, 1963.

HUGHES, H. STUART. *The United States and Italy.* Rev. ed. Cambridge, Mass.: Harvard University Press, 1965.

INSOLERA, ITALO. *Roma moderna.* Turin: Einaudi, 1963.

JEMOLO, ARTURO CARLO. *Chiesa e Stato in Italia negli ultimi cento anni.* Rev. ed. Turin: Einaudi, 1952.

———. *Italia tormentata.* Bari: Laterza, 1951.

———. *Società civile e società religiosa.* Turin: Einaudi, 1959.

KISH, GEORGE. *Life in Europe: Italy.* Grand Rapids, Mich.: The Fideler Company, 1964.

KOGAN, NORMAN. *The Government of Italy*. New York: Thomas Y. Crowell Company, 1962.
———. *Italy and the Allies*. Cambridge, Mass.: Harvard University Press, 1956.
———. *The Politics of Italian Foreign Policy*. New York: Frederick A. Praeger, 1963.

LA CAVERA, DOMENICO. *Liberali e grande industria nel Mezzogiorno*. Florence: Parenti, 1961.
LA MALFA, UGO. *La politica economica in Italia 1946–1962*. Milan: Comunità, 1962.
———. *Verso la politica di piano*. Naples: E.S.I., 1963.
LANDOLFI, ANTONIO. *Il Partito socialista oggi e domani*. Milan: Azione Comune, 1963.
LAPALOMBARA, JOSEPH. *Interest Groups in Italian Politics*. Princeton, N.J.: Princeton University Press, 1964.
———. *The Italian Labor Movement: Problems and Prospects*. Ithaca, N.Y.: Cornell University Press, 1957.
———. *The Politics of Economic Planning in Italy*. Syracuse, N.Y.: Maxwell School of Citizenship and Public Affairs, 1964.
LA PIRA, GIORGIO. *Per una architettura cristiana dello Stato*. Florence: Fiorentina, 1954.
LAURA, ERNESTO G. (ed.). *La censura cinematografica*. Rome: Bianco Nero, 1961.
LEONE, GIOVANNI. *Cinque mesi a Palazzo Chigi*. Milan: Mondadori, 1964.
———. *Testimomanze*. Milan: Mondadori, 1963.
LEVINE, IRVING R. *Main Street, Italy*. New York: Doubleday & Company, 1963.
LEWIS, NORMAN. *The Honored Society: A Searching Look at the Mafia*. New York: G. P. Putnam's Sons, 1964.
LIUZZI, GIORGIO. *Italia difesa*. Rome: Volpe, 1963.
LOMBARDINI, GABRIELE. *De Gasperi e i cattolici*. Milan: Comunità, 1962.
LUTZ, VERA C. *Italy, a Study in Economic Development*. London and New York: Oxford University Press, 1962.
LUZZATTO FEGIZ, PIERPAOLO. *Il volto sconosciuto dell' Italia*. Milan: Giuffrè, 1956.

MACK SMITH, DENIS. *Italy: A Modern History*. Ann Arbor, Mich.: The University of Michigan Press, 1959.
MAGLIANO, ANGELO. *La borghesia e la paura*. Florence: Vallecchi, 1957.
MAGRI, F. *La Democrazia Cristiana in Italia*. 2d ed. Milan: La Fiaccola, 1960.
MAMMARELLA, GIUSEPPE. *Italy After Fascism*. Montreal: Mario Casalini, 1964.

MANFREDI, ANTONIO. *Alto Adige segreto.* Milan: Ricciardi, 1964.
MANNUCI, CESARE. *Lo spettatore senza libertà.* Bari: Laterza, 1961.
MARANINI, GIUSEPPE. *Miti e realtà della democrazia.* Milan: Comunità, 1958.
————. *Ordinamento giudiziario e indipendenza della magistratura.* Milan: Comunità, 1962.
MAURO, WALTER. *Letteratura sotto inchiesta.* Rome: Canesi, 1963.
MAXWELL, GAVIN. *The Ten Pains of Death: A Vivid Portrait of the People of Modern Sicily.* New York: E. P. Dutton & Company, 1960.
MELIS, RENATO. *Sindicalisti italiani.* Rome: Volpe, 1965.
MENNELLA, CRISTOFORO. *Ricerche e centrali nucleari in Italia.* Turin: Internazionale, 1965.
MEYNAUD, JEAN. *Pianificazione politica.* Milan: Comunità, 1963.
————. *Rapport sur la classe dirigeante italienne.* Lausanne: Etudes de Science Politique, 1964.
MONTINI, GIOVANNI BATTISTA (POPE PAUL VI). *The Christian in the Material World.* Translated by MICHAEL M. McMANUS. Baltimore: Helicon Press, 1964.
MORANDI, RODOLFO. *Democrazia diretta e ricostruzione capitalistica 1945-1948.* Turin: Einaudi, 1960.
————. *Il Partito e le classi 1948-1955.* Turin: Einaudi, 1961.
MORRIS, JAMES. *The Road to Huddersfield: A Journey to Five Continents.* New York: Pantheon Books, 1963.
MOSCATI, RUGGIERO. *Il ministero degli affari esteri 1870-1961.* Milan: Giuffrè, 1961.
MOTZO DENTICE D' ACCADIA, CECILIA (ed.). *Legislazione scolastica e autonomie.* Bari: Laterza, 1964.

NAVACCO, DOMENICO. *Inchiesta sulla mafia.* Milan: Feltrinelli, 1964.
NEGRO, SILVIO. *Roma non basta una vita.* Venice: Neri Pozza, 1962.
————. *Vaticano minore.* Venice: Neri Pozza, 1963.
NELSON, LOWRY. *Land Reform in Italy.* New York: National Planning Association, 1956.
NENNI, PIETRO. *Una battaglia vinta.* Rome and Milan: Leonardo, 1946.
————. *Dialogo con la sinistra cattolica.* Rome: Avanti, 1954.
————. *La legislatura fallita 1953-1958.* Rome: Avanti, 1959.
NEUFELD, MAURICE F. *Italy: School for Awakening Countries.* Ithaca, N.Y.: The New York State School of Industrial and Labor Relations, 1961.
————. *Labor Unions and National Politics in Italian Industrial Plants.* Ithaca, N.Y.: The Institute of International Industrial and Labor Relations, 1954.
NICOLINI, FAUSTO. *Croce.* Turin: U.T.E.T., 1962.

OMODEO, ZONA, EVA, and SERINI, PAOLO. *Adolfo Omodeo: Lettere 1910-1946.* Turin: Einaudi, 1963.

PACIFICI, SERGIO. *A Guide to Contemporary Italian Literature.* New York: Meridian Books, 1962 (paper).
PACOR, MARIO. *Confine orientale.* Milan: Feltrinelli, 1964.
PANTALEONE, MICHELE. *Mafia e politica.* Turin: Einaudi, 1962.
PAPI, UGO. *Programmazione indicativa.* Milan: Giuffrè, 1962.
PARTITO COMUNISTA ITALIANO. *Trenta anni di vita e di lotte del PCI.* Rome: Riuniti, 1952.
PARTITO DELLA DEMOCRAZIA CRISTIANA. *Atti dei Convegni di San Pellegrino.* 3 vols. Rome: Cinque Lune, 1962–64.
PASSARIN D' ENTRÈVES, ETTORE. *Gli ultimi quarant' anni.* Bologna: Zanichelli, 1961.
PASTORE, GIULIO. *I lavoratori nello stato.* Florence: Vallecchi, 1963.
PERMOLI, P. *Lezioni sull' antifascismo.* Bari: Laterza, 1960.
PERTICONE, GIACOMO. *La formazione della classe politica nell' Italia contemporanea.* Florence: Sansoni, 1954.
―――. *L'Italia contemporanea.* Milan: Mondadori, 1961.
PICCARDI, LEOPOLDO. *La storia non aspetta.* Bari: Laterza, 1957.
POGGI, GIANFRANCO. *Il clero di riserva.* Milan: Feltrinelli, 1963.
POZZANI, SILVIO. *L'economia italiana: Situazioni e problemi.* Milan: Comunità, 1961.
PRYCE, ROY. *The Italian Local Elections, 1956.* ("St. Antony's Papers," No. 3.) New York: St Martin's Press, 1957.
PULLINI, GIORGIO. *Il romanzo italiano del dopoguerra 1945–1960.* Milan: Schwarz, 1961.

QUARONI, PIETRO. *Ricordi di un ambasciatore.* Milan: Garzanti, 1954.
―――. *Valigia diplomatica.* Milan: Garzanti, 1956.

RAGGHIANTI, CARLO LODOVICO (ed.). *Scuola secondo costituzione.* Florence: La Nuova Italia, 1964.
REALE, EGIDIO. *Egidio Reale e il suo tempo.* Florence: La Nuova Italia, 1961.
REALE, EUGENIO. *Nascita del Cominform.* Milan: Mondadori, 1958.
REVEL, JEAN-FRANÇOIS. *Pour l'Italie.* Paris: Julliard, 1958.
RICHELMY, CARLO. *Diplomazia in castigo.* Rome: Canesi, 1963.
―――. *I preti in Italia.* Rome: Gherardo Casini, 1956.
ROMEO, ROSARIO. *Breve storia della grande industria in Italia.* Bologna: Cappelli, 1961.
ROMITA, GIUSEPPE. *Memorie.* Pisa: Nistri-Lischi, 1960.
―――. *Dalla monarchia alla repubblica.* Pisa: Nistri-Lischi, 1959.
―――. *Panorama socialista.* Rome: Opere Nuove, 1956.
ROSSI, ERNESTO. *Il malgoverno.* Bari: Laterza, 1954.
―――. *I nostri quattrini.* Bari: Laterza, 1964.
―――. *I padroni del vapore.* 2d ed. Bari: Laterza, 1965.
―――. *Settimo: Non rubare.* Bari: Laterza, 1952.
――― (ed). *La Federconsorzi.* Milan: Feltrinelli, 1963.

Rossi, Nerino. *Cinque anni difficili.* Bologna: Cappelli, 1958.
Rossi-Doria, Manlio. *Dieci anni di politica agraria nel Mezzogiorno.* Bari: Laterza, 1958.
————. *Rapporto sulla Federconsorzi.* Bari: Laterza, 1963.
————. *Riforma agraria e azione meridionalista.* Bologna: Agricole Bologna, 1948.
Ruini, Meuccio. *Come si è formata la costituzione.* Milan: Giuffrè, 1961.
————. *Rievocazione-studi-ricordi.* Milan: Giuffrè, 1961.
Ruocco, Maria. *L'educazione sessuale in Italia.* Florence: La Nuova Italia, 1964.
Russo, Giovanni. *Chi ha più santi in paradiso.* Bari: Laterza, 1964.

Saitta, Armando. *Storia e miti del '900.* Bari: Laterza, 1960.
Salvadori, Massimo. *Resistenza ed azione.* Bari: Laterza, 1951.
Salvatorelli, Luigi. *La guerra fredda 1945-1955.* Venice: Neri Pozza, 1956.
Salvemini, Gaetano. *Clericali e laici.* Florence: Parenti, 1957.
————. *Italia scombinata.* Turin: Einaudi, 1959.
Santarelli, Enzo. *La revisione del marxismo in Italia.* Milan: Feltrinelli, 1965.
Saraceno, Pasquale. *Iniziativa privata e azione pubblica nei piani di sviluppo economico.* Milan: Giuffrè, 1959.
————. *L'Italia verso la piena occupazione.* Milan: Feltrinelli, 1963.
————. *La mancata unificazione economica dell' Italia a cento anni dall' unificazione politica.* Milan: Giuffrè, 1961.
Sartori, Giovanni. *Il parlamento italiano.* Naples: E.S.I., 1963.
Sauvage, Tristan. *Pittura italiana del dopoguerra.* Milan: Schwarz, 1957.
Scalfari, Eugenio. *Rapporto sul neocapitalismo in Italia.* Bari: Laterza, 1961.
————. *Storia segreta dell' industria elettrica.* Bari: Laterza, 1963.
———— (ed.). *Le baronie elettriche.* Bari: Laterza, 1960.
Scoccimarro, Mauro. *Il secondo dopoguerra.* Rome: Riuniti, 1956.
Scott, Walter G. *Gli investimenti stranieri in Italia.* Milan: Feltrinelli, 1961.
Sebilleau, Pierre. *Italie des contrastes.* Paris and Grenoble: Arthaud, 1961.
Sela, M. *I congressi nazionali della Democrazia Cristiana.* Rome: Cinque Lune, 1959.
Seniga, Giulio. *Togliatti e Stalin.* Milan: Sugar, 1962.
Settembrini, Domenico. *La Chiesa nella politica italiana.* Pisa: Nistri-Lischi, 1964.
Sforza, Carlo. *Cinque anni a Palazzo Chigi.* Rome: Atlante, 1952.
Sforza, Marco Cesarini. *Uomo politico.* Florence: Vallecchi, 1963.
Società Italiana per L'Organizzazione Internazionale. *Italy and the United Nations.* New York: Manhattan Publishing Company, 1959.

SPADOLINI, GIOVANNI. *Il papato socialista*. 3d ed. Milan: Longanesi, 1964.

SPINELLI, ALTIERO. *L'Europa non cade dal cielo*. Bologna: Il Mulino, 1960.

SPREAFICO, ALBERTO, and LAPALOMBARA, JOSEPH. *Elezioni e comportamento politico in Italia*. Milan: Comunità, 1963.

STURZO, LUIGI. *Italy and the Coming World*. Translated by BARBARA BARCLAY CARTER. New York: Roy Publishers, 1945.

————. *Politica di questi anni*. Bologna: Zanichelli, 1954.

SULLO, FIORENTINO. *Lo scandalo urbanistico*. Florence: Vallecchi, 1964.

TAMBRONI, FERNANDO. *Il senso dello Stato*. Milan: Bompiani, 1960.

————. *Un governo amministrativo*. Rome: Les Problèmes de l'Europe, 1960.

TARANTINI, DOMENICO. *Processo allo spettacolo*. Milan: Comunità, 1961.

TARCHIANI, ALBERTO. *Dieci anni tra Roma e Washington*. Milan: Mondadori, 1955.

TAVIANI, PAOLO EMILIO. *Saggi sulla Democrazia Cristiana*. Florence: Vallecchi, 1961.

TOGLIATTI, PALMIRO. *Nella democrazia e nella pace verso il socialismo*. Rome: Riuniti, 1963.

————. *Linea d'una politica*. Milan: Milano-Sera, 1948.

————. *Il Partito Comunista Italiano*. Rome: Riuniti, 1961.

TOMASI, TINA. *La formazione della classe dirigente*. Rome: Armando, 1965.

TORELLI, MILZIADE. *Quirinale alla ribalta*. Milan: Le Stelle, 1960.

TOSCANO, MARIO. *Pagine di storia diplomatica contemporanea*. Milan: Giuffrè, 1963.

TREMELLONI, ROBERTO. *Le strade del benessere in uno stato efficiente*. Milan: Istituto Lombardo di Studi Sociali, 1958.

TUPINI, GIORGIO. *I democratici cristiani*. Milan: Garzanti, 1954.

VALENTINO, NINO. *L'elezione di Segni*. Milan: Comunità, 1963.

VALIANI, LEO. *L'avvento di De Gasperi*. Turin: De Silva, 1949.

————. *Gli sviluppi ideologici del socialismo democratico in Italia*. Rome: Opere Nuove, 1962.

————. *Tutte le strade conducono a Roma*. Florence: La Nuova Italia, 1947.

VALITUTTI, SALVATORE (ed.). *Scuola pubblica e privata*. Bari: Laterza, 1965.

VANONI, EZIO. *Discorsi sul programma di sviluppo economico*. Rome: Istituto Poligrafico dello Stato, 1956.

VAUSSARD, MAURICE. *Storia della Democrazia Cristiana*. Bologna: Cappelli, 1959.

VILLARI, ROSARIO. *Mezzogiorno tra riforma e rivoluzione*. Bari: Laterza, 1962.

―――――. *Il Sud nella storia d'Italia*. Bari: Laterza, 1961.

VINCIGUERRA, MARIO. *I partiti politici italiani dal 1948 al 1955*. Rome: Centro Editoriale dell' Osservatore, 1955.

VOTAW, DOW. *The Six-Legged Dog: Mattei and ENI*. Berkeley, Calif.: University of California Press, 1964.

WEBB, LEICESTER C. *Church and State in Italy, 1947–1957*. New York: Cambridge University Press, 1958.

WEBSTER, RICHARD. *Christian Democracy in Italy, 1860–1960*. London: Hollis & Carter, 1961.

WEISS, IGNAZIO. *Politica dell' informazione*. Milan: Comunità, 1961.

―――――. *Il potere di carta*. Milan: U.T.E.T., 1965.

WISKEMANN, ELIZABETH. *Italy*. London and New York: Oxford University Press, 1947.

ZAMPAGLIONE, GERARDO. *Italy*. New York: Frederick A. Praeger, 1956.

Index

Acerbo Law, 76
ACLI (Christian Association of Italian Workers): denounces "dialogue," 208; helps southern immigrants, 154 n.; and trade unions, 50; *see also* Catholic Action Society, Italian
Action Party, 6, 225; disappearance of, 38; origins of, 28; republicanism of, 34; resignation of, 8, 46
Africa, trade with, 144
Africa, North, 157
AGIP (Italian General Petroleum Agency), 66, 106, 107
Agip-Nucleare, 135
Agnelli, Gianni, 209
Agnelli, Giovanni, 156
agriculture: agrarian pacts, debate over, 121–22; conflict over reforms, 7–8, 76; decline of, 214; difficulties of, 67; exodus from land, 149; fluctuations in, 65–66; growth of, 142; improvement in, 201; land expropriation, 153; land reform in Sicily, 149; peasants, 57–59, 92; policy change in, 149–50; reform of, 57–62; reforms resented, 70; sharecropping, 121–22, 184, 203; and social status, 70–71; weakness of reforms, 149; wheat prices, 134
Air Force, Italian, 25
Albania, 14, 21, 23, 25
Alexander, Sir Harold, 13
Algeria, 126 n.
Allied Commission, 8, 31, 37, 38
Allied High Command, 9
Allied Military Government: blocks CLN, 32; lire in circulation, 43; and partisans, 9; removes controls, 35; resists purge, 31
Alps, boundaries in, 18–19
Alto Adige; *see* South Tyrol
Amendola, Giorgio: on Communist weaknesses, 205–6; supports Socialist candidates, 207; thesis of, 208; and workers, 223

Andreotti, Giulio, 165
anti-Fascism: among bureaucrats, 35; decline of, 87–88; effect of armistice terms on, 7; in Genoa, 170–71; opposition to King, 6; and peace treaty, 27
Apulia, 25, 58
Argentina, 157
Army, Italian, 5, 25
Asia, trade with, 144
Assolombardo (Lombard Business Association), 88
atomic power: dispute over, 134–35; regulation of, 80
Augusta, 226
Austria: boundary claims by, 15; feeling against, 20; and South Tyrol, 20–21, 160–61
Autostrada del Sole, 148
Azzariti, Gaetano, 119

Badoglio, Pietro: backed by Togliatti, 34; escapes from Rome, 5; forms political government, 6; and parties, 28; proclaimed head of government, 4; rejected as Prime Minister, 7
Balkan Peace Zone, 132
Bank of Italy, 44, 197, 199, 211
Bari, 139, 226
"Basic Principles" (editorial), 169, 192–93
Basso, Lelio, 138, 176
Belgium, 144
Berlin air-lift, 54
Bishop of Prato, 124
Bo, Giorgio, 168, 213, 223
Bologna, 222
Bolzano; *see* South Tyrol
Bonomi, Ivanoe, 14; becomes Prime Minister, 7; recognizes CLNAI, 9; resigns post, 8
Bonomi, Paolo, 134
Brenner Pass, 4
Brindisi, 226
Budapest, 124, 128